WORDS,
WORKS, AND
WAYS OF
KNOWING

WORDS, WORKS, AND WAYS OF KNOWING

❖ ❖ ❖ ❖ ❖ ❖

The Breakdown of Moral Philosophy in
New England before the Civil War

Sara Paretsky

with a preface by the author and an afterword by

AMANDA PORTERFIELD

THE UNIVERSITY OF CHICAGO PRESS *Chicago and London*

Sara Paretsky is the author of, most recently, Brush Back.
A prolific crime and mystery novelist, she received her
PhD in history from the University of Chicago in 1977.

The University of Chicago Press, Chicago 60637
The University of Chicago Press, Ltd., London
© 2016 by Sara Paretsky
Afterword © 2016 by The University of Chicago
All rights reserved. Published 2016.
Printed in the United States of America

25 24 23 22 21 20 19 18 17 16   1 2 3 4 5

ISBN-13: 978-0-226-33774-6 (cloth)
ISBN-13: 978-0-226-33788-3 (e-book)
DOI: 10.7208/chicago/9780226337883.001.0001

Library of Congress Cataloging-in-Publication Data
Names: Paretsky, Sara, author.
Title: Words, works, and ways of knowing : the breakdown of moral philosophy
in New England before the Civil War / Sara Paretsky ; with a preface
by the author and an afterword by Amanda Porterfield.
Description: Chicago ; London : The University of Chicago Press, 2016. |
Includes bibliographical references and index.
Identifiers: LCCN 2015037376 | ISBN 9780226337746
(cloth : alk. paper) | ISBN 9780226337883 (e-book)
Subjects: LCSH: Ethics—Study and teaching—New England—History. | Andover
Theological Seminary—History. | Learning and scholarship—New England—History.
Classification: LCC BJ68.A53 P37 2016 | DDC 170.974/09034—dc23
LC record available at http://lccn.loc.gov/2015037376

♾ This paper meets the requirements of
ANSI/NISO Z39.48-1992 (Permanence of Paper).

FOR COURTENAY

All other things to their destruction draw,

Only our love hath no decay;

This, no tomorrow hath, nor yesterday,

Running it never runs from us away,

But truly keepes his first, last, everlasting day.

JOHN DONNE, "The Anniversarie"

CONTENTS

PREFACE

I was ten when I read my first work of history: Mark Twain's *Personal Recollections of Joan of Arc*. True, it's a romantic and sentimental version of the saint, but Twain did read all the original source material. His passion for Joan spoke to my own young experience and yearnings. *Personal Recollections* didn't make me want to be a historian, but it did make me long for a vision as great as hers and the passion to see it through to the end, even — or especially—if the end were a pile of faggots in the old market of Rouen.

Almost everything I've ever written has been part of this thirst for a vision, what the physicist Frank Wilczek calls "a longing for the harmonies."[1] It's the feeling you get from looking at the night sky, if you're lucky enough to see the stars hang down like living jewels, when you long to reach up and become part of that infinite jeweled space. The intensity of the feeling is part of adolescence, but the yearning has never completely left me, even in later age.

V. I. Warshawski, the detective I created in 1982 and who appears in seventeen of my novels, is a woman of action, but hers is an ardent spirit. Her passion for trying to right wrongs comes from a deeper thirst for creating a just world, a world of harmonies. In the novels, people mock her as "Doña Quixote," or as Joan of Arc, but I don't write about her mockingly. She is the mirror of my own desires.

My novels also reflect another aspect of my life: the struggle to find a voice of my own, and to help other women gain the power to speak and to take up public space.

How the dissertation I wrote in the 1970s fits into the larger body of my postgraduate writing is a question that I've had to think hard about. I came to the liberal theologians at the Andover Theological Seminary (today the site of Phillips Andover Academy) for a number of reasons. In part, I was drawn to religious thinkers because the saints and ascetics of Christian history seemed to have the same longings that I did. As an undergraduate, I used to study in the underground stacks in my university's library. In that cave-like, quasi-monastic atmosphere, I read Calvin's *Institutes of the Christian Religion*, the biographies of early Reformers like Thomas Cranmer, and the sermons of John Donne.

Still, why did I write a dissertation about men struggling with intellectual challenges to their religious beliefs? Why not take on Teresa of Avila, for instance, or, in the secular world, someone like Elizabeth Barrett Browning?

I grew up in eastern Kansas in a family that valued the written word above almost any other good. We also were hearty eaters, so very often we read and ate at the same time.

I also grew up in a family that did not think the accomplishments or dreams of girls and women were worth attending to. I had four brothers whose education was important, but the expectations for me were limited to an old-fashioned model of circumscribed domesticity. I was expected to stay home to care for the house, the parents, the small brothers, and, despite winning a number of important scholarships, was essentially commanded to attend the University of Kansas.

I decided if I had to stay in Kansas for the academic year, I'd spend my summers elsewhere. I was as tired as Charlotte Brontë of a life "confined to making puddings and knitting stockings."[2]

The summer of 1966, I came to Chicago to work for the Presbytery of Chicago as a volunteer in the Civil Rights Movement. That was the summer that Martin Luther King, Jr., and his family moved into a tenement on the South Side while they tried to pry the city of Chicago out of its entrenched racist housing, employment, and other policies (these included barring blacks from most of the city's public beaches).[3]

With two other college students, I was assigned to a mostly Polish and Lithuanian neighborhood only a few blocks from where Dr. King was living. We found ourselves with a front-row seat to some of the most violent confrontations of the Civil Rights Movement.

We were working with kids aged seven to eleven, and we took them all over the city by the L train, to the museums, the beaches, the ballparks. After hours, we were sent to meetings of the local white citizens council, the local alderman's constituency meetings, Black Power meetings, and to schools and stock exchanges and slaughter yards.

Although it was a summer of violence, it was also a time of hope: the possibility of change seemed real and exciting. Our work that summer and our engagement with the city gave me a deep attachment to Chicago. When I finished my undergraduate degree in January 1968, I came back; Chicago has been my home now for almost fifty years.[4]

Because of my experience of Chicago during the race riots of 1966, I wanted to earn a PhD in US history. I wanted to try to understand the background of the violent divisions in the country. I had applied to a number of universities, but in 1968 I had taken a job as a secretary in the Social Science Division at the University of Chicago. Thanks to Emma "Bickie" Pitcher, with whom I worked, I received a Ford Foundation Fellowship and started graduate work at Chicago in the fall of 1968.

In Kansas, as an undergraduate, I was becoming a feminist. I started school a few months after the Civil Rights Act of 1964 became law. Our dean of women, Emily Taylor, was a strong feminist who made the best use of Title VII legislation to promote the position of women in Kansas. Later, as the director of the Office of Higher Education in the Department of Education, Dr. Taylor mentored women administrators, grooming them to become university presidents.

Under Dr. Taylor, I chaired the first University of Kansas Commission on the Status of Women. Our research was cited by the Department of Labor's Office of Federal Contract Compliance as they established guidelines for universities.

When I began graduate school, it was without the support of the people and institutions that had helped me begin to find a voice. My choice of dissertation topic was inevitably guided by the faculty, and the faculty's interests were largely intellectual and extremely misogynist: women played almost no role, either in their own scholarly work or in their vision of the history profession.

In a meeting of entering students, we were told that women could memorize and parrot things back, but that we were not capable of original work. Like the other women in the room, I sat meekly, not reacting. (The following spring, I wrote a play that my fellow students acted out for the faculty, satirizing their confused reaction to women students, so I can't have been totally passive. As a result of that drama, the history graduate students elected me as their president, figuring I was reckless enough to speak up for all the students, men as well as women. Some years later, a member of the European field committee told me I frightened the faculty, but unfortunately their fear made them dig their heels in rather than change their attitude toward women.)

The misogyny was relentless. We women students formed a caucus that tried to persuade the faculty to consider women scholars for assistant professor openings. The department chairman told us the history department would not "dilute its standards" by adding women to the faculty. The search committees refused to read books or articles by potential women candidates, to attend lectures these women gave at meetings of the American Historical Association, or even to look at the vitae we Chicago students prepared. Some of the junior faculty applauded the efforts of our graduate student women's caucus, but, without tenure, there was little they could do beyond offer moral support.

Women's history was in its infancy in the late sixties and early seventies; no one on the faculty wanted to supervise a dissertation in that area. When Hilda Smith boldly wrote about seventeenth-century English feminists, one department member actually went to her dissertation defense in order to harangue her committee into failing her. Her friends sat on the floor outside, waiting for the verdict. When she passed, we could hardly believe it.

At the end of my first year, the dozen or so other women who had started the American Field Committee program with me dropped out. I persevered not because I was better or more dedicated, but because I didn't have a default plan for my life—I wanted to be a scholar and a university teacher.

The path from a personal passion or interest to a finished dissertation is seldom direct, and in the case of this work, it was even less so. Calvin and his followers continued to interest me, and I spent part of my coursework on the Calvinists who settled New England in the early seventeenth century.

I was also reading about the abolitionist movement. I wrote my master's thesis on the radical abolitionists, many of whom had connections to Andover Theological Seminary.

At the same time, I was studying Victorian science. I began to see that Darwin, who I had assumed upended millennia of Bible-centered interpretations of nature, was actually a link in a longer chain of research. New scholarship in geology and philology, centered chiefly in Edinburgh and in German universities, had started raising difficult questions for Christian scholars as early as the eighteenth century.

As a person who was both a social activist and a contemplative thinker, I was drawn to the struggle Calvinist scholars faced in trying to reconcile their internal conflict between faith and science.[5] In 1970, I submitted a dissertation proposal. I wanted to tie together the intellectual work taking place at Andover and the Calvinist scholars' influence on social justice movements, including abolition and suffrage, and at the same time, look at the way American intellectuals were affected by the new learning in Europe.

In hindsight, it's easy to see that my proposal was for a project that a mature scholar would have covered in six or seven books. However, my committee chair, George Stocking, accepted it without commenting on it or questioning me very deeply.

Stocking told me he didn't want to see work in progress, only a finished dissertation. I went away and happily began reading and writing, and after

Preface

a year, I turned in a draft. Stocking then explained to me that my proposal was unworkable and that the draft barely dented the surface of the topic.

When I asked why he had accepted the proposal, he said he never expected me to do any work on it. I asked for more direction, but Stocking said I needed to figure out how to make the topic manageable on my own. I asked the department for a new committee but they were adamant against making a change.

I repeated the process two more times. Each time, Stocking refused to look at work in progress and then rejected the finished draft. My fellowship had ended. I began working part-time in publicity and marketing.[6]

Finally, with help from my third reader, Don Scott—who had been denied tenure and had moved to the East Coast—I was able to shape the topic into a manageable piece of work. Neil Harris kindly read portions of the work. His critique of my writing improved not only the finished dissertation, but all my subsequent writing.

I completed the final draft in 1976. Stocking took eighteen months to read and approve it, and I was finally able to submit it to the department for a degree in 1977.

It was while I was working on this last draft that I stumbled on some exciting family papers. These belonged to the Park family in Nashville, Tennessee, descendants of one of the founders of Andover, Edwards Amasa Park. When the Park family moved from New England to Tennessee, they brought with them four trunks of letters and journals belonging not just to Park but to other faculty members.

I read letters between faculty wives; the Andover faculty would often travel to Germany and Edinburgh for study and the women corresponded across the Atlantic. I learned that many of the wives were significant scholars in their own right, and that translations of Hebrew or Greek documents I had read were actually created by Andover women, but published under their husbands' names. One woman, daughter of the first Andover professor of theology, was a novelist. The women also wrote in touchingly matter-of-fact language about disease and death in their midst: "A mild winter in Boston," one wrote. "Only three children have died."

One of the key figures in this dissertation, Edward Hitchcock—who taught geology at Amherst and lectured at Andover—was committed to women's education. His most notable student was Emily Dickinson. Although Amherst didn't allow women in the classroom, Hitchcock made it possible for Dickinson to study geology with him privately.

By the time I saw the Park family papers, I didn't have the energy to undertake a new study of the world of the Andover Calvinists. I hope that other scholars will study the archive and show the wide role that women played in the intellectual ferment of the nineteenth century.

While I was completing my dissertation, I was also looking for jobs. The department provided no help in the job search.[7] I arranged only one interview on my own, which didn't pan out. After graduation, I worked in the corporate world for ten years.

My reading-eating family all had a passion for crime fiction, which I shared. While I was selling computers to insurance agents, I kept reading crime fiction. I grew weary of the depiction of women in most English-language mysteries as either vamps or victims, and I began to dream of a detective who would reflect the experience of my generation: women doing jobs that only recently had opened for us. Women who could have a sex life without it defining them as wicked. Women who could solve their own problems. Five years after I got my PhD, I published my first detective novel, *Indemnity Only*.

V. I. Warshawski brings together the many different strands of my life—the struggle for justice, the struggle for a voice, the struggle to have my work and other women's work treated with respect. At the same time, the process of thinking and writing about her allows me to go into what Melville called "the silent grass-growing" space where creativity thrives. In that space, he added, you can "spread and expand yourself, and bring to yourself the tinglings of life that are felt . . . in the planets . . . and the Fixed Stars."[8]

Despite the difficulties I experienced as a graduate student, I am proud of my University of Chicago PhD, and I am proud of this piece of work. I had many experiences at the university which were deeply meaningful. I also acquired skills which still stand me in good stead.

The university's librarians, first at the Divinity School and later, when it opened, at Regenstein, were an engaged, knowledgeable resource for all history students. It was they who guided me to the collections and figures that were central to my research.

I had the privilege of studying with John Hope Franklin, Daniel Boorstin, and Neil Harris, all significant scholars, creative thinkers, and fine writers. As president of the history graduate students, I represented students from the Social Science Division in seminars with President Edward Levi, who was meeting with students and faculty to discuss the future of the university. Levi, who went on to serve as Gerald Ford's attorney general, was a deep and provocative thinker; it was exciting to sit in those seminars.

My years of research and reading gave me the skills to understand the context and shape of historical events. I have a better understanding of contemporary American problems—religious, social, and political—because of my studies.

Finally, through my time in graduate school, I became wedded to the need for thorough and unbiased research. It's considered a hallmark of my fiction, and whenever my books are praised for it, I credit the University of Chicago for teaching me to value it.

ACKNOWLEDGMENTS

I have incurred many debts to many people in the process of writing this dissertation. It would be impossible to list them all here, and I intend no disrespect to those whose names I omit. I can only mention those whose help had the most immediate bearing on completing this rather arduous work.

I am obligated to no one more than Donald M. Scott, now at North Carolina State University. Don has given me persistent advice and encouragement. His own knowledge of this period and the New England ministers is superb; he first imbued me with an appreciation for their minds and aspirations. Even after leaving Chicago for North Carolina, Don continued to direct this essay. I would probably still be working on it if not for his help.

George W. Stocking and Neil Harris, both of the University of Chicago, also gave me valuable help. I would like to thank Neil for editing parts of this dissertation. I have not read any better writer of history and am grateful to him for sharing some of his skill with me. To George I owe not so much help with this essay, but the discovery of the excitement inhering in historical research, and much appreciated assistance in the early stages of my graduate study.

Librarians did more to make this work possible than any other single group. I want to mention in particular Harvey Arnold, formerly Divinity School librarian at the University of Chicago. Mr. Arnold knew American religious bibliography by heart and directed me to my most important sources. I am grateful, too, to Tom Owens, also of the University of Chicago libraries; to Julia Kellogg at Phillips–Andover Preparatory School; and to the librarians at Yale and Andover-Newton Theological Seminary, who all gave me much cheerful assistance.

Drs. Charles and Jane Park, in Nashville, Tennessee, very generously opened their home to me, allowing me to use their fascinating collection of Park family papers. I would also like to thank the Ford Foundation for their fellowship assistance.

The technical assistance is in some ways the least important part of a humanities dissertation. A work like this is a very lonely experience. No one but the author is really familiar with the exact problems or sources she is working on. One spends long hours alone, progress is slow, encouragement and advice difficult to obtain. Without the support of good friends, I do not think my spirits could have sustained the ardor of this labor. In particular, I owe much to Kathleen Dunkum, whose love carried me through many difficult times and still supports me. Isabel Thompson has done more for me than I can say; few people are ever fortunate enough to have such a friend. The other members of the Agnes Bletch Collective—Helen Bergman Dittmer, Marilyn Martin, and Mimi Lowinger—also gave me much cheer in dark times. Emma B. Pitcher, now Dean of Students in the University of Chicago's Graduate School of Business, has been a good friend and constant supporter of this dissertation; I also owe to her many kind offices in obtaining a graduate fellowship for me, and for smoothing many bureaucratic paths within the University.

I must also mention my mother, Mary Edwards Paretsky. This dissertation is dedicated in part to her, as a substitute for her own uncompleted work. To my father, David Paretsky, I owe much which cannot be detailed or repaid.

I cannot close without grateful thanks to Carol Jean Brown, who typed the manuscript. She did a beautiful job, and won my everlasting respect for the way in which she threaded between footnotes, text, and bibliography.

INTRODUCTION

❖ ❖ ❖

New England religious orthodoxy has fallen into ill-repute over the years. Its descendants crop up in the twentieth century as fundamentalists, a strongly anti-intellectual group. But it is possible to go back to New England in 1810 and find a quite noteworthy band of intellectual Calvinists. They joined together to found a seminary at Andover, Massachusetts, which produced respected and reputable scholars. They tried to take in the compass of human learning: classics, languages, biblical studies, philosophy, and even natural science, in addition to the orthodox theology which they preached.

The men who founded the seminary belonged to a new type of Christian intellectual. Unlike their predecessors, for whom all paths of knowledge led to theology, these men explored learning for the sake of scholarship as well as religion. Because their work revolved around twin centers of faith and knowledge, this new type can be called the Christian scholar.

A number of factors contributed to their appearance. One was the Congregational tradition of an erudite ministry, which drew its clergymen naturally to study. Another came from the institutionalization of ministerial education at the turn of the century. The theological seminary at Andover provided both an impetus and the time for its early faculty members to concentrate on the emerging disciplines of philology and textual criticism.

While a devotion to these new fields became common to New England professors, not all devotees were Christian scholars. For the Liberals at Harvard, religion had lost the ability to regenerate the hearts of men; in its place they put literature. As Lewis Simpson points out in *The Man of Letters in New England and the South*, the Liberals "set up an image of the Boston ministry as an order with a distinctive vocation to literature."[1] The Unitarians and Transcendentalists came out of the Boston literary societies inspired by that calling. Christian scholars emerged from Orthodoxy.

Although such scholars appeared at most New England colleges, notably Yale, Amherst, and Brown, it was at Andover that a tension between faith and learning became most apparent. The colleges taught law, geology, and literature, as well as theology. So much energy went into so many areas of study that it is difficult to see the effect of a knowledge explosion in biblical studies on collegiate faculties. At Andover, all work centered on theology and the Bible. Changes in any aspect of these two fields immediately came to the faculty's attention and was reflected in their work. Andover can be used as a microcosm for a process going on throughout New England.

The Christian scholars' work took place in the larger setting of New England intellectual activity. Andover engaged in many joint ventures with Yale, Harvard, Brown, and Amherst. Despite theological differences, all five schools relied on the unity of reason and revelation; all understood perception as taught by the Scottish realists; and all analyzed natural science and philosophy from Baconian principles.

The Congregationalists had created a great synthesis of all branches of thought. This was not a self-conscious act, but stemmed from their perception of God's immanence in the entire Universe. They called the science which defined human response to the immanent Deity moral philosophy.

Loosely speaking, moral philosophy taught "men their duties and the reasons of [them]." A University of Pennsylvania catalog defined it that way in 1790. They added that moral philosophy included duty to humanity (ethics); the subdivisions of ethics which treated man's physical and mental equipment (physiology and psychology); and the existence of God and the immortality of the soul (natural theology). Moral philosophy also included duty to the family (economics), and to the state (politics).[2] In short, moral philosophy stood for all ideas on mind, nature, society, and religion which the Calvinists studied. It was taught as a separate course at almost every college in this country up to the Civil War.[3]

During the first half of the nineteenth century, this great synthesis broke down. After the Civil War, the great colleges of New England— Yale, Amherst, Brown, Williams—passed into the control of men still Christian, but no longer Calvinist. Andover followed the same course. However, the men who took over these schools were not strangers to New England, heretics who sprang up like the gourd in the night. They were students of the Calvinists themselves, but they had no use for their teachers' theology or philosophy.

The take-over of institutions by men hostile to their predecessors has been documented by Daniel Day Williams, in *The Andover Liberals*, and Laurence Veysey, in the *Emergence of the American University*.[4] The present study traces the process up to the point of take-over. It explores the intellectual events which stripped moral philosophy of the vitality it held for the Christian scholars.

A number of forces undermined this intellectual system. Prominent among them were German progress in biblical and linguistic studies, and English advances in geology. Yet a study of the Christian scholars quickly reveals their intense interest in these fields. Their system did not collapse from the onslaught of new knowledge. On the contrary, they embraced the new developments in European learning eagerly, reinterpreting them through the filter of New England orthodoxy. Ultimately, their very eagerness for involvement in the frontiers of learning caused their downfall. Their students remained interested in new European ideas and methods, but discarded evangelical Calvinism.

The first chapter sets the stage for the Christian scholars. It describes Andover's founding, and explores in greater detail the intellectual system to which its early faculty subscribed. The seminary was not established as a center of learning but to promote evangelical Christianity; Christian scholars appeared as a by-product. The seminary's founders were responding in part to the Liberals' take-over of Harvard; they wanted to train young men to defend orthodoxy.

The metaphor of the seminary as fortress can also be seen in another way: it protected the faculty from the onslaughts of the world. It provided them with a sanctuary in which they pursued scholarship. Despite their firm espousal of the need for preachers, they did not enjoy pastoral life. A parish meant distracting duties, and a life lived perpetually in a fishbowl.

In 1846, the New Haven preacher Leonard Bacon expressed a degree of bitterness towards scholars who were protected from the bitter winds of the world. Participating in the ordination of Yale's President-elect Theodore Dwight Woolsey, Bacon mourned Woolsey's inexperience. He would make a better president and minister, Bacon proclaimed, had he known the harshness of life in a parish ministry, where men learned "to endure the harness of a good soldier of Christ."[5]

The seminary drew its early faculty from men committed to orthodoxy. It tried to find great preachers. But the trustees also found men who wished to exchange the unpleasant realities of parish life for the challenges of literature. They developed Andover into a center of learning almost despite the wishes of her trustees. Chapter two describes how true scholarship came to Andover with a brilliant young New Haven preacher, Moses Stuart. Stuart undertook the study of Hebrew and German with a driving energy. He quickly became an authority in the new science of biblical criticism. He used his expertise to defend orthodoxy from the Liberals at Harvard, proving the value of European studies to Congregational New England.

The debates with the Liberals, or Unitarians, as they came to be called, took place primarily between 1819 and 1824. They have been the subject of much scholarly attention, primarily from people eager to pin-point the end of New England Calvinism. Chapter two explores these debates from another viewpoint, seeing in them the strengthening of intellectual Calvinism. They convinced Andover's trustees, and many other Congregation-alists, that the new learning had merit. They provided the impetus for the flowering of intellectual Calvinism in the 1830s and '40s.

Chapter three discusses the mature expression of Christian scholar-ship at Andover in the 1840s. Stuart's students had come of age and as-sumed prominent positions on the faculty. Chief among these men were Edwards A. Park and Bela Bates Edwards, who taught theology and sacred literature, respectively. The controversies with the Unitarians had died down; Park and Edwards spent most of their time pursuing common inter-ests with men at Harvard and Yale, traveling to Germany, and maintaining a series of erudite scholarly journals.

The distance between the seminary faculty and parish ministers widened in this period. While Edwards claimed he directed his literary activities primarily to parish ministers, most of his readers were fellow professors. Furthermore, more and more of the faculty had little or no parochial ex-perience. Park served as pastor of a church for two years; Edwards never tended a parish. Stuart was hired in 1810 because of his brilliant preaching, Edwards in 1836 for his proficiency in Hebrew.

The young faculty were acutely aware of the seminary's mission to train evangelical preachers. However, they also stressed the value of the intellect for Christians, a bold proclamation in revival-conscious New England. Park summarized the new faculty's beliefs in his famous 1850 sermon, "Theology of the Intellect and That of the Feelings."

Chapter four shows the intricate manner in which Christian scholars combined new European learning with moral philosophy. Developments in history and philology took most of their attention. Andover produced some notable biblical scholars in this period, including Edward Robinson, whose Palestinian journals are still read today.

German biblical critics in the 1840s were primarily Hegelians. They treated the Bible as a myth, and were alarmingly materialistic. Andover men saw their job as one of christening dangerous German ideas to make them useful for New England. However, in the process, the Christian schol-ars jettisoned their total literal reliance on sacred scriptures. Unconsciously, they tied biblical interpretation to historical research, rather than the eye of faith. The process created major cracks in the system of moral philosophy.

Chapter five traces a similar process in natural science. It describes a group of Christian scientists, educated at Andover and Yale, who main-tained close ties to these institutions. Edward Hitchcock and Benjamin Silliman, geologists at Amherst and Yale, were the best known scientists among this group. Their work in geology broke ground for the new science in America. They conducted the earliest surveys of Connecticut and Massa-chusetts, helped explore New York, collected fossils which they recognized as vestiges of life far earlier than that recorded in the Bible.

At the same time, Hitchcock and Silliman were evangelical Christians anxious to demonstrate the divine Designer's presence in the rocks. "Scientific reputation was not the culmination of my ambition," Hitchcock wrote late in life, "but the higher object of making science illustrate the Divine Glory."[6] Hitchcock contributed numerous articles to Andover's literary journals which tried to unite the God of revelation with the God who had created a universe untold millennia earlier. The Christian scientist, like the Christian scholars, ended up evaluating the Bible by disciplines alien to it. The scholars used human history, the scientists natural history, but both separated the Bible from other fields of study.

The final chapter describes the outcome of this separation after the Civil War. Park's and Edwards' students, sent to Germany to enjoy the best fruits of European study, abandoned New England Calvinism. They returned to Andover as faculty members, and drove their seniors from the seminary. They abandoned the great synthesis integrating New England theology with philosophy and natural science. Instead, they subordinated the Bible to the new God, evolution. New England theology had been a consistent, well-reasoned system. The new men, known as the Andover Liberals, discarded reason for emotion. Where an earlier generation always turned first to the Bible to understand a Christian response to life, the Liberals used the Bible as a last resort. Whatever common human emotions declared to be true, was true, they said. If the Bible disagreed, they abandoned the Bible.

Those who still relied on the sacred text were no longer welcome at Andover, or other major New England schools. They retreated first to Oberlin, and then to the Bible colleges of the South, where they kept up a vain rear-guard action against evolution, and the new theologies which were tied to it. They were soon ignored by those in the major institutions such as Harvard and Yale. Andover itself, vitiated by controversies over the new theology in the 1890s, could no longer attract enough students to support itself. In 1908, exactly a century after its founding, the seminary merged with its early enemy, Harvard. Today, it maintains a separate campus in Newton Center, Massachusetts, but awards degrees through Harvard's Divinity School. The old seminary buildings in Andover are used by Phillips Academy there.

The choice Edwards, Park, and Hitchcock faced was between tying the Bible to other modern disciplines, or not participating fully in the world of scholarship. They took the first option, which meant opening New England

Calvinism to attacks from those who mythologized the Bible. The second choice would have kept Christians from participation in the knowledge explosion of the 1840s. Either decision ultimately spelled the end of intellectual Calvinism. But the Christian scholars chose to explore and embrace the new worlds unfolding before them. They enriched those worlds. While we no longer remember their names, their impact is present in every institution where they taught, from the Pacific Theological Seminary in Berkeley, to the Chicago Theological Seminary on Chicago's south side, to Yale, Brown, Amherst, and the other great centers of New England learning.

The Background of the Christian Scholar

But how are men to call upon him in whom
they have not believed? And how are they to believe in him
of whom they have never heard? And how are they to hear
without a preacher? And how can men preach
unless they are sent?
— *Romans 10:14*

In his 1852 apology for the New England divinity, the Calvinist E. A. Park praised his theological forebears for the virtues, both practical and intellectual, which they brought to their work. "We might extol them as diligent readers," Park said. The theologian Samuel Hopkins (1721–1803) studied twelve hours every day "for more than half a century," while his contemporary Nathaniel Emmons "remained like a fixture in his parsonage study, and like his brethren read 'the books which are books.'" Still another eighteenth-century Calvinist, Dr. West, "sat near his library so long, that his feet wore away the wood-work in one part of his room, and left this enduring memorial of his sedentary habit."[1]

These men followed a Congregational impulse going back to the time of Elizabeth I, the desire for a learned ministry. Hopkins, Emmons, and West all attended college. West, in particular, was an outstanding classical scholar.[2] Nathaniel Emmons had an "ardent thirst for knowledge" and so "gained his father's consent that he should commense a course of classical study."[3]

Adept as they were in classical literature, it was not as important to these Christians as their souls' salvation. For Sprague and other historians, a biography always centered on its subject's sense of a saving conversion. Hopkins, in his autobiographical sketch, devoted considerable attention to his own religious awakening.[4] Since every other decision of his adult life, including his career as a minister, related directly or indirectly to his conversion, it is not surprising that he devoted almost a fifth of his autobiography to it. The rest of the essay concerned problems relating to his career. Nowhere did he mention the classical scholarship in which he was so competent. He did not consider it important, except as a tool in understanding the Bible.

Hopkins' *System of Doctrines*, the theological system he published near the end of his life, made heavy demands on its readers' intelligence, but it was not an abstract exercise. The New England theologians were practical. They wanted to bring men to a sense of sin and show them the means of grace. Hopkins' views on regeneration, which differed from older New England Calvinist thought, evolved during several decades of practical experience in revivals and pamphlet wars.[5] He first published his ideas on the causes of sin in a controversy with Jonathan Mayhew.[6]

Hopkins and his contemporaries unified literature and theology by subordinating one to the other. Well versed in philosophy, particularly in the work of Locke, they incorporated his ideas into their theological thought. They did not produce separate literary or philosophical treatises. The assumption that other areas of knowledge could be integrated into theology remained with Hopkins' heirs when they founded Andover in 1808.

Hopkins developed a following among a large group of Massachusetts clergy. They continued to refine his ideas, and to quarrel with the Old Calvinists. However, around 1805, the two groups began discussing uniting in founding a theological seminary. The Liberals' take-over of Harvard posed a serious enough threat to Orthodox Calvinism that the two parties thought it time to settle their differences and join against the University's influence. In addition, they found the existing structures for ministerial education inadequate and hoped to improve them.

Jedidiah Morse, a Trinitarian Calvinist in Charlestown, and a member of the Harvard Board of Overseers, first considered the need for a separate institution. Hopkinsians and Old Calvinists ought to unite against the dangers emanating from Cambridge, he urged in his journal *The Panoplist*. A letter to him from Yale president Timothy Dwight in July, 1805, shared Morse's fear of the waxing Liberal influence at Harvard. Dwight wrote his approval of Morse's proposed institution, voicing his concern over the continued separation of the two parties in the controversy with the Liberals. The Harvard presidency stood vacant. Dwight feared that that position, too, would be filled by a Liberal, adding that "the election of Mr. Ware has occasioned very serious sensations" in Connecticut.[7]

Henry Ware's election to the Hollis Chair of Divinity in 1805 had occasioned considerable sensation in Boston, too. As a Liberal Congregationalist, Ware denied that "Jesus Christ is God, equal to the Father." Since the Hollis Professor's duties included instructing aspirants to the ministry in a fifth year of study (after they completed the regular college course), Ware's election was a serious blow to the Trinitarians.

The following year, as Dwight had feared, another Liberal was named president. Samuel Webber's election to that office particularly galled Eliphalet Pearson, who had been acting president and not unnaturally hoped for the permanent position. Pearson, the Hancock Professor of Hebrew, was a Trinitarian Calvinist from the town of Andover some thirty miles north of Boston. He had been principal of Phillips Academy there until coming to Harvard. When he resigned his chair to protest Webber's election, Andover voted to show their support for him by giving him a house.[8]

Convinced that "the interests of evangelical religion, so perilled [sic] at the University, called for some new and more vigorous efforts for their defence,"[9] Pearson supported Morse's seminary scheme. Pearson persuaded the wealthy Samuel Abbot of Andover to draw up a will leaving the bulk of his estate to Phillips Academy to establish a chair in theology. Some people thought Pearson unscrupulous in his efforts to get money for the seminary;[10] others said that the whole seminary scheme was designed "to provide for the ex-Professor."[11]

Pearson and Morse were Old Calvinists. At the same time that they were trying to establish a chair of Christian Theology at Phillips, the Hopkinsians were planning a seminary at Newbury Port, Massachusetts, about a day's ride from Andover. One of their leaders, Dr. Samuel Spring, hoped to preserve the special doctrines of the Calvinist minority by establishing a school whose graduates would preach them. He persuaded three of his wealthy parishioners to endow such an institution. Leonard Woods (1774–1852), pastor of the Newbury Port Church, agreed to fill the chair of Christian theology.

Spring's motives were only partly doctrinaire: he also sought a better way to teach young men preparing for the ministry. In the eighteenth century, ministerial aspirants had attached themselves to some divine whom they admired. He would form a small school whose members met several times a week for discussion. Leonard Woods' training with Charles Backus followed this pattern.

Backus met with students once a week on Wednesday night, when he questioned them on the meaning of a previously assigned passage in Scripture. One evening, for example, the topic was St. John's assertion that "God is love." "Mr. Church," Backus asked, "how is it consistent with this love, that God should make any miserable?" The student answered that "the good of the whole intelligent creation requires that the Sin should be punished."

Other questions followed, on the most perfect example of this love (in Jesus Christ), the nature of the atonement, and so on. In this catechetical fashion, students learned the details of the New England theology. They had a similar session on Sunday evening; once a week Backus lectured to them. This was the extent of their formal training. Everything else they learned through private reading.[12]

The number of men holding such schools was decreasing by the end of the eighteenth century. Spring himself had conducted one, but no longer had the energy to do so. He sought a more reliable vehicle for theological instruction than the part-time attention of a busy parish minister.[13]

Interest in founding a seminary coincided with an intense concern among pious Christians for the cause of missions. When Spring tried to get money from the wealthy Newbury Port merchant William Norris, Norris told him that his money was going to missions. Woods pointed out that training ministers of the Gospel would be the best possible gift to the cause of missions, and Norris promptly pledged $10,000 to the seminary.[14] Abbot left his money to Phillips because he desired "the defense and promotion of the Christian Religion, by increasing the number of learned and able Defenders of the truth of the Gospel of Christ."[15] In later years he was fond of pointing at the seminary he had helped build, saying, "I hope it will be the means of saving millions of souls."[16]

Morse found out that the Hopkinsians were planning a seminary through Leonard Woods, who edited his evangelical journal, *The Panoplist*. Morse immediately saw the opportunity for the joint Old Calvinist-Hopkinsian school he desired. Through Woods, who was Spring's protégé (Woods edited another periodical, *The Massachusetts Home Missionary Journal*, for the Hopkinsian), he began urging the latter to unite with the Old Calvinists at Andover. The Newbury Port group were afraid, as Spring said, "of being swallowed up and making a grave for Hopkinsianism by union."[17] The Hopkinsian raised every conceivable objection to union, including legal questions which Morse had to clear up in the Massachusetts General Assembly. After almost two years of negotiations, Spring finally signed a set of "Principles of Union" with Pearson, on the condition that Woods be the first professor of Christian theology.

The "Principles of Union" announced that the two groups would prepare a creed for the seminary to which its faculty had to swear annually.[18] Faculty and students could belong either to Presbyterian or Congregational churches, but they had to affirm the teachings of the Westminster Shorter Catechism. In addition, the Hopkinsians would construct an associate creed for the professors they appointed. The founders hoped that requiring an annual avowal of these doctrines would preserve the school from the kind of change that had occurred at Harvard. Abbot, in fact, made his bequest contingent on the chairholder's espousal of all the points in the Shorter Catechism.[19]

The divergent types creating Andover shared one object: the defense and promotion of Orthodox Congregationalism. One might fancifully picture the seminary as a fortress for defending orthodoxy. The faculty made up the first line of fortifications, guarding the New England divinity through the time-honored means of sermons and pamphlets. At the same time, they engaged in a new activity: the mass training of young men to preach the Gospel in foreign lands and the western United States.

The Seminary's commitment to evangelism can be seen in the careers of its graduates. Of the 981 men graduated between 1811 and 1850, 255, or 23 percent, spent some part of their careers in home or foreign mission work. They passed the rest of their working lives in settled pastorates in the United States. Sixty-seven, or 7 percent, devoted their entire lives to foreign missions (two were shot in Sumatra) and 53 to home missions. In all, 38 percent of these men spent all or part of their careers in missions. Of the remaining, 438, or 44 percent, worked only as parish ministers; 95 served as both ministers and teachers; 60 taught either in academies or colleges; and 78 served as agents for various evangelical societies.[20]

These figures argue powerfully that training ministers and missionaries, not educating scholars, was the seminary's primary goal. Indeed, only a handful of intellectuals of any note came out of Andover. Christian scholars emerged among the faculty as a side effect of trying to equip their students with the best skills available for confronting heathenism, paganism, Romanism, or heresies bred closer to home.

The trustees did not focus on skill in language and literature in choosing their faculty. Because they were to serve the cause of God in so many different ways—teaching, preaching, studying, conducting polemical debates—the trustees sought ministers of unimpeachable orthodoxy and proven energy to teach at their seminary. The faculty were educated as well as possible in the New England colleges of the 1790s, but they were not scholars. Indeed, as Eliphalet Pearson's short career at Andover demonstrates, the seminary had no use for scholars in its early days.

Pearson had been a Hebraist at Harvard for twenty years before coming to Andover. In the *Annals of the American Pulpit*, he is remembered as a perfectionist in language study who was dissatisfied with less than that high standard in his students.[21] This attitude stood him in poor stead at Andover. Woods said of him that "his manner of teaching and his idea of government and social intercourse were not agreeable to pious young men" preparing to preach.[22] The seminarians, enthusiastic in their call to the ministry, valued their devotional exercises and spent a lot of time at them. The free style of these gatherings embarrassed Pearson. He found the students more eager for their prayers than for the study of sacred literature.[23] A high degree of mutual dissatisfaction resulted in Pearson's resigning his office at the end of a year. Although he remained president of the Board of Trustees until his death in 1826, he did not take much interest in seminary affairs or in the gospel ministry. He devoted the rest of his life to historical researches.

Pearson was a scholar, but not a Christian one. His concern with the ultimate questions of religion was not tied to the studies he prosecuted; his tenure at the seminary, where these questions held the central place, was an unhappy one. Other early members of the faculty were Christians, but not Christian scholars.

Among the three initial chairholders when the seminary opened, only Pearson had any pretence to scholarship. Neither Leonard Woods, Abbot Professor of Christian Theology, nor Edward Griffin, the Bartlett Professor of Sacred Rhetoric, studied literature for its sake alone. Nor did the seminary want men who did.

The trustees expected the professor of sacred rhetoric to be a model of oratorical ability. As a teacher he was to present the principles of Christianity "homiletically and rhetorically," teaching young men to prepare and deliver sermons. The Bartlett professor also addressed the important question of how to conduct revivals of religion. He was not to teach the principles of exegesis or the doctrine of revelation: these were the province of the Brown and Abbot professors. The Bartlett professor's job was to "assist" young men "in teaching those doctrines in a proper manner to others."[24] It was of utmost importance that a man renowned both for his orthodoxy and his oratorical abilities be found for the chair.

Edward Griffin, the first Bartlett professor, had studied theology with Jonathan Edwards the younger in New Haven. Under Edwards he developed a firm belief both in revivals and orthodox Calvinism, ideas which he practiced during his tenure at the First Presbyterian Church in Newark from 1801–1809. He was hired by Andover because of his reputation for powerful preaching. The pulpit ministry remained his first love, and he shortly resigned his chair to become pastor of the Park Street Church in Boston. Griffin's extreme religious opinions made him unpopular throughout his career, even leading to charges of extravagance at evangelical Andover; his departure did not distress the seminary.[25]

The trustees next selected Ebenezer Porter of Washington, Connecticut, to fill the Bartlett chair. In his Washington pastorate, Porter had assisted a number of theological students in preparing for the ministry. These young men helped bring his reputation to Andover. In addition, Porter's preaching and character were of the highest calibre. At the time that he came to Andover, he had turned down a call from the prestigious First Church in New Haven. During his tenure at Andover, the University of Vermont, South Carolina College, Hamilton College, Middlebury, and Dartmouth all asked him to be their presidents. He believed so firmly in the seminary's twin goals of training missionaries and defending orthodoxy that he refused all these offers, along with the divinity professorship at Yale, to remain at Andover.

Porter had no more than the usual acquaintance of his day with classical literature. The trustees hired him for his character and preaching, not for his learning. Nor did he, while at Andover, become a scholar: he subordinated study to his work as a preacher and a teacher of preachers.

One of his students characterized him as reading

history and biography with this view—to have read them as a preacher—to have read them as I imagine Cicero would have recommended, who would have the orator know every thing— but subordinate all knowledge to his life task . . .[26]

The trustees zealously watched over the school in its early days. No matter how able any man's scholarship might be, his religious opinions were much more important. The story of the Rev. James Murdock is a case in point. Murdock assisted Porter in sacred rhetoric from 1819 to 1824 and served as the first professor of ecclesiastical history from 1824 to 1828. The trustees forced him to resign in 1828, after an extended controversy which went all the way to the Supreme Court of Massachusetts. Murdock had written that the Atonement was symbolic, not actual,[27] contradicting the Westminster Shorter Catechism. After leaving Andover, Murdock moved to New Haven, where he studied church history on his own.

Leonard Woods had the longest tenure of the early professors and achieved one of the widest reputations. He came to the seminary at its opening, remaining in the Abbot chair until forced to resign in 1846 at the age of 72. One suspects from the accounts of the seminary's founding that Pearson and Morse found him a pleasant, disingenuous figure through whom they could bring the Newbury Port money to Andover. As a compromise candidate for the Abbot professorship, he was acceptable to both Hopkinsians and Old Calvinists, an indication of how ill-defined his theological views were.

Because his desire for unity among the Congregationalists was stronger than his devotion to any particular doctrine, he straddled beliefs of both groups. He held conservative ideas on innate depravity and allied himself with Old Calvinists on the means of regeneration.

Woods exemplifies the educated minister of his day. He attended Harvard, where he came under conviction concerning matters of religion in 1794. After three years of indecision, he decided to prepare for the ministry. He studied for three months with Dr. Charles Backus, then read the masters of Puritan theology on his own for a year. Like most of his contemporaries, his self discipline was prodigious. Rising before dawn, he prayed and studied until noon, then took some exercise before reading again until late afternoon. He made it his business to keep up with Congregational journals as well as the Bible and ecclesiastical history.[28] He was well acquainted with the Common Sense philosophy which was the hallmark of New England thought during this period and used it to address theological questions.

Woods was not an innovative thinker. Like the older style of educated minister, he read Edwards, Calvin, and other masters, hoping to clarify their thought in his own writing, not trying to develop original ideas. He did not act from lack of interest in modern intellectual events: throughout his life he kept abreast of the changing currents in foreign and American biblical scholarship. He read Greek, Latin, and German, and could, of course, read the Scriptures in Hebrew, but he used these skills only as tools in the cause of evangelical religion. Evangelism bounded his universe. During his life, Woods edited two journals and founded a third.

All three were directed at home missionaries. His other publications were limited to his disputes with the Unitarians on depravity, with Taylor on the will, and to his Andover lectures, which he published as a systematic theology. Woods was never a profound student of any subject.

Devotion to the gospel ministry characterized all the early faculty at Andover. Yet Moses Stuart (1780–1852), who replaced Pearson as Brown professor in 1810, added another dimension to his calling, taking advantage of the facilities Andover offered a serious student of literature. Using the seminary library, publishers in the town of Andover who were devoted to the seminary's cause,[29] and time spent primarily in teaching and reading, he became one of the foremost biblical scholars in America.

Stuart was born in 1780 into a Connecticut farming family. Like many other ministers, he originally contemplated another profession. He was admitted to the New Haven bar in 1802, where a brilliant career was prophesied for him. However, instead of going into practice, he accepted a teaching position at Yale, and there fell under the influence of the powerfully persuasive Timothy Dwight. Stuart was converted and licensed to preach in 1803. In 1806, he accepted a call to the First Church in New Haven.[30]

When Pearson resigned from the Brown professorship, the trustees traveled throughout New England and the Middle Atlantic states, listening to preachers of note in order to find a suitable successor. In his three years at the First Church, Stuart had developed a considerable reputation as a pulpit orator of great skill: two hundred persons were joined to the church during that time. Dr. Spring's choice settled on Stuart. Spring approached Dwight, who told him that the young man could not be spared. "We want no man who can be spared," Spring retorted, and prevailed on Stuart to seek the approval of his church for dismission.[31]

When he came to Andover, Stuart knew Greek and Latin, but his acquaintance with Hebrew stopped at the alphabet and a few psalms. Indeed, he scrupled to accept the invitation because of his ignorance. "If I go to Andover, I must go there in the first place, as your pupil," he wrote Pearson in the fall of 1809. "My knowledge of Hebrew at present amounts to nothing . . ."[32]

In hiring an unqualified young man of proven energy and talent to fill a new professorship, the trustees followed a practice common in this period. The difficulty of finding an able scholar who was also an evangelical Christian would have been enormous, whereas a man who did one thing well could probably do anything well. Similarly, when Dwight sought someone for the newly-created chair in chemistry at Yale in 1802, his choice lighted on another lawyer, Benjamin Silliman. Silliman, like Stuart, rapidly made up his deficiencies, and became a leading authority in natural science.

Stuart's energy and intellect were prodigious. During his first three years at Andover, he taught himself Hebrew and put together a grammar for teaching his students. He imported Hebrew type, setting up the first American press for printing Hebrew manuscripts.[33] His Hebrew grammar, first published in 1813, went through eight editions before his death, and was reissued until 1928. At the same time that he was mastering Hebrew, Stuart discovered that Germans were the modern experts in hermeneutics and taught himself their language.[34]

Stuart died in 1852. During the intervening forty years he wrote some 2,000 folio pages, including sermons, political essays (he was vigorous in the anti-slavery movement), commentaries on the Epistles, and many different works on Hebrew and Old Testament scholarship. He was enthusiastic about the seminary's sending out missionaries to the world, but his own calling was to study: he privately thought the parochial ministry a handicap to a bright young man. When Edward Everett of Harvard, with whom he studied German, was called to a parish ministry, Stuart urged him not to accept it. He wrote to

> take the liberty to express my doubt, whether you ought to stop in your present course, so much short, as your parochial duties will compel you to do. You will be obliged to cut off many pleasant studies, which at your time of life, will be a severe trial.[35]

There is no telling what drove Stuart to his initial interest in biblical scholarship. It may have been the proximity to Harvard, where the new Dexter professor, Andrews Norton, was using German critical methods to further the Liberal cause. Stuart certainly used Hebrew scholarship and philology in general to defend Calvinism against the Liberals. He also used philology as an aid to piety: his moving sermons on the Lord's Supper were often built around a philological discourse. And he studied languages and literature from an interest he found inherent in these subjects.

As the German scholar August Tholuck wrote of Stuart in 1834, his studies never diverted him from the fundamental doctrines of the Calvinist confession.[36] At the same time, however, they did change some of his attitudes. He came to reject, in part, a literal interpretation of the Bible which was fundamental to Calvinist thought. This erosion was subtle and by no means through-going. When geology explicitly threatened the authenticity of the Scriptures, Stuart insisted on their literal truth. But when discussing the authenticity of various texts, he came to believe that only the Bible's meaning was inspired, not its actual words. He also questioned the authorship of some of the Psalms, parts of Isaiah, and Genesis, which he thought Moses had compiled from different ancient accounts, not written himself.

The opening of Andover pleased almost no one but its founders. Hopkinsians like Dr. Emmons feared that their peculiar doctrines were not spelled out clearly enough in the Creed. Strict Calvinists thought the Creed conceded too much to the Hopkinsians, and would have been better satisfied with a separate Calvinist institution.[37] And as Morse had made no secret of his desire to use Andover to "bring about a *counter-revolution* in our University,"[38] Harvard opened fire on the school before it was a month old.

Much of the hostility centered on the seminary's creed. The Old Calvinists required the faculty to swear to the Westminster Shorter Catechism; the Hopkinsians added some doctrines of their own in an associate creed which the associate faculty (the Brown and Bartlett professors, whom they appointed) had to affirm. Seminary statutes required that each professor, "on the day of his inauguration," make "and subscribe the solemn declaration of his faith in divine Revelation and in the fundamental doc-trines of the Gospel of Christ" as expressed in the Shorter Catechism.[39] In the early years of the seminary, the faculty adhered strictly to the creed. Murdock was fired not because he lacked piety, but because his teaching on the atonement differed from the Shorter Catechism. Even in later years, the professors still had to make an annual profession to the trustees and a public confession every five years.[40]

The creed was written as part of the defensive fortress of Orthodoxy; the Liberals attacked it as a medieval vestige. Writing in their organ, the *Monthly Anthology and Boston Review*, for November, 1808, they said that the document aroused "their most solemn objections." The existence of a creed would constrict the inquiry after truth by forcing the inquirer to subscribe to a limited set of religious principles. Doctrines should be evident directly from the Bible, the Liberals contended. To bolster them with a creed meant that Andover did not have faith that Jesus and the Apostles had made a full statement of Christianity.[41]

Worse than this, the Anthology wrote, the creed went against the spirit of individual conscience which was the bulwark of Protestantism. Andover's confession of faith was "a yoke too galling to be endured by any man, who has felt the difficulty of investigating truth, a yoke which neither we nor our fathers were able to bear." They saw an "institution rising among us [in this age of religious liberty] which would have disgraced the bigotry of the Dark Ages."[42]

The language typifies the intemperate debating style of the times, but the charge is not without interest. Initially the creed did not trouble the Seminary faculty. They swore to it faithfully every year and avowed it publicly every five. But as Stuart became more engrossed in his biblical studies, the document began to confine him. The trustees did try to "limit the inquiry after truth," as the Liberals put it, so that they could adhere to the creed. Stuart was forced at one point to fight for the right to study German literature.

The Andover faculty shared a common intellectual ground with New England schools of every theological persuasion. All relied on three major assumptions on how to organize knowledge of the universe. The first, and most important of these predicated a fundamental unity between reason and revelation.

When Levi Frisbie accepted the first Alford Professorship of Natural Religion, Moral Philosophy, and Civil Polity at Harvard in 1817, he agreed to demonstrate the existence of a Deity, or first cause, to describe the duties of man to his maker, and of men to each other, interpreting the whole with remarks, showing the coincidence between the doctrines of revelation and the dictates of reason in these important points; and lastly, notwithstanding this coincidence, to state the absolute necessity and vast utility of a divine revelation.[43]

It is difficult to distinguish these ideas from those professed at Andover at the same time. Consider the charge to the Andover faculty for the discussion of natural theology. The seminary constitution required the Abbot professor to include this topic in his lectures on Christian theology. He should demonstrate the existence, attributes, and providence of God; the soul's immortality; the "obligations of man to his Maker"; and the social duties of men to each other. The whole discussion should be

> interspersed with remarks on the coincidence between the dictates of reason and the doctrines of revelation . . . ; and, notwithstanding such coincidence, the necessity and utility of a divine revelation stated.[44]

The Liberals did not question the reality of divine revelation. They resisted efforts to overthrow it by rationalism, biblical criticism, or geology. They set themselves in strong opposition to the Deists, those who accepted natural religion but not revelation.[45] Henry Ware, the Hollis Professor of Divinity whose election precipitated Andover's founding, was amazed that "some of the German divines do not believe in miracles and yet believe in Christianity."[46] They might reject certain scriptural passages as interpolations, but the Liberals were not rationalists. The difference between the Alford and the Abbot professors was one of emphasis: at Harvard, reason had greater authority in interpreting revelation than Andover gave it.

The relation between reason and revelation lay at the heart of the thorniest controversies in the early nineteenth century. According to the Orthodox, the Liberals raised human thought above the divine Word. Leonard Woods engaged in a fierce exchange with Yale's Nathaniel William Taylor on the same grounds. Taylor had challenged the traditional Calvinist doctrine of total depravity, asserting that men could keep from sinning, although it was certain that they would not. Woods claimed that this doctrine undermined scriptural authority.

In a series of "Letters to Young Ministers" written for the Spirit of the Pilgrims (a New Haven publication) in 1832, Woods outlined what he considered the appropriate balance between reason and revelation. He believed that Taylor had upset this delicate relationship in order to establish a false doctrine. For the Protestant, Woods wrote, "the word of God is the only and sufficient rule of our faith and practice." If we are inquiring into the truth, as soon as we ascertain "what God teaches us in his word, we have come to the end of our inquiry; — we have attained to the knowledge of the truth."[47]

From this biblical basis, Woods developed an argument on the inability of sinners to repent without prevenient grace. In contrast to Taylor, who said that the unrepentant possessed the ability to receive the truths of the Gospel, the Andover theologian cited passage after passage in which the Scriptures testified only to "the sinner's inability to render holy obedience unto God."[48] Woods believed, as had his Calvinist forebears, that unless a person "is renewed by the Spirit of God, it is impossible for him to cease from sin or to do that which is spiritually good."[49] The heart must be renewed first, before the sinner can obey God. Men like Taylor might wish to believe that obedience could come first, Woods said, but that is not taught anywhere in Scripture. The minister who professed to sinners that they could fulfill their obligations to love God by their own ability taught false doctrine.[50]

Woods insisted that any doctrine must be found complete in revelation. For this reason, much of the six letters was devoted to Scriptural quotation. Furthermore, Woods believed that Taylor had subverted revelation by a too-heavy reliance on reason. Woods said emphatically that the understanding had no role to play in interpreting Scripture, let alone the role Taylor gave it in deciding what was true and false doctrinally. Our reason teaches us that Scripture is to be believed, he wrote, but beyond that we must accept what the Bible says whether it seems rational or not. "If that reasoning, which is strictly *philosophical*, may ever be used on the subject of religion," Woods asserted, "it must be for the purpose of illustrating and enforcing a doctrine . . . already made known . . . and vindicating it against objections."[51]

The same volume of *Spirit of the Pilgrims* containing Woods' "Letters" also printed a review of Yale President Jeremiah Day's ordination sermon, "The Christian Preacher's Commission." This sermon, which drew the heartiest editorial praise (and Taylor was one of the editors) also addressed the reason-revelation problem. Day believed that "the truths which [the minister] has derived from [Scriptures] he is bound to make the subject of his communication to his hearers. Nothing else will accomplish the design of his ministry."[52] The difference between Woods and the Yale position lay in the fact that the latter allowed reason to modify passages which "seem to demand" an "assent to what is intuitively or demonstratively false."[53] Nonetheless, both Taylor and Woods agreed that reason was only a tool in the study of revelation.

The New England divines expressed their ideas on reason and revelation, on man's corrupted will, or on the operation of moral agency in the language of Common Sense philosophy. Known also as Scottish Realism or Scottish philosophy, this system formed the second part of the New Englanders' common intellectual ground. The Scot John Witherspoon, who became president of the College of New Jersey in 1763, introduced Common Sense into America. Thirteen of Witherspoon's students became college presidents, others professors in New England and the South, and through them the philosophy gained a rapid following throughout the country.[54] Men like Timothy Dwight saw Common Sense as the best defense against the increasingly popular—and atheistical—French ideologues.[55] Others valued it as an irrefutable way to prove the existence of God. As Sydney Alstrom writes, the philosophy became "a vast subterranean influence" underlying all American theology.[56]

The importance of Scottish Realism for New England theology lay in two points. It created a duality of subject and object in which mind was an active and matter a passive power, and it stated that moral sense was inherent in the human mind.

Beginning with Locke, English philosophy had wrestled with the problem of perception. How do you know when you look at this page that it really exists? Your experience of reality takes place in your mind, in the realm of ideas. You have an idea of the page, but, Locke would argue, no satisfactory way to connect that idea to the external reality which is this piece of paper.

The connection between ideas and reality continued to absorb British philosophers. Hume, late in the eighteenth century, pushed Locke's train of thought remorselessly. He insisted that if all experience existed only ideally (in the realm of ideas), then there was no ground for belief in external objects at all. Nor could one believe in cause and effect. Only custom or habit makes us believe that when one billiard ball hits another, for example, the motion of the first ball causes motion in the second, Hume wrote.[57]

The Common Sense philosophers revolted against this extreme idealism. They were Newtonians, and Newtonian physics demanded a real world in which billiard balls hit each other and transmitted motion. The realists restored belief in external objects by dividing perception into two coinciding parts: the subject or mind which looks, and the object which is perceived.

Thomas Reid (1710–1796), the Scottish philosopher most read in this country, developed his thought by observing how most people view the world around them. Only philosophers question their own existence, he said. Most people know they exist by relying on their common sense.[58] Similarly, if you are looking at this page, or smelling a rose, your common sense tells you they exist. Philosophically speaking, two phenomena coincide to

Chapter I

create the rose's smell. The first is the conscious mind which has the idea of the scent, the second the rose, which provides it.

An important corollary to this duality of subject and object lay in Reid's belief that mind was the active power in perception. Matter, he wrote, was a passive instrument in the hands of an intelligent being.[59] Such an argument offered incontrovertible proof for the existence of God as the prevenient active intelligence responsible for the matter we see around us.

The Scottish school observed the actions of the conscious mind in developing a general sense of how most people behave. They considered a common pattern of behavior evidence of certain *a priori* principles or affections in the mind. These constituted axioms. Like the basis for Newton's mathematics, axioms of thought or behavior required no proof. For Americans, one of Reid's most important axioms was that man's moral sense exists *a priori*.[60] Inherent moral sense allowed the construction of a system of ethics without needing to prove its necessity for a fallen creation.

The weakness of Scottish philosophy lay in its unquestioning acceptance of a parallel between physics and philosophy. The realists believed they could base moral philosophy on axioms of human thought, using the inductive method derived from Bacon and Newton. They believed, too, that those giants supported such an application. They quoted Bacon, who had applied induction to natural science, on its use in philosophy. The Scots also quoted Newton's Optics, in which the great physicist had written, "if natural philosophy in all its parts, by pursuing this method [induction], shall be at length perfected, the bounds of moral philosophy will also be enlarged."[61]

The Scots considered the use of induction a characteristic innate in the human mind. When Reid wrote that "by our constitution we have a propensity to trace particular facts and observations to general rules,"[62] he meant that inductive reason was a natural human act. Everyone he observed reasoned intuitively by induction. It underlay all correct human thought.

At Andover, Common Sense did not assume major articulated importance until the 1840s. But Woods, Dwight, Ware, Taylor, and every other major figure of any religious persuasion at the turn of the century defined their theology in the language of Common Sense. While every theological school put the realists to a different use, the Scots provided a common language in which New Englanders discussed philosophy and religion.

In his essay on "New England Theology" written in 1852, Park praised the eminent New England divines Dwight and Appleton for their facility in Common Sense. After lauding the heroes of New England theology for their learning, Park said that their true merit lay not in their scholarship, but in their practical approach to life. They were "adepts in the philosophy of Reid,

Oswald, Campbell, Beattie, Stewart . . ." A philosophy which developed "the fundamental laws of human belief," Park added, had been a great aid to the divines in developing practical ethical axioms.[63]

Park relied heavily on Reid and on Reid's disciple, Dugald Stewart, for the development of his own work. He considered Stewart's writings almost beyond praise.[64] Park came to the Scottish philosophers early in life, but their application to theology he learned from the Yale theologian, Nathaniel William Taylor (1786–1858).

Timothy Dwight had used Reid and Stewart in his famous defense of orthodoxy against the French atheism which he saw as the chief enemy at Yale in the 1790s. The duality between subject and object gave him the necessary rational handle for confronting a rational atheism. His results, in the shape of revivals of religion, were spectacular, but the philosophy must be thought of as the nearest weapon he could pick up for the purpose he required, not as inhering in his work.

For Dwight's star pupil, Taylor, who became professor of didactic philosophy at Yale in 1822, Scottish philosophy assumed a fundamental role in defining Congregational theology. Taylor used the separation of perceptor and object to amplify Edwardsean theology's division between the understanding and the will. He suggested a three-fold partition of the mind, in which sensibility was an uncorrupted neutral point to which the truth of the Gospel could appeal. Once activated by the Gospel, sensibility could influence the totally corrupted understanding and will. Through this division, Taylor removed the necessity to sin, since if part of the mind were uncorrupted, man had the power not to fall. Sin was certain, he said, but not necessary.[65]

Taylor saw to it that Stewart was put on the required reading list at Yale.[66] At Andover, students read Reid, Stewart, Smith, and Butler. At Harvard they read the same authors. Scottish realism had been introduced at Princeton in the 1760s and continued to be taught there.[67]

Taylor's definition of moral agency, derived from Common Sense reasoning, roused Woods to write the "Letters to Young Ministers" discussed earlier. The Andover theologian rejected Taylor's conclusions, but not Scottish philosophy. Woods relied on induction and the parallel between natural and mental science in his own discussion of moral agency. He and Taylor both agreed that the sinner has an obligation to love God. They disagreed on how the heart could be stirred to that love. In defining man's duty to love God, Woods said that it was so "evident and certain that . . . it does not need proof . . . There is nothing more evident." How did he know it was self-evident? By observing what happened when the "mental facilities [are] in a right state, . . . the eyes of . . . understanding open, [the] conscience awake." In this condition, a man will hear

> the first and great command: "Thou shalt love the Lord thy God with all thy heart, and with all thy soul, . . ."
>
> These remarks disclose an important principle, namely, that the feeling of obligation is founded in the very constitution of the human mind.[68]

To uncover the principle of obligation, Woods used his own introspective experiences, along with his knowledge of what happened to other sinners he had seen converted. Such observation lay at the heart of Common Sense: the natural behavior of the majority of people gave the key to what was real and what imagined or false. Woods' experience showed him that obligation "was found in the very constitution of the human mind." The observation of human behavior became an appealing tool for placing biblical theology on a scientific basis.

Common Sense relied explicitly on what the Scots thought was the method of Bacon and Newton. Baconianism was also implicit in the way New England divines looked at natural science. The "Baconian" approach to science formed the third common intellectual premise for New England intellectuals in this period.

In *American Science in the Age of Jackson,* George Daniels states that most Americans who thought about the topic in the first half of the nineteenth century called themselves Baconians or Newtonians. They did not, however, stop to define what these titles meant to them.[69] In practice, New England science boiled down to Cuvier's dictum of observation, nomenclature, and classification, with an attempt so to arrange the facts of science that the laws of nature were revealed.[70]

Woods agreed with this definition. Neither he nor the Scottish realists distinguished between the method they attributed to Bacon and Newton and inquiry into the human mind.[71] "What we wish to know," Woods told his Andover classes, "are the simple facts that exist, and the general laws which these facts obviously develop and clearly prove . . ."[72] Theology, human nature, and natural science all operated according to laws educible through observation and induction. When Andover became involved in biblical studies, the faculty assumed that the sciences of philology and criticism followed discernible laws just as did theology.

Natural theology, or "the evidences of the existence and attributes of the deity collected from the appearances of nature,"[73] represented the ultimate synthesis of the different aspects of New England thought. The coincidence between the dictates of reason and the doctrines of revelation was nowhere more clearly demonstrated than in natural theology. Here, too, the Baconian method as defined by Scottish realism uncovered the laws of nature, revealing the divine Designer behind them. At Andover, Yale, and Harvard, natural theology also included moral philosophy. In this capacity, it defined the duties of men to each other and to God.

The English archdeacon William Paley (1743–1805) wrote what Americans considered the best text on natural theology. As much as they disliked his moral philosophy, New England divines praised his *Natural Theology*. At Harvard, the work was used without reservation.[74] While a number of Calvinist scholars, including Park and Amherst's Edward Hitchcock, hoped to write a better text, they considered Paley's one of the best available.[75]

The Andover catalog for 1828 listed the books used in studying this discipline. Paley's work is the only which directly addressed the evidences of nature. Other authorities, such as Timothy Dwight, discussed the moral aspects of natural theology, including the attributes of God and the proofs of his existence.[76] Because the divines were more interested in moral philosophy than in the evidences of nature, the former was taught as a separate course at most colleges. Seniors studied it with the college president as the culmination of their college career.

Paley treated comparative anatomy to establish the evidence of a contrivance so ingenious that it necessitated a contriver. From astronomy Paley found the laws which circumscribed the Deity as well as his universe.[77] The method he used was analogical. There were parallels among all aspects of nature, from the thinking man who produced a watch, to the thinking Deity who produced a universe. Through analogy, one could understand the operation of parts of the universe not directly available to observation.[78]

A Unitarian writer, James Brager, pointed out in 1835 that because analogy was used in both natural science and natural theology, the latter could be considered as scientific as physics.[79] Natural science, natural theology, Common Sense philosophy all looked at observable analogous phenomena. From them could be deduced laws of nature, laws of God, or laws of human thought.[80] Without ever really studying natural science, the Christian scholars would claim the ability to distinguish true from false science according to its agreement with the natural laws they understood. This attitude became particularly important later in the century, when new sciences no longer seemed to lead smoothly and directly back to the Designer.

In treating depravity, Woods lectured that the discussion must be based on known facts, not metaphysical speculation. No hypothesis or argument "not founded on facts, can be admitted in the science of the mind any more than in the science of physics," he reasoned. "Any hypothesis in natural science, which is not supported by the evidence of facts, we regard as a dream of the imagination. We should do the same in mental science."[81] The facts were found first in Scripture, second in axioms of human behavior.

As the Andover faculty began to develop the tools of scholarship, they approached the newly developing sciences of philology and historical criticism in the firm belief that they had a method which illuminated every area of human thought. Based on Baconian principles, this method unveiled physics, moral agency, or the existence of God with equal ease. While Harvard might be at odds with Andover, or Andover with Yale, on the issue of depravity, no one doubted that the method elucidated all available facts and uncovered the general laws behind them. The Christian scholars were in many ways a new phenomenon, but they did not represent a radical departure from the past. Instead, they used the tools of thought which lay at everyone's hand in New England.

CHAPTER II

Reason, Revelation, and the Rise of Biblical Criticism

❖ ❖ ❖

Every age and country have their coterie of Virorum Obscurorum,
who place the safety of the church and society in ignorance; . . . But such men
and Providence are always at war with each other . . . Freedom of thought, with
ample room for expansion, is the law of nature, and whenever this is tramelled
by the interposition of human authority, the elements of the spiritual
world produce a storm, and clear the atmosphere.
— *Barnas Sears, "German Literature; —Its*
Religious Character and Influence"

"A quarter of a century's reading of German authors" has moved (me) "farther off . . . from heresy, than when I came to this seminary," Moses Stuart asserted in 1841.[1] He was writing an open letter to the Baptist scholar Barnas Sears on their common problem, hostility to the German scholarship they both loved. Both Sears and Stuart were trying to grapple with the vast body of German biblical criticism and convert it to the needs of evangelical Christianity. But to many of their peers, the Germans were a source of every imaginable theological crime.[2]

The problem lay in the attitude many German scholars had towards the Bible. They believed it was no different from other books, that it had been written by men over a period of time, and that its contents were a matter for historical, not theological criticism.

In the early nineteenth century, German scholars were the undisputed leaders in biblical studies. They had almost single-handedly developed the field of textual criticism in the eighteenth century; anyone interested in that area of study had to know the great German scholars. The father of modern criticism was J. D. Michaelis (1717–1791), Professor of Oriental Languages at the University of Jena. Michaelis applied a linguistic analysis developed by the English to the New Testament. In 1750, he published a critique of the New Testament which questioned the authenticity of many of the Epistles, as well as of Mark's and Luke's gospels.[3] His successor at Jena from 1770–1790, Johann Gottfried Eichhorn, followed the same method in studying the Old Testament. He scrupulously analyzed the language of the Pentateuch. By isolating passages with archaic expressions, he found two different names for God, Yahwe (Jehovah), and Elohim, depending on the age of the passage. On this basis he identified two separate hands in the composition of the Pentateuch. The work itself, Eichhorn decided, was compiled over several centuries, perhaps even a millennium.

Eichhorn's students rapidly expanded his linguistic analyses. Their work involved an ever-deeper understanding of Hebrew, Greek, Syriac, and other biblical languages. Gesenius (1786–1842), who did important textual work on the prophets, was primarily a Hebrew scholar. He compared texts to find the oldest forms of words; by examining their roots, he tried to discover the evolution of the language. Knowing the oldest forms of words helped him determine the oldest sections of the Bible.

Many of the German critical writers denied that the texts with which they worked were either inspired or revealed. They studied the Bible as they did Greek mythology: for the light it threw on the minds of primitive people. They demonstrated that the books of the Bible were generally the composite work of numerous authors over many generations, and found errors committed by copyists during the millennia before printing was invented. On these grounds, the Germans rejected the claim that the Bible we now read was the work of men writing at the dictate of God. Not only that, they interpreted accounts of divine intervention in human affairs as the subjective view of the biblical authors.

Such opinions aroused many American Congregationalists. Like Woods, they insisted that the Bible contained nothing that was not divinely inspired, and that it was the only rule of faith and practice. They wished to guard themselves not so much from the Germans, as from the Liberals, but they saw a strong German influence at work in Harvard.

Stuart wrote scornfully in 1841 that "the Unitarians of [1810] were, as a mass, . . . guiltless in respect to the sin of German study."[4] But the Liberals had really brought the awareness of German scholarship to Boston. In particular, the Liberals early saw in textual criticism a means for refuting certain passages which contradicted their peculiar beliefs about Jesus.

The Liberals did not deny Jesus' divinity. They said he was the Son of God, but not the Word who was with God from the beginning. The doctrine of the Trinity was a fourth-century imposition on the simple message of the Gospel, they claimed. They also rejected, on rational and hermeneutical grounds, the imputation of Adam's sin to other men, and the doctrine of election. Grace was generally available to everyone, they said, for a good God would not condemn his own creation to eternal death.

Until they discovered German criticism, the Liberals had rested their case on their intuitive, Common Sense ideas about the character of God. Textual criticism gave them the scientific tool they needed to prove their case. In 1806, the brilliant young Liberal scholar Joseph Stevens Buckminster (1784–1812) made the first American pilgrimage to Germany for the sole purpose of studying textual criticism.

The son of a Calvinist minister, Buckminster began reading works of the English Unitarians while a student at Harvard in 1802. Becoming convinced that Jesus was not equal to the Father, he went through a period of estrangement from his own father. To help resolve theological tensions at home, the son began a course of biblical studies. He read John Locke's critique of the epistles, and Michaelis. Far from convincing him that the Liberal ideas were wrong, these authors persuaded Buckminster that many Calvinist theological points were backed up by poor translations, mistakes in copying, or later interpolations. By the time he accepted a call to the Liberal Brattle Street Church in 1805, Buckminster was convinced that America's most urgent need was for a good library of critical works.[5]

In 1806, Buckminster's health, threatened by epilepsy, declined so seriously that his congregation sent him to Europe to rest. There he spent a happy year acquiring some 3,000 books, many on biblical literature. On his return, he persuaded Harvard to sponsor an American translation of the best German work on the New Testament.

In 1810, a Boston merchant named Samuel Dexter bequeathed $5,000 to Harvard for a lectureship promoting "a critical knowledge of the Holy Scriptures." Buckminster was the Fellows' natural choice for first lecturer. He decided that his most important task was to get German materials into American hands as fast as possible. Unfortunately, a fatal attack of epilepsy cut short his myriad plans in the summer of 1812. However, he had roused the Boston literary societies in which he was a prominent member to an interest in criticism, and had convinced the Harvard Fellows of its importance.

Channing succeeded Buckminster as Dexter lecturer. He had no inclination for scholarship, but preferred preaching: he held the position a scant year before returning full time to the pulpit ministry.[6] In 1813, the Fellows appointed Andrews Norton, then editor of the militant Liberal *General Repository and Review*, to the lecturership. Unequal to Buckminster as a scholar, Norton had a fine appreciation for the use of criticism in aiding the Liberal cause. In the lead article of the *Repository*'s first issue, Norton defined differences between Liberals and Orthodox in their use of the Bible. The Orthodox, he wrote, believed that God had immediately and miraculously superintended the composition of the Scriptures. They interpreted the Bible differently from other documents, making no allowance "for the inadvertence of the writer, and none for the exaggeration produced by strong feelings." They would not analyze language to find "peculiarities of expression of the writer or of the age or country to which he belonged," Norton complained, and "pay but little regard to the circumstances in which he wrote, or to those of the persons, whom he addressed."[7]

Since the Liberals interpreted the Scriptures as they did other ancient writings, Norton contended that they would free the Bible from creedalism and restore its true meaning.[8] Norton continued to press Buckminster's arguments about doctrines antithetical to Liberal beliefs. "By the removal of a very few passages," he wrote, Christians could get rid of "that doctrine, which places Jesus Christ on an equality with the God and Father of us all." Passages showing man's inability to repent without the infusion of irresistible grace could be similarly expunged, leaving the New Testament a consistent "body of doctrines and precepts . . ." acceptable to rational men.[9] Since Norton believed in the divinity of Jesus, his special moral character, his resurrection from the dead, and the promise of life everlasting,[10] most of the New Testament could remain as it was. However, by accepting or rejecting doctrines as they pleased rational men, Norton had left the Liberals without much defense against an accusation of Rationalism. Stuart eventually put this intellectual weakness to good use.

When Norton published his "Defense," Stuart was working hard to make up his deficiencies in Hebrew at Andover. A compulsive worker, Stuart set out to teach himself Hebrew as soon as he had settled down at the seminary. At the same time, he was mastering hermeneutics, since his appointment required him to offer lectures on interpretation. According to his own recollections in 1841, he constantly encountered references to German works as he studied both Hebrew and interpretation.[11] This was what convinced him that the heart of modern biblical studies lay in Germany.

Because Andover always had a jealous eye on Harvard, Buckminster's work may also have sparked Stuart's interest in German. Whatever the cause, Stuart decided to learn the language, and read through Luther's version of John's gospel with a dictionary. When Buckminster died, Stuart bought Eichhorn's four-volume *Introduction to the Old Testament* at the auction of his library.[12]

As Stuart mastered foreign languages, he shared his knowledge, including his copy of Eichhorn, with Edward Everett, then a Harvard classicist. Everett proposed to translate the master; Stuart heartily approved.[13] Such was his interest in critical studies, that it overrode any antipathy to Liberalism. In fact it never occurred to Stuart that in helping Everett he might aid

Harvard's cause. Instead, he freely shared all the fruits of his labor, including his newly-completed Hebrew grammar.[14]

Stuart's grammar just began his active scholarly career. His main interest turned more and more towards hermeneutics, but Eichhorn's work convinced him that a thorough knowledge of Hebrew was essential for a proper understanding of the Bible. He did not start preparing lectures on hermeneutics until 1814, while he continued to perfect his Hebrew. He probably began delivering these lectures immediately, but did not complete a formal set of fifty until 1819. These he revised and polished through 1822.[15] As his critical powers became increasingly sophisticated, he stopped writing out his lectures. Thus we have the complete set on Old Testament hermeneutics, but nothing on the New Testament.[16]

The lectures reveal a dilemma Stuart struggled with between what he studied and what his heart taught him. Like Woods, he held that the Bible's truth was established by the heart, independent of reason. Yet his reason caused him to use German historical methods to prove the validity of the texts. He tried to get around this problem by treating criticism in a Common Sense manner, as a science with axioms that needed no proof.

"The fundamental principles of hermeneutics are established independently of religious opinions," he told his classes for some thirty-five years. "They result from the laws of our nature, or from the principles of our reason."[17] Hermeneutics was a science, he often said, just as much as physics. While theologians still quarreled about Revelation, he added, there were fewer and fewer grounds for such disagreements: the rational laws of interpretation made it possible to uncover what the text really meant. If the meaning of the text could not be found through "an appeal to reason," Stuart argued, then "a particular internal revelation to every individual becomes necessary."[18]

Nowhere was the balance between reason and revelation more difficult to maintain than in criticism. Stuart tried to walk a tightrope between them. That the Bible was a revelation of God he emphatically affirmed.[19] Not only that, but it was the heart, not the mind, which enabled men to accept its truths. "The Bible contains not a little, which is intended to apply to the . . . moral & religious feelings and sympathies," Stuart reminded his students. "Grammatical and historical exegesis cannot penetrate the interior of such passages." The only way to understand what the Bible said was to "possess those feelings and sympathies."[20]

None of those criticisms which Norton directed against the Orthodox in 1812 could be leveled at Stuart. Lecturing on "The Principles of Exegesis," Stuart laid down two major rules for his students to follow. The first was to interpret any writer's language "agreeably to the *usus loquendi*, or customary sense of words, in the language in which he writes." The second urged students to take account of "the views, opinions, and circumstances" of those for whom the "work was originally designed."[21] These two principles were intended to stop the interpretation of words out of context. Since most words allow a variety of translations, one could take a small passage and translate it to fit a particular doctrine. Stuart wanted his students to know the range of meanings any word might have, and pick the one best fitting the general sense of an entire passage. He sought in this way to circumvent the kind of special translations indulged in by the Liberals to make the Bible fit their doctrines. He also opposed those who attempted to make allegories out of such factual tales as Abraham's bigamy. The Bible was the history of a people, he lectured, and much of it had to be understood simply as history, important because God had intervened in it.

In 1832, Stuart amplified his exegetical principles in an essay for the *Biblical Repository*, an Andover review. "If the Bible is not a book which is intelligible in the same way as other books are," he wrote, "then it is difficult indeed to see how it is a revelation."[22] Since a revelation is a communication, Stuart argued, it ought to be as comprehensible as ordinary speech. The trouble with treating the Bible as such a document lay in the difficulty of learning Hebrew and Greek, the problem of textual inaccuracies, and the problem of ascertaining authorship of different books. But Stuart was confident that true understanding awaited anyone with the patience to learn both language and critical methods.

Much of Stuart's early published work was grammatical. He wrote his Hebrew grammar to make up deficiencies in Hebrew instruction available at the time. He considered it a poor beginning and would not even put a copy in the seminary library.[23] However, he set to work immediately on revising and enlarging the grammar. Immersing himself in the best European scholarship, he produced three improved editions by 1828, by which time he was turning his attention to related Semitic languages.

In 1829, Stuart published a *Chrestomathy* (literally, "simple instruction") for Hebrew, designed to help students prepare for admission to the seminary. Stuart considered this language the most important tool any Christian could have for understanding the Bible;[24] at his insistence, the trustees for a time made knowledge of it mandatory for entrance to the seminary.

The *Chrestomathy* illustrates Stuart's general approach to exegesis. It presents progressively more difficult passages from Scripture in Hebrew, each one numbered and accompanied by a corresponding note in the second half of the book. For the simpler passages, Stuart carefully explained the grammatical forms, reasons for the vowel points, and the general family of words and forms to which each word in the sentence belonged. As the passages became more complex, Stuart expanded his exposition. Every word mentioned in a chapter or verse he deemed worthy of exploration to arrive at the fullest knowledge of that passage's meaning. Where Adam and Eve ate from the tree of knowledge, attaining the sense of good and evil, and were expelled from Eden, Stuart began with an analysis of the place-names in the verse. He called on modern Arabic and studied its place-names for roots close to the ancient Hebrew. Comparing the two, he tried to decide where Eden was most probably located. Next, Stuart subjected the tree of knowledge to a lengthy exposition. In deciding what "knowledge of good and evil meant," Stuart referred the reader to German authorities on the subject, to other passages in the Bible using the same words, and finally gave his own interpretation.[25] In every instance, Stuart held true to his belief that the Bible does not have hidden messages. Unless we are given a specific cue for interpreting the Bible allegorically, it must be understood literally.[26]

Stuart thought of hermeneutics as an abstract science, grammar the tool for studying it. In his lectures, he spent some time outlining the rules of interpretation to his classes, trying to persuade them of the validity of using reason to study Sacred Scripture. To placate the wary, he insisted that hermeneutics was the science "which prescribes the rules of interpreting language,"[27] not of interpreting the Bible. Once he knew what the language meant, the interpreter understood the Bible. Accuracy of communication was Stuart's main message: we need biblical studies to hear the Bible's message as the ancients did.[28]

Because hermeneutics was a science, Stuart obediently followed it, even when it led him, like Eichhorn, to question the accepted author of a book. For instance, the Book of Chronicles was written several centuries after the events it relates, Stuart deduced.[29] But the findings of his science did not shake his belief in the Bible. That aspect of Baconian science which urged its adherents to "order, name, and classify" forbade theorizing. Stuart regarded himself as a fact-gatherer and looked to time to settle all discrepancies between the faith he believed and the facts he uncovered.

Stuart did not ignore the problems his hermeneutical work revealed, but he believed that he had a talisman in the New Testament, a document above criticism against which Old Testament claims could be examined. He first developed this argument in his Andover lectures on the Old Testament canon, in which he refused to give up the Old Testament chronology.

To establish the appropriate chronology, Stuart first considered the approximate age of biblical texts. Eichhorn believed that the Prophets, including Moses, were later in origin than standard chronology claimed, probably around the time of the Second Temple (c. 350 B.C.). The German scholar thought religions developed from primitive to sophisticated forms, until the revelation of Christ appeared to address man's highest moral sense. According to Eichhorn's system, the prophecies belonged to a more advanced state of religion than was possible at the time of the exodus from Egypt.[30]

Stuart objected that religion was exempt from this kind of developmentalism. Moses "burst forth from all the gross absurdities of Egyptian polytheism," Stuart told his students, not because of "the slow, cautious, gradual progress of the children of nature toward the most exalted acquisitions of spiritual knowledge," but with "the presence and special aid of the Divinity." To explain the law which Moses gave, or the prophecies of Isaiah without reference to "supernatural assistance" went "against the universal experience of all nations," he added. To do so created "a mystery more difficult of explanation than the common supposition, that the Hebrew writers were divinely inspired."[31]

The acceptance of divine intervention in history implied acceptance of the chronology of events as recorded in the Old Testament. As for the canonicity of the Law and the Prophets, Stuart believed the New Testament established it beyond question. If Christ or the Apostles referred to an Old Testament book, that conferred immediate canonicity upon it to Stuart. To believe otherwise raised the possibility that Christ was a deceiver.[32] If Jesus mentioned a prophecy of Isaiah's, and Isaiah had not so prophesied—had not even lived, except as a composite person—how could we accept Jesus as Lord? The New Testament justified the Old, but if a book accepted commonly as part of the canon were not mentioned in the Gospels or Epistles, Stuart could still find New Testament authority for it. For example, Jesus never referred to the book of Nehemiah, but he did twice call Jerusalem the "holy city." As this was Nehemiah's name for the city, Stuart claimed that Jesus was sanctioning that book as part of the canon.[33]

Stuart relied heavily on the argument that Christ did not deceive. It was this belief which enabled him to hold two opposing views on disputed passages, for he could see their errors and yet maintain that they were somehow true. Such difficulties were apparent, not real, he said: he hoped for time and greater knowledge to clear them up.

Despite his realization that the biblical texts contained many errors, if only superficial ones, Stuart demonstrated the authority and genuineness of every Old Testament book. In his Andover lectures, he went through the canon in order, discussing who the author of each book was, how we know when it was written, and whether the events recorded had actually occurred. Structural or literary questions, such as dating the book of Job by its poetic forms, he left to Porter.[34] He did not try to demonstrate that the books were inspired, because that "belonged to the Professor of Christian Theology."[35]

Stuart treated the Pentateuch as one book. In lecturing on it, he discussed two major questions which the Germans had raised: was the Pentateuch some 3,400 years old, as tradition demanded; and had Moses written it?

In his notes, Stuart drew up in parallel columns the two hands Eichhorn discerned from the two names for God, Elohim and Jehovah. The creation story, which appears twice, once in some detail using Elohim, and again, briefly, using Jehovah, was the clearest example of two different sources combined in one book. Stuart did not doubt that both strains existed. The passages he gave his classes to copy showed that Genesis could "easily be divided between the records with Elohim and [those with] Jehovah . . ."[36]

Such a division might at first startle "the mind of a pious man," Stuart told his students. Yet since it was true, the critic had to find some explanation for it. There could be no doubt that Moses, or at least someone similar, was the author of that part of Exodus dealing with his own history, for only "a resident of Egypt . . . would give such a minute account of ancient Egyptian manners and customs, as appears in the books of Genesis & Exodus."[37]

Stuart suggested that Moses had actually woven together the Elohist and Yahwist accounts in Genesis. Naturally, Moses was not an eye-witness of creation nor of early Hebrew history. He must have had ancient written sources at his disposal, the scholar reasoned. Where he found the two accounts differed, he inserted both of them; when one was more copious, he used it. Stuart thought the most likely explanation was "two original records, blended by Moses,"[38] but he also suggested that Moses might have relied on oral tradition. After all, only five links in the genealogical chain separated Adam from Moses, and the tales could easily have been passed from father to son among a people which relied more on oral than on written history.[39]

The strongest arguments Stuart found for Mosaic authorship came from external testimony. "We have seen that Jesus uniformly considered this book as the work of Moses," he reminded the young men, "that all the testimony we have on this subject is in favor of this tradition; and that no ancient or express testimony to the contrary has ever been produced." And finally, he added the passionate plea with which he defended the Old Testament all his life. "The critic who admits the Iliad of Homer, or the history of Herodotus to be genuine," he argued, "on the ground of uniform tradition among the Greeks, must admit . . . Genesis to be genuine, on the ground of uniform tradition among the Jews."[40] All the external testimony on which Stuart relied was actually either internal to the Bible, or inherent in the Judeo-Christian tradition. The New Testament was the only document external to the Old whose authority he quoted to verify the latter's authenticity. And the New Testament authority depended entirely on a faith in Christ as the Messiah who fulfilled Old Testament prophecies.

Stuart gave short shrift to German arguments that the Pentateuch, particularly the last three-and-a-half books, were of comparatively recent origin. Eichhorn accounted the ancient words in Genesis as vestiges of older manuscripts. Stuart argued that these archaisms were the best evidence of the text's antiquity: a more recent writer would have obliterated them.[41] He also considered the external evidence which upheld the account's Mosaic authorship proof of its antiquity: Christ would not have deceived us in so important a matter.[42]

In book after book, Stuart found discrepancies which called their accepted authors and times of composition into doubt. Joshua, for instance, threw "many difficulties" in the way of "supposing that the book was brought to its present form at the time [of Joshua]."[43] Some passages referred to events which took place later. Names and phrases appeared "which are of much later origin than the time of the conquest of Canaan."[44] Internal evidence on many psalms so strongly contradicted David's authorship that Stuart found it "astonishing, that it ever should have been proposed."[45] In Nehemiah, the Andover critic discerned three separate accounts woven together by a later hand, rather than the work of one fifth-century prophet.[46]

In his 1814 discussion of Chronicles, Stuart expressed a perplexity over biblical studies which he never resolved. He was convinced that this book was written about a century-and-a-half later than tradition allowed. Many discrepancies occurred between the genealogy tables in Chronicles and those in Genesis, which could only mean, Stuart concluded, that the records had been lost during the Babylonian captivity and reconstructed later. The events in Chronicles supposedly took place before the captivity. To doubt the date of authorship, or the accuracy of the recorded events, could easily cast doubt on the divine inspiration of the texts. Stuart told his students that these findings could be "derogatory to the credit due to the Sacred Scriptures or to inspired books." But he added that anyone who thought so "would be doing eminent service to the cause of sacred literature if he would substitute a better method of accounting for the difficulties that exist." No one could deny the discrepancies between Genesis and Chronicles, and no one could "solve them . . . except in such a way" as Stuart had.[47]

Stuart could not bring himself to face the implications of his work. Even after arguing as he did about Chronicles or Joshua or Psalms, he still insisted that the works were divinely inspired. After pointing out that Joshua was completed at a much later time than the book describes, Stuart added "that it bears every desirable mark of genuineness and authenticity."[48] Stuart seems to have kept two parallel tracks of thought in his mind, the first the fact-gathering dictated by Baconian science, and the second his traditional faith in literal biblical truth. "All sacred Scripture is given by inspiration of God," he told his classes. The gospel authors assure us that the Old Testament was so inspired by "the appeals, that are made to them as deciding every question, . . . the express declarations, that God speaks in them; [and] that the Holy Ghost speaks in them . . ."[49]

Stuart believed he could learn from the Germans without being affected by their theology. He admitted that Eichhorn's "theological views are such as ought to be regarded with horror," but added that he had "not perused any writer of equal ability."[50] But he kept himself free from Eichhorn's influence by running his mind on separate tracks. The trustees and other seminary faculty seemed less certain that Stuart would not harm himself nor the Seminary. During the period 1813–1819, Stuart recalled, "some of my best and most confidential friends were no doubt in a state of real alarm respecting me."[51] He said he was accused of having "secretly gone over to the Germans, [and of] leading the seminary over" with him. Not only was he charged with "encouraging our young men in the study of deistical Rationalism," but it was "whispered about . . . that it was all the other Professors could do, to keep the Seminary from going over into Unitarianism."[52] Woods, too, was troubled by Stuart's opinions, fearing that "in regard to the plenary inspiration of the Scriptures, Professor Stuart . . . dissented somewhat from the common doctrine . . ."[53]

The real fear at Andover was not whether Stuart might become a Rationalist, but a Unitarian. The primary use both Andover and Harvard made of all European scholarship was to apply it to the American scene. The debates with the Unitarians in which Stuart and Woods both engaged between 1819 and 1822 were the great battleground on which the modern German weapons were first employed. The debates hinged on the degree to which reason could dictate the authority of the Bible. The Unitarians took a stand perilously close to the Germans, and Stuart and Woods responded to that. The use of reason underlay the terms of the argument, which raged around whether the Bible actually supported Trinitarianism.

Harvard and Andover had carried on a sniping war since the seminary's opening. For years, the Orthodox had tried to bring matters to an open contest, in hopes of pushing the Liberals out of the Congregational polity. The Liberals were using their position within Congregationalism to take control of Boston-area churches. They would gain a majority in a congregation, then vote to have its confession of faith made non-Trinitarian. This loss of property infuriated the Orthodox even more than Liberal doctrines did. The Orthodox hoped that if they forced them to become a separate religious group, the Liberals would lose their legal ability to take over Congregational property. The Liberals resisted these efforts equally strongly.

Jedidiah Morse began open battle in 1815. He took a chapter from an English work on Unitarianism and published it under the title *American Unitarianism*. In it he accused the Liberals of concealing their heterodoxy under the Congregational name. He identified them closely with the English Unitarians and demanded that they dissociate themselves from the Orthodox.[54]

The Liberals responded with great vehemence. Accepting the divinity of Jesus as they did, they refused to be identified with Unitarianism.[55] However, as one of their apologists, George Ellis, pointed out, "the title Unitarian was forced upon those who now bear it."[56] In 1819, Channing made the great apologetic statement of Liberalism in his famous Baltimore sermon, "Unitarian Christianity." There he took the Unitarian label, trying, as Ellis said, "to make it as intelligible as possible," although it was "at best a definition of one of [their] doctrinal tenets."[57]

In Baltimore, Channing said three things were equally important for understanding the Bible: hermeneutics, reason, and a sense of what is fitting in nature. The Bible was not supernaturally inspired, he stated. It was the work of men acting in history. But it was the second of "God's successive revelations to mankind." The trouble was, Channing argued, that men mistook revelation for inspiration. Many passages have only a local and temporal significance, no longer applicable to modern people. Channing included most of the Old Testament in this category. The historical context of the books and idiosyncrasies of their authors were part of the Bible as much as the religious truths it taught. The responsible interpreter had to separate the truths from the context, so as not to generalize a peculiarly local concern.[58]

Channing found reason particularly important for interpreting the Bible. While his sense of Old Testament history did not differ radically from

Stuart's, his use of reason did. The Bible, he said, was addressed to rational men whose reason disposed them to a correct understanding of the text. If the Scriptures seemed to teach a doctrine that contradicted man's rational sense, that doctrine should be abandoned. The idea men had of God's character was as important an exegetical tool as grammar, Channing argued: passages which upset our sense of the divine nature were probably later interpolations. In particular, that statement in John's Epistle which reads "There are three that bear witness in heaven, the Father, the Son, and the Holy Ghost; and these three are one" Channing found beyond doubt to be a later interpolation.[59]

Channing believed, like Eichhorn, that religion showed a progressive sophistication of revelation. He and the other Liberals tended to undervalue the Old Testament in comparison with the New. Channing considered that the dispensation of Moses was "imperfect, earthly, obscure," compared with that of Jesus Christ who was "the only master of Christians." Christ's teachings had "divine authority" for Channing, who professed to make them "the rule of [his life]."[60]

The Orthodox found the Trinity supported by passages like the one from John quoted above, and by Old Testament prophecies. By letting his reason decide on which scriptural texts were authentic, and by discounting the Old Testament, Channing put together the Unitarian position. He said that the Trinity had no justification in Scripture, nature, or reason. In nature, a unity has "one being, one mind, one person," he asserted, and the unity of God was "no different . . . from the oneness of other intelligent beings."[61] Both reason and nature argued against the Trinity, and Scriptural passages supporting the doctrine were obvious interpolations.

Channing mustered the same arguments against Christ as very man and very God. This belief abused and confounded the language of Scripture, he urged, which "labour[s] to express [Jesus'] inferiority to God the Father."[62] While Jesus was divine, he was by no means God. The atonement, consequently, represented a ministry of reconciliation, not the sacrifice of God himself for a fallen humanity.[63] A sacrificial atonement "threw darkness over all our conceptions of intelligent natures," Channing concluded.[64]

Channing's sermon demanded a response from the Orthodox. Andover, their fortress, was looked to by the rest of New England to see how she would handle this first challenge.[65] Because Channing's sermon had relied more on hermeneutics than theology, Stuart rather than Woods undertook the first response. Close on the publication of the Baltimore sermon followed Stuart's *Letters to the Rev. Wm. E. Channing, containing remarks on his sermon, recently preached and published at Baltimore.*

As Brown points out in the *Rise of Biblical Criticism*, the real difference between Channing and Stuart lay in the use they assigned reason as an interpreter of Scripture.[66] Despite the fact that Stuart's reason took him down the same critical paths as Channing, he refused to suspend belief in certain texts because they "taxed his credulity," as the Unitarian put it. Stuart forced himself to accept as authentic some passages which he knew were interpolations. On the other hand, Channing weakened the entire theist case, at least in its scriptural base, by insisting that unappealing passages were false.

Stuart chose to answer three points raised by Channing: "The Principles of interpreting Scripture; The unity of God, and, The divinity and humanity of the Saviour."[67] He decided that if he established a common interpretative ground with Channing, the latter would have to agree with a grammatically proven doctrine of the Trinity.

The first question to ask in interpretation, as Stuart often had reminded his students, was "What did the original writer mean to convey?"[68] To understand this, "the language of the Bible is to be interpreted by the same [philological] laws . . . as that of any other book." If they did not use these tools, he asked, how could "men ever come to agree in what manner the Scripture should be interpreted, or feel any assurance that they have attained . . . the meaning of its language."[69]

Behind these grammatical laws lay Stuart's belief in the authority of the Bible. It was "to our reason that the arguments which prove the divine origin of Christianity are addressed." But once reason had assented to that revelation, the Bible had to be accepted as authoritative, as "orthodoxy in the highest sense of the word." One either accepted or rejected divine authority: "philosophy has no right to interfere here," Stuart stated.[70]

Channing had written that he admitted "without reserve or exception" any doctrines "seen . . . to be clearly taught in the Scriptures." But he had also insisted that before one accepted a doctrine as a valid part of Scriptures, it had to agree with one's sense of what God is. Stuart thought that the "sole office" of reason with respect to Scripture was as "interpreter of Revelation"; Channing used it as a "legislator."[71] On these grounds, Channing rejected much of the Old Testament. And when he found Christ's equality with the Father expressed by St. John, he did not "hesitate to modify, and restrain, and turn from the most obvious sense [these later passages], because this sense is opposed to the known properties of the beings to whom they relate."[72]

Stuart responded that if John taught anything that revolted against nature and reason, one ought to reject the whole of his writings as deceitful.

But suspending the laws of exegesis for one passage took away any reliable standard for interpreting the entire Bible. Anyone could pick any idea of God he liked, and simply say that passages opposing it were either later interpolations, or were applicable only to a narrow time period, not for all men and all times. "The simple question," Stuart repeated, was what John originally said,

> not what your philosophy may lead you to regard as probable . . . If I believed . . . as you do, that a Saviour with a human and divine nature is "an enormous tax on human credulity," I should certainly reject the authority of John. To violate the laws of exegesis in order to save his credit, I could regard as nothing more than striving to keep up a fictitious belief in divine revelation.[73]

Brown claims that the Andover scholar really ignored the Unitarian arguments, that he wrote as a theologian, not a biblical scholar because he relied ultimately on faith, not textual evidence.[74] Two-thirds of Stuart's *Letters* contained a grammatical discussion of those biblical passages affirming the Trinity and the man-God nature of Christ. If the Unitarians felt competent to answer this eminently hermeneutical argument, they did not indicate it. Channing, whether from dislike of polemic or from the sense of his own inadequacies as a scholar, asked Andrews Norton to reply to Stuart for him. By that time, the Dexter lectureship had become a professorship in sacred literature. Norton was Stuart's counterpart at Harvard in terms of position. But he did not attempt a hermeneutical argument against Stuart. He contented himself with reiterating that "we may reject the literal meaning of a passage, when we cannot pronounce with confidence what is its true meaning."[75] He shifted the field of argument from textual criticism to philosophy. His reply to Stuart discussed the meaning of "person" and attacked the doctrine of the Trinity. Such an argument was by its nature inconclusive. Woods, who answered Norton, had fifteen centuries of Trinitarian philosophy at his command. He rehashed these arguments for Norton. Henry Ware, the Hollis Professor, replied with another set of standard positions, and the debate continued inconclusively along well-trod theological paths, making no further use of hermeneutics.

Channing had put the Unitarians in the ambiguous position of having a divinely authorized text whose statements were subject to the laws of nature and human reason. Unlike the Germans, who used critical methods to decide what parts of the text were original, Channing used his own good sense. Stuart noted in the 1846 edition of his *Letters* that he had not understood the fundamental difference between himself and Channing in 1819;

otherwise he would have argued for the authority of Scriptures, not the validity of orthodox Christology.[76] Channing certainly was not reasoning as a biblical scholar in his arguments: he believed what appealed to him regardless of the textual evidence.

Traditional historiography has given inordinate weight to the importance of the Unitarian debates, particularly the pamphlet warfare between Henry Ware and Leonard Woods following Norton's reply to Stuart. People like Haroutunian, in *Piety Versus Moralism*, have looked at the Calvinist-Unitarian conflict as a fight between progress and repression. Haroutunian sees the Calvinists as representatives of a medieval mindset, and the Unitarians as modernists.[77] Haroutunian, Foster in his *Genetic History*, and, more recently Howe, in *The Unitarian Conscience*, all believe that the Unitarians out-argued the Calvinists, and that the debates put the seal on their declining intellectual authority.

Such an attitude ignores the pre-eminence Calvinist scholars held in schools other than Harvard before the Civil War. The debates did harm the Calvinists. As Mead shows in *Nathaniel William Taylor*, they brought into the open the dissension between Andover and Yale, with a divisive effect on parish life. But the debates strengthened Calvinist scholarship by proving its utility in the defense of orthodoxy.

The net effect at Andover was two-fold. In the first place it convinced the Orthodox that German critical study was essential to their defense. Secondly, it concretized the position of Christian scholarship, strengthening the belief of Orthodox intellectuals that all sciences could be integrated into New England theology. Stuart's *Letters* went through three editions in a month, convincing his colleagues that he had been right in studying German. "His friends confessed their error in resisting his German progress," Park recorded in his memorial sermon. The "venerable" Porter told Stuart, "'you could not have written that volume without your German aid. You are in the right in this matter and your friends are in the wrong; take your own way in the future.'"[78]

The trustees were not so easily satisfied. In 1825, they appointed a committee to investigate "the degree of attention which the students gave to the writings of lax and infidel writers and commentators." They believed that a number of students had lost their faith through studying German authors.[79] The committee, composed of two trustees, and Justin Edward, the seminary president, did not find enough benefit in German authors to outweigh their obvious detractions. Still, the three men recognized that the German authors were the greatest authorities on criticism and language. They urged Stuart to produce some comparable works to obviate the need to rely on

German sources.[80] They further suggested that he and Woods "frequently" remind students "of the inestimable value of religious truth" and of "the reverence, meekness, simplicity, and submission which should attend all their inquiries at the Divine oracle."[81]

Stuart argued that if one gave up German, just because it was used by heretics, the seminary should also exclude geometry.[82] He insisted that German was essential to biblical studies, and would not agree that learning it was more dangerous than reading English—for Hume was an English author just as malign as Michaelis.[83] Nonetheless, Stuart did proceed with his monumental *Defense of the Old Testament Canon*, which tried to "embrace . . . whatever is most valuable in the literature and criticism of the German writers" while excluding "their eccentricities and errors."[84] But Stuart did not stop using German authors in his own research or in teaching. He could not, in honesty, abandon what he knew was the best source for critical studies.

Stuart never went to Germany himself, but all of his most important pupils did. Barnas Sears, a classical scholar who later became president of Brown, traveled in Germany from 1838 to 1840. Sears helped Edwards Park plan the first of Park's several German tours in 1842.[85] Edward Robinson (1794–1863), the most important Hebraist Andover ever produced, spent many years in Germany. Robinson married the daughter of a Halle professor, and his father-in-law proved helpful in getting a European audience for Andover scholarship.[86] The list goes on to include all of the second generation of Andover faculty: Edwards, Phelps, and Stowe, in addition to Park.

Familiarity did not relax the anxious fears of many outside the seminary. Sears still was apologizing for German literature in 1841,[87] while Providence Christians worried about the faith of one of their young men whom Park sent abroad in 1853.[88]

The Andover faculty were not oblivious to the dangers of German theology. They were even appalled by it. Robinson frequently expressed his fears of the consequences of German scholarship. The Germans had betrayed the heritage of the Reformation, he wrote in 1831, rejecting the principle that "the Bible was the only and sufficient rule of faith and practice."[89] Nonetheless, he thought it important to emulate them, for they had resources both in men and libraries to develop scholarship as Americans could not.[90]

Stuart and Robinson both hoped, unavailingly, that critical studies would become as important in America as in Europe. Robinson began two journals, the *Biblical Repository* in 1831, and the *Bibliotheca Sacra* in 1843, both designed to promote biblical studies. Neither succeeded; both were converted into general theological journals. Stuart, delivering Andover's commencement address in 1846, urged young men to pursue their biblical studies, no matter what climate they labored in. He urgently addressed the need to refute the rationalist heresies emanating from Europe. "Let it be seen that Truth has intelligent and learned and skillful defenders, as well as error," he besought.[91] These pleadings were in vain. As Brown points out, to the bulk of American clergy, biblical studies was just one more demand on their time and deserved no more attention than home missions, revivals, temperance, or the host of other activities in which they engaged.[92]

While the majority of Congregational ministers remained indifferent to biblical studies, the field assumed increasing importance at Andover. The trustees, while not completely happy with Stuart, did agree to require Hebrew of entering students in 1827. The requirement was dropped a decade later, but in 1836, the trustees hired Bela Bates Edwards to assist Stuart in Hebrew.

Far from destroying the power of intellectual Calvinism, the Unitarian debates strengthened it. Everyone connected with Andover began advocating some degree of involvement in biblical studies. The seminary continued to share the broader concerns of Congregationalism for salvation, conversion, and missions. But the faculty began interpreting their mission as somehow different from that of the educated pastor. Increasingly, they saw themselves as channels for carrying new intellectual skills from the European centers of learning to the American ministry.

CHAPTER III

The Christian Scholar
Comes of Age

❖ ❖ ❖

That a man can be at the same time an eminent scholar
and an eminent Christian, is difficult, but not impossible . . .
The way to attain both is very simple . . . Make it your supreme object
to live for the glory of God, in the salvation of men . . . The perfection of
human character consists in the harmonious cultivation of the physical,
intellectual, and moral powers. Neither can be neglected without guilt.
All are necessary to the highest usefulness.
— Bela Bates Edwards, "Life of Henry Martyn"

As Americans took increasing advantage of German education, Calvinist intellectuals underwent a minor renaissance in the 1830s and '40s. Characterized by a sophisticated use of European scholarship and a preference for academic over parochial ministries, this movement had its major expression at Andover.

Andover lay at the center of a network of Christian scholars in this period. Moses Stuart's students graced almost every college faculty in New England, providing an intellectual community which collaborated on literary ventures. "No teacher in the land ever attached to himself so many theological pupils," Park wrote in his 1852 eulogy of the master. While Andover alumni totaled 1,100 in that year, "the number of [Stuart's] scholars has been more than fifteen hundred." They came from Canada as well as the twenty-six states to pursue special studies with Stuart. Seventy went from Andover to be "the presidents or professors of our highest literary institutions."[1] The *Bibliotheca Sacra*, published at Andover, was the public voice of this scholarly network.

Some of Stuart's more famous pupils included Francis Wayland, prominent moral philosopher and president of Brown University; Edward Hitchcock, one of the fathers of American geology and president of Amherst; and Leonard Bacon, outstanding pastor, abolitionist, and man of letters. As Stuart's driving interest lay in biblical studies, his most important pupils were famous in this area. Thirty of those students who became missionaries translated the Bible into various foreign languages,[2] others became prominent scholars at home. Edward Robinson was the best known of Stuart's students, but other prominent men included Bela Bates Edwards, Calvin Stowe, W. G. T. Shedd, and Edwards Park on the Andover faculty, and Barnas Sears and Horatio Hackett on the faculty at nearby Newton Center. All these men contributed often to the *Bibliotheca*, and corresponded regularly with Park and Edwards, who edited it.[3]

The career of Horatio Balch Hackett (1808–1875) followed a pattern typical of Andover-educated participants in the Calvinist renaissance. He attended Andover from 1830 to 1833, with a year's interruption as a Greek tutor at Amherst. E. A. Park was his contemporary at Andover, while Bela Bates Edwards had been Hackett's own Greek tutor when he was an Amherst undergraduate. His early acquaintance with these two men, later so prominent on the Andover faculty, kept Hackett involved in Andover's affairs after his graduation.

While Hackett was at Andover, Robinson served as Professor Extraordinary of Sacred Languages and Literature there.[4] Hackett assisted him in preparing a Greek grammar for publication. Through Robinson's influence, the younger man came to Francis Wayland's attention at Brown. Robinson recommended Hackett highly, and the latter went to Brown in 1835 as professor of Latin and Greek. In 1838, he became professor of Hebrew.[5]

While still at Andover, Hackett became convinced that adult baptism was the only baptismal mode justified by Scriptures. He was received into the Baptist communion in 1835. In 1839, he accepted a call to the Baptist seminary in Newton Center, Massachusetts, as Professor of Biblical Literature and Interpretation, a post he held until his death. The proximity of Newton Center and Andover encouraged his involvement with his alma mater. He augmented Andover's Greek department in 1848, and collaborated with Edwards in preparing a number of manuscripts on Hebrew. Only his Baptist convictions kept Andover from offering him the Brown professorship in 1852.[6]

In 1841, Hackett made the first of three European tours to deepen his knowledge of sacred languages. German study had become a routine part of education for the second generation of Christian scholars, and Hackett followed their pattern by studying with the pietist critic August Tholuck at Halle and Neander in Berlin.

Hackett's own work also followed a pattern typical of the Christian scholars. He translated some books from the New Testament with notes and commentaries, translated a number of German grammars and essays on sacred subjects, and wrote essays and study guides for Hebrew, Chaldaic, and Syriac. Like Robinson, he traveled in the Holy Land, publishing "illustrations of Scripture" drawn from his journeys.[7]

The literary collaborations between Andover faculty and those of other institutions were not limited to alumni like Hackett. Perhaps the most prominent "outside" scholar who worked with Edwards and Park was Theodore Dwight Woolsey (1801–1889), a grandson of Timothy Dwight. Woolsey, associated with Yale throughout his life, was elected president in 1846. Up to that time, he had been a brilliant classical scholar. As professor of Greek at Yale, he produced the best American editions of Plato and the early Greek dramatists. After 1846, he devoted himself to international politics and political science, becoming an authority in these new fields, too.

Like many other Congregationalists, Woolsey was "subject to periods of acute consciousness of sin and moral responsibility that depressed him at intervals all his life."[8] This consciousness resolved him against ordination: he wrote his father of his "utter repugnance" to the ministry. Unlike most of the other Christian scholars Woolsey was not ordained until the office of the president required it. Even then, his doubts of his fitness for the office continued.

Woolsey determined as a young man to "gain a minute and thorough knowledge of the Greek language, and to lay foundations for an acquaintance such as few in America possess with classical literature . . ."[9] He may have believed that the ministry would deter him from studying language as thoroughly as he liked. The question of unworthiness for the ministry vexed many Christian scholars. To what extent it was a psychological excuse for doing what they preferred is impossible to say.

In 1842, B. B. Edwards began corresponding with Woolsey, whom he had never met. Woolsey's edition of the *Gorgias* had just appeared, and Edwards was eager to start an acquaintance with a potential contributor to his periodicals.[10] When Edwards took over the *Bibliotheca* from Robinson in 1844, Woolsey contributed a number of articles on Greek and Latin. Edwards begged him to sign his name to these, as the Yale professor's reputation would add to the prestige of the new journal. Their correspondence blossomed into a personal friendship between the men and their wives, who visited each other in New Haven and Andover. Woolsey helped Mrs. Edwards financially when Edwards died in 1852.[11] Through Woolsey, Park and Edwards met and began working with a Yale-based network of educators, including Noah Porter.[12]

The Andover scholars did not limit their literary collaborations to working with evangelical Trinitarians. Park and Edwards also cooperated with

Unitarians from Harvard. Cornelius Conway Fenton (1807–1862), a noted Harvard classicist, joined Edwards and Sears in writing a volume of *Classical Studies*. Edwards himself sat on Harvard's Greek examining committee for ten years. Park delivered the Dudleian lecture at Harvard in 1845, on the "Perils of Romanism." Harvard men contributed more and more to the *Bibliotheca* as time passed. Unlike Woods and Stuart, Park and Edwards were not concerned with refuting Unitarianism. The intellectual interests the two groups shared were more important to both sides than party divisions.

As an institution, Andover's focus shifted slightly from a defensive bastion of Trinitarian Congregationalism to an active center of Christian scholarship in this period. Under the prodding first of Stuart, then Robinson and others, Andover built up one of the largest institutional libraries in New England. While her 6,000-volume collection lagged far behind Harvard's 30,000, only Yale (8,500) and Bowdoin (8,000) had larger libraries.[13] Considering the seminary's youth compared with these established colleges, this was a large collection, arguing a strong institutional commitment to the library. Every faculty member who went to Europe considered it part of his commission to enlarge the seminary's collection.[14] The trustees, too, worked to build it up. A note from Samuel Armstrong, the treasurer, to fellow trustee Samuel Farrar on expenditures for ordering books shows them taking an active part in the ordering. "I am looking daily for the additional books from England," Armstrong wrote in 1833, which will "Make in all $1000 for the Library." Robinson had given him a list to purchase, but Armstrong chose to "finish the Eng. [*sic*] order in the first place."[15]

The trustees in the 1830s began to cherish Andover's reputation for scholarship. In 1837, trustee William Bannister (a state senator), had written Farrar that "there is much dissatisfaction in this Theo. Sem'y on account of the deficiency—even failure—of instruction in Prof. Stuart's department." Bannister feared that Andover's declining reputation in that field would cause enrollments to drop "if some remedy" were not "seasonably applied." He urged Farrar to consider hiring a young man to augment Stuart's work.[16] Bela Bates Edwards took up his new duties the following September.

Neither the Andover faculty nor Christians at other schools forgot their primary purpose: to train ministers for promoting the gospel of Christ. All the Andover-trained scholars combined piety with literature. As Hackett's biographer points out, his "professional interest in the scholar's spoils of interpretation was subordinate to his interest . . . in the plain meaning of Scriptures, by which his race was to be judged . . ."[17] This balance between classical and religious interests was apparent in many other Andover graduates. Calvin Stowe (1802–1886), who attended Andover from 1825–1828 and served as Professor of Sacred Literature from 1852–1864, always carried pocket copies of the Greek New Testament and Dante's *Divine Comedy* (in Italian); they were under his pillow when he died.[18] Barnas Sears (1802–1880), a Baptist like Hackett, taught Christian theology at Newton Center. He also published a German grammar, essays on how to teach Latin, and a study on the current state of classical studies.[19] Like Hackett, both Stowe and Sears studied in Germany for several years.

At Andover itself, the balance between scholarship and piety existed in each faculty member: Ralph Emerson (1787–1863), who taught church history; W. G. T. Shedd, who succeeded him; Stowe; Austin Phelps, who taught sacred rhetoric after 1848; and of course, Edwards and Park, all wanted their scholarly gifts to aid evangelical Christianity. While each man combined these twin aspirations, each separately embodied one more than the other in fulfilling the seminary's mission. Edwards was a by-word for scholarship, Park for pulpit rhetoric. Phelps was a brilliant preacher; Shedd and Stowe outstanding scholars.

Park and Edwards dominated the faculty in the 1840s and '50s. The two met at Andover as students, where they struck up a warm and lasting friendship (Park met his wife through Edwards in 1835[20]). Before the two became colleagues, Edwards confided his editorial ambitions to his friend; afterwards they shared many literary tasks. Their families grew up together, and Edwards' only daughter married Park's surviving son.

The two close friends provide a symbolic picture of the relationship between the seminary's pursuit of scholarship and its defense of orthodoxy. Both tied religion to their understanding of modern science, Edwards through philology (which we will discuss in chapter 4), and Park in theology.

Edwards (1802–1852) exemplified the life of a Christian scholar. He was involved in a range of activities, so many that the number he did well is amazing. He taught at Andover for fifteen years. He was active in many social action groups, including the American Education Society, the American Home Mission Society, the temperance movement, and missionary efforts. He edited four different journals, spoke or read ten languages, and took an active part in the life of his wife and their surviving child Sarah. He was a strong advocate of women's rights in education.[21]

Edwards had "a living enthusiasm for good letters," Park wrote. At the same time, he strove to be a model of Christian charity, while obsessed with a sense of sin so profound that even on his death bed he shrank from claiming divine grace. His last prayers were uttered in the tones of a "stricken, bruised, crushed penitent," Park recorded. As one of his students, later professor of Greek at Dartmouth, recalled Edwards, he "was a *religious* teacher of *inspired* truth."[22] Putnam said that he sought to raise his students "above the mere curiosity of the scholar to the serious, the submissive, and the devout temper of the Christian."[23] Park, Hackett, and others remembered Edwards as "that disciple whom Jesus loved," a common characterization for any particularly well-loved friend. His outstanding quality seems to have been a sweet and pious temper, which his students strove to emulate.

The youngest surviving child of Ann Bates and Elisha Edwards, B. B. Edwards grew up in an indulgent, over-protective household which encouraged both his introspection and his excessive shrinking from public life. When he was fourteen, his parents sent him away to school. He was so homesick there that he hired a chaise and returned home, only to be sent away again. Similarly, when he underwent his intense conversion in 1823, he sought refuge with his parents while struggling with this crisis. His mother's death in 1826 plunged him into a two-year depression. Even in an age where displays of strong emotion were encouraged, Edwards' effusions were thought unusual. Park wrote that they were excessive and "not to be commended."[24]

Edwards attended Amherst College from 1821 to 1824. In 1825, he entered Andover. In 1826, he agreed to work as assistant secretary for the American Education Society, an organization he served until his death. In 1826, he was also acting as Greek tutor at Amherst. These combined activities took so much time that he dropped his Andover studies until 1829. At that point, he tried to curtail his secretarial duties somewhat in order to complete the theological course. Ordained to the ministry in 1831, Edwards never served as a pastor: he was a poor public speaker and shrank from exposing himself in that way. In 1837, Andover hired him to teach Hebrew, but he continued laboring for the American Education Society, as well as the Home Mission Society. The pulmonary condition which killed him caused him to take a year's vacation in Europe in 1846–47, where he involved himself in major British and German intellectual movements. Elected to the Brown Professorship in 1848, he labored incessantly at the seminary despite his worsening health until he died in 1852.

While Edwards' deep piety shone through all aspects of his life and work, his was, as Park noted, a contemplative style of Christianity. His chief preoccupations were intellectual, and most of his adult time was spent in two intellectual pursuits: editing scholarly journals and studying biblical and classical languages and literatures.

It was with the American Education Society that Edwards began his literary work. Founded in 1815, this society was devoted to educating "pious young men for the gospel ministry."[25] It solicited contributions to support a scholarship fund, figuring that the income each year from $1,000 could maintain one man in a college or a seminary.[26] As assistant secretary, Edwards' duties included visiting recipients of scholarships, examining their piety and financial eligibility, conducting the Society's correspondence, and assisting the Secretary, the Rev. Mr. Cornelius, in keeping records.[27] Visiting beneficiaries at Amherst in 1832, Edwards "inquired of the officers concerning our young men; saw about thirty-five of them individually . . . ; gave an address to them; preached a sermon to the students."[28]

The record-keeping Edwards did ultimately had the most effect on his career, for it led him to begin his editorial work. With Cornelius, he ran the *American Quarterly Register* for the Society from 1828 through 1832. He remained on the editorial staff until 1842. In the *Register*, Edwards gathered statistics on different aspects of American education. Tables showed the size of college enrollments and of school libraries. He compiled lists of ordinations and installations from different denominations. The journal also supplied occasional information about colleges and seminaries, reported revivals and numbers of conversions in them, and printed inspirational advice from such prominent teachers as Ebenezer Porter.

While Edwards remained interested in these statistical details, it was the *American Quarterly Observer* which provided the model for his lifelong editorial plan. He began the *Observer* independently in 1832 and ran it until 1835, when he merged it with the *Biblical Repository and Classical Review*. He really wanted a periodical with a wider coverage of intellectual topics than the *Quarterly Register* allowed. He outlined his hopes to Park late in 1832. He wanted to include

> the discussion of Politics—Christian Economy—the general Principles
> of our Benevolent Societies—geographical and statistical articles in
> connection with the propagation of Christianity—Mental Philosophy
> in its relation to moral—independent Christian Reviews of the most
> important new publications—and perhaps a condensed analysis of
> literary and other intelligence.[29]

Edwards believed he had a peculiar ministry to parochial pastors. He considered it his duty to disseminate culture to them.[30] Tours he made for the American Education Society convinced him that the standards of biblical scholarship in the country were very low. To raise them, he wanted to familiarize Americans with German thought. Above all, he hoped to improve "the mental and moral culture of . . . pastors" and "foster the continued interest of [the] clergy in good learning."[31] Edwards believed that a periodical possessing "intellectual power" which reached 2,000 ministers could ultimately "illuminate the conscience, and arouse and direct the mind, of the whole country."[32]

In 1835, he took over the *Biblical Repository* from Robinson, changing it from its exclusive focus on critical studies to a general theological review. He gave up the editorship in 1838 to devote himself full-time to teaching, but in 1844 he again took over one of Robinson's castoffs, the *Bibliotheca Sacra*, which he edited until 1852. He merged the *Bibliotheca* with the *Repository*. Both periodicals investigated the topics he had outlined to Park in 1832.

While pursuing his literary career, Edwards also spent a lot of energy on his other major interest, languages. In 1826, he was invited to become professor of Greek at Amherst. He turned down this offer, but continued to study biblical languages and literatures. He made an effort "to read a portion of Greek every day," his friend Hackett recalled.[33] In 1839, to understand Hebrew better, he began studying Arabic, and eventually grew quite proficient at it. He read German as a matter of course, learned French, and studied Italian. In addition, he had considerable knowledge of Chaldaic and Syriac. Hackett wrote in his memorial that "no teacher in this country has ever surpassed him as a grammarian."[34]

In addition, Edwards genuinely loved classical learning. He rewarded himself at the end of his daily labors by reading Virgil or some other classical poet. Homer was his favorite: the rest of his books were shipped back to Andover during his final illness in Athens, Georgia, but the blind poet remained with him until the end. During his European tour, Edwards met Tholuck, Mueller, Neander, and other scholars, but his greatest joy came from revisiting the scenes of classical antiquity in Rome.[35]

Like Woolsey, Edwards was so consumed by a sense of sin that he would not undertake a parish ministry. He wrote his father in 1830 that "as I am borne on towards the Christian ministry, I shrink back almost with terror."[36] His scruples arose, he claimed, from his fear that salvation would elude him as a minister. "Chrysostom says, that he thinks but a few ministers are finally saved," he wrote his father after preaching for the first time. He added that "Augustine, when they wished to ordain him, asked with much solicitude, if they wished that he should perish."[37] Similar self-doubts kept him from becoming a missionary, a career he considered the most noble and essential of all Christian vocations; or from devoting himself body and soul to the anti-slavery cause. This cause affected him deeply, he recorded, almost to the point of distracting him from his professional duties, but he would not serve it with the bulk of his time.[38]

In fact, like Woolsey, Edwards followed those professional activities which he most enjoyed. He stated that he did those things which would keep him humble and stifle his desire for public acclaim. On those grounds he refused the Amherst professorship in 1830 to continue working for the American Education Society. In 1837, the search for humility led him from the Society to the Andover faculty. It was more than coincidence that he found his greatest joy in the literary work which he also saw as his professional duty. Defending Christian scholarship at one point, Edwards wrote that a person could be absorbed by study from three different causes. He might do it from love of the Savior, or in deference to some secret resolution. Finally, he added, "it is possible [that a scholar] finds *happiness* in the *employment* of his faculties, that he would be wretched if he were not earnestly engaged."[39] Edwards probably studied from all three motives, but the last statement was a cry from the heart. He found true happiness in learning.

Edwards Amasa Park (1808–1899), who characterized Andover's commitment to orthodoxy in this period, was also an able scholar. Like other orthodox young men who came to Andover, he early learned from Stuart that biblical studies could enhance, not impair, the effectiveness of Christian witness.[40] Park learned German, became well-versed in biblical languages, and studied in Germany. He made three trips abroad in all, the first and most important in 1842–43. His exposure to a range of German thought, including that of the Hegelians (whom he deliberately sought), had a lasting impact on his own work.

However, it was Park's considerable skill as a pulpit orator that led Andover to hire him in 1836. His wide fame in the New England of his day came not from his scholarly attainments, which never formed a major part of his professional life or work, but from the power of his preaching and the logic with which he reinterpreted Edwardsean Calvinism for the 1850s.

Park is generally known as the last of the consistent, or Edwardsean Calvinists. In his own day many found him radical, for he abandoned much of the determinism of the older Calvinists. But he was forced into retirement in 1881 because his views were considered obsolete by his young post–Civil War colleagues.[41] Indeed, while he had planned for years to write a systematic theology when he retired, he decided that his ideas would find too little acceptance for him to make the effort.[42]

All Park's upbringing and education pushed him into the role he ultimately assumed as defender of the faith. The second of four sons born to

Abigail Ware and Calvin Park, he grew up in a household dominated by intense piety and erudite religious discussion. His father was professor of moral philosophy at Brown, and directed the education of his sons, who all became Congregational ministers. Park recalled in later life that by the age of ten he was already "something of a theologian," due to the rigorous religious training he received from his father.[43] He entered Brown at fourteen, graduating as valedictorian in 1826. At that point, he went to teach in Weymouth, Massachusetts, hoping to decide what to do with his life.

All his thoughts from his earliest years had been directed to the questions of sin and Salvation; he was very worried about the state of his soul. He believed his heart was hard, that he had no real sense of sin, let alone of grace, and could not even call himself a Christian. Fearing that his interest in religion was more intellectual than experiential, he could not bear to prepare for the ministry which he wanted as his life's work. He considered medicine, but decided finally "if [he] could not preach honestly, [he] could not do anything honestly."[44] He subjected himself to a rigorous self-examination and concluded that he did indeed believe and love the doctrines of the Bible. He even accepted those "commonly disliked and opposed by men, concerning God's character and sovereignty, his decrees of election, his attitude towards sin."[45] He decided that he was, in fact, a Christian and ready for a ministerial career. These reflections, recorded some seventy years after the fact, are the only record we have of Park's conversion. It seems to have been much less intense emotionally than that of Edwards.

Park spent the year following his conversion studying theology at home. In 1828, he enrolled at Andover, where he finished the three-year course in 1830. During this period, he published his first theological article, defending orthodoxy against Unitarianism. It was part apology, part polemic, but chiefly an effort to find a common ethical ground for the two parties. While the article merely restated some common Calvinist positions, its efforts to mediate philosophically between the sects foreshadowed Park's later ecumenical efforts.[46]

On his ordination, he accepted a call to Braintree, Massachusetts, where he had a successful two-year ministry. He presided over a moderately successful revival, and his preaching began to attract attention. He received calls from several prominent Boston churches, but declined them, for he began to be strongly interested in education.

At the end of his second year in Braintree, Park pleaded poor health and was dismissed from his charge. He took off a year for rest and introspection. At its end, he went to Yale to listen to Nathaniel Taylor.

Already dissatisfied with Woods' anthropology, Park quickly accepted

Taylor's views on depravity and regeneration.[47] Park himself had grown up adept in Scottish philosophy under his father's tutelage. Taylor's use of it impressed him profoundly. Scottish realism became a hallmark of Park's theology as he developed it over the next fifteen years.

In 1836, Park's reputation as a pulpit orator brought a call from Andover to serve as professor of sacred rhetoric. Park seized this opportunity to move into education. Once at Andover, he went from strength to strength, achieving a dominant position in the seminary. In 1847, he was elected to its most prestigious chair, the Abbot professorship of Christian theology, because the trustees believed his reputation was bringing many students to the school.[48]

His renown came not only because of his great skill in the pulpit and his printed essays in the *Bibliotheca*, but also from his personal ambition. From earliest childhood, Park had been highly competitive. The stress his father placed on intellectual achievement fostered keen rivalry among the sons. This spirit still cropped up in relations between Edwards and his elder brother Calvin when the former was at Braintree. The older man was studying there as a resident licentiate.[49] He wrote Edwards that he would leave Andover if Edwards returned there. Calvin tried to push his brother into accepting a job in Bangor, Maine, to remove him from the Andover area. The younger man turned it down as being too remote from the center of theological action.[50]

The Park brothers' rivalry carried over into Edwards' approach to his colleagues once on the Andover faculty. Park had early alienated Woods by his conversion to Taylor's theology. Relations between the two men became increasingly strained as Park's influence grew both inside and out of the seminary. Friction between Park and other members of the faculty often arose because he took more than his share of preaching opportunities and other occasions for public attention.[51] Park's ambition also led him to assume a kind of deanship over the rest of the faculty. He served as their spokesman from the late 1840s until 1868.

When Park achieved his fondest wish by getting elected to the Abbot chair, it caused more tension with Woods and his supporters. Park had served as temporary Abbot professor in 1846–47, due to unspecified turmoil in the seminary during which Woods had been forced to step down.[52] Later, Park wrote Edwards of a sympathy meeting got up in New Haven for the older man. Park was worried by the public feeling Woods had roused; one gets the impression that he may have forced the older man to resign,[53] but the details are unfortunately lost.

One of the trustees, Dr. Daniel Dana, backed Woods and opposed Park against the vote of the others. Dana protested Park's election because in accepting Taylor's views, Park had "repudiated the doctrine of original sin" explicitly laid down in Abbot's will as a condition for holding the professorship.[54] Woods supported Dana, seeking a legal opinion on whether Abbot's heirs could reclaim the endowment. Stuart, too, sided with Woods. His acrimony towards Park was heightened by the latter's refusal to print some of his articles in the *Bibliotheca*.

The opposition was unsuccessful. Edwards rejoiced from England both on his friend's appointment, and the failure of his enemies. "The Abbot Professor meant not so, but a higher Power over-ruled all for good," he exulted. "I am glad because the Trustees were compelled to yield to the popular view."[55] Park's ambitions had placed him where he wanted to be. From the Abbot chair he dominated the seminary and much of New England Congregationalism for three decades.

Park probably began to formulate his own theology in 1834, when he heard Taylor lecture. His ideas had jelled by the time he gave his inaugural address as Abbot professor, and did not change noticeably for the rest of his life. Adapting to the intellectual climate of the day, he used Common Sense and natural theology to present religious truths as both objective and scientific.

Woods, too, had based theology on Common Sense and the analogy between religious and scientific thought. The difference between Park and his predecessor lay in Park's use of Scottish philosophy and natural theology as apologetic tools. Woods took for granted that hypotheses in theology were established on the same factual basis as those in physics. He didn't try to explore the underlying similarities or differences of the two fields. Park, on the other hand, had to establish theology self-consciously as a science grounded in Baconianism. In face of rational attacks on the Bible at home and abroad, Park felt compelled to restructure the principles by which Christians thought about the sacred book. If principles could be established in such a way as to compel atheistic support, Park believed Christians would then have the tools to prove the truth of the inspired volume.[56]

Park believed that such compelling grounds could only be found in a Baconian natural philosophy. He used Common Sense to put theology on the same footing as other natural sciences. He argued that any science was a "system of ultimate truths which, in conformity with the fundamental laws of belief, are proved by subordinate facts."[57] Theology's axioms included the necessary existence of God as the cause of created matter, the necessary unity of God, and so on. The facts included such things as perfect natural contrivances which betokened their divine designer. The geometrical perfection of beehives, for example, existed long before Newton uncovered the mathematics behind them. Abstract reason exhibited by unthinking bees constituted proof of their creation by a thinking being, Park contended.[58] Baconian methods proved the existence of God in this fashion, and gave theology a scientific basis in Park's mind.

Park next used natural theology to prove the Deity's benevolence. Like Paley, he relied on the fitness of means to ends as one sign of divine benevolence. Further, the common experience of all men proved for Park that one could, indeed, claim benevolence as an attribute of a Creator who so wondrously adapted means to ends.[59] Relying on common human perception was, of course, one of the pillars of Scottish reasoning. In discussing benevolence, Park also covered the immortality of the soul: God, as a skillful contriver, would not make a being as short-lived as man appears to be. Instead, he lives on forever after death. Park also explained the necessity for sin and pain in a benevolent deity's world.[60]

Park now came to the trickiest part of his argument, which involved using natural theology to prove the divine inspiration of Scripture. He hoped to prove their truth from necessity, rather than faith, in order to compel atheistic acquiescence. The Bible attested to the existence of a benevolent God from beginning to end, Park believed. Because we have separate proof from natural theology of a benevolent deity, the Scriptures were necessarily true and constituted one of the facts in the science of natural theology.[61] From that position, Park discussed divine inspiration, jumping without noticing it from the assertion that the Scriptures were true to the fact that they had been divinely inspired.

Park always used a four-step argument based on the inductive method to prove his scientific truths. In his lectures, he used moral philosophy to prove the existence of God; natural theology to prove his benevolence; his benevolence to prove the truth of the Bible; and the Bible to prove the truth of Calvinist doctrines.[62] He also preached a cycle of sermons in the winter of 1844–45, using natural theology in the same manner to prove all of modern Calvinism.[63]

In this fashion, Park tied theology to modern science. Where Woods only drew parallels between Christian doctrines and Newtonian mathematics, Park forced his faith to rely on modern science. If the Common Sense interpretation of natural philosophy should turn out to be untenable, then theology would have no reliable foundation, either.

Yet Park believed firmly in the faith once delivered by the early New England saints. While he spent much of his public energy mediating between Calvinism and other denominations, in the classroom he tried to prepare young men to uphold the faith of their fathers. His own beliefs were strongly enough defended that he could explore many different ideas, including rationalism and Unitarianism. But he thought it an important part of his duties to buttress the minds of his charges with Trinitarian Congregationalism before they were exposed to the world. They read Channing, Hume, Monbodo, and other dangerous authors,[64] but only under close supervision. For every year that we have notes of Park's class lectures, he followed the same format with similar wording. Each doctrine was subjected to a rigorous examination. Park went through every conceivable argument which could be raised against it, and responses to those arguments. Beginning with the existence of God, Park outlined all the incorrect proofs first. For instance, proof of God's existence as an innate idea was invalid, and Park listed four objections to it, answers to the objections, and responses to the answers. When he came to his own proof for God, derived from moral philosophy, he also listed all objections, this time to give the students weapons for answering opponents.

Park's concern with his students' faith did not stop with their intellectual ability to defend it. Both he and Edwards kept a keen eye on the young men's religious state. Reporting once to the trustees, Park complained about heretical tendencies in the Middle class. Some were "Transcendentalists; some, Free Will Baptists; one . . . is about as near to Swedenborgianiam as anything."[65] In the same year, Edwards was relieved to report on the junior year's spontaneous involvement in devotions. They attended "monthly concert on Sabbath eve," with missionary meetings on Mondays, a religious conference every Wednesday, "several prayer meetings" on Saturdays, and "four prayer meetings" each month "without faculty members present."[66]

The Andover of the Calvinist renaissance differed markedly from the school founded by Abbot and Bartlett in 1808. The change lay not so much in doctrinal modifications, although these were great, nor increased erudition—for Stuart was a formidable scholar—but in the school's growing cosmopolitanism. Where Stuart struggled for a copy of Eichhorn's work, Edwards corresponded easily with Germany's top biblical scholars. Not only did he visit them, but they asked him to write for their theological journals.[67]

Park continued to defend orthodox doctrines, but his opponents lay outside Andover's network of scholars. His greatest public debate before the Civil War was with Princeton's Charles Hodge on the freedom of the will.[68] With Andover's early foes, the Unitarians, Park stood on terms of great cordiality. Indeed, Harvard granted him an honorary divinity degree.

Park used the *Bibliotheca Sacra* as a forum for ecumenism, hoping to ease some of the barriers between different parties of Christians. He asked representatives of different denominations, including Baptists, Episcopalians, Methodists, and even Roman Catholics, to explain their important distinctive doctrines. When the Methodist Daniel Day Whedon contributed such an article in 1862, he wrote Park of the positive benefits coming from his editorial policy. Whedon was gratified by the "manly & liberal course which" Park "struck out." He added that "as editor of the Meth. Qu. [*sic*] Review I have followed suit."[69]

It was through the *Bibliotheca* that Park and Edwards best expressed their dedication to the community of Christian scholars. Taking over the journal from Robinson in 1844, they merged it with the old *Biblical Repository,* and continued it along the same editorial lines.[70] Leonard Bacon had described the *Repository* in 1843 as "modeled . . . after the type of German rather than English journalism." It was a "rich repository of essays and disquisitions on various points in theology and kindred sciences, with here and there a valuable contribution on some topic of general literature." Bacon added that it was "a work chiefly for professional men."[71] The *Bibliotheca,* following in the *Repository*'s path, became known as the most erudite theological journal in New England.[72] Its articles were signed to show that it was a clearing-house for discussion, not a party organ.[73] The quarterly format was another signal of its intellectual, rather than polemic intent, for party journals tended to use the monthly. Coming out only every three months seemed to add a certain ponderousness to a journal.[74]

Insofar as Andover had a house organ, it was the *Bibliotheca.* All the faculty took a hand in it. Park and Edwards were editors-in-chief, but Stowe, Emerson, Phelps, and men of non-professorial rank like E. R. A. Taylor all assisted. The type of articles Edwards solicited reflected the seminary's commitment to scholarship and its involvement with German learning in particular. He seldom printed essays on doctrinal disputes. The first volume contained translations of nine German papers on interpretation, language, or theology; a discussion of Aristotle's life by Park; various exegetical articles by Stuart and Edwards; and a long treatise on the history of monasticism by Ralph Emerson. Robinson, Woolsey, and Sears also contributed essays.[75]

As time passed, the *Bibliotheca* continued to present much of German scholarship to the American clergy. It reviewed the most important new grammars and lexicons; published philological discourses; printed such daring ideas as those of the Hegelian Christians. In 1845, Edwards wrote Park that he did not want to print extreme theological views which might alienate people "till our publication . . . is larger."[76] And with the exception of Park's responses to Hodge in the 1850s, the *Bibliotheca* did not get involved in controversy.

The yearning at Andover for a high standard of American letters and literary institutions was reflected time and again in the *Bibliotheca*. The first volume[77] opened with an article by Edward Robinson on "The Aspect of Literature and Science in the United States as Compared with Europe." The stress which Edwards and Park placed on literature is apparent from the prominent position they gave this article, as well as from the prestige of its author.

Robinson praised many aspects of American schools. In particular, he lauded the high level of literacy here, extending to all classes of society: in Europe, he wrote, literacy was an upper-class privilege.[78] Yet with all the advantages Robinson saw in the United States—its strong practical science, its active public men, the democratic political institutions—he "pine[d] away with longing, when he regard[ed] the infinite distance" between American libraries and those of Europe. The article pleaded for money to build up American libraries.

Gone were the days when Stuart had to defend scholarship as an aid to orthodoxy. Robinson made no apology for his desire. He simply wanted Americans to develop the tools which would enable those with intellectual aspirations to stand on the same footing with European scholars.

Park and Edwards expressed similar longings in an article on "Theological Education in the United States." They, however, did claim that "profound and varied learning" would aid theological science. "Such learning leads the mind away from the common temptations of life," the two wrote, and "tends to elevate the minister above those degrading sins to which the indolent and the ignorant are exposed."[79] Not only would learning aid the theologian, the two believed: it was his duty to develop his intellect. Erudition would inspire him "with humility [for] his safety lies in confining himself to his appropriate duties; and of these duties, the diligent occupation of his intellect is one."[80] Indeed, if a clergyman developed his intellect, he would be better able to discharge "the practical duties of his office."

The needs which Park and Edwards saw in American theological education demonstrate further the sophistication of Andover compared with her early years. Stuart had written that when he came to Andover in 1810, there was scarcely anyone in America competent to teach Hebrew.[81] Park and Edwards did not complain about the level of Hebrew training in the country. Instead, they worried that the Hebrew of American theologians was inadequate because these men had not studied "Chaldaic, Syriac, Samaritan, Arabic, and Ethiopian dialects, [so] as to be able to derive from them any valuable illustrations of the meaning of Hebrew words and phrases."[82]

When Andover was established, it was to protect orthodox doctrines from the dangers emanating out of Cambridge. By the time Park and Edwards were collaborating on the *Bibliotheca*, this cause was forgotten in their larger desire to develop a high standard of scholarship in America. They protested the number of theological seminaries, for the multiplication of schools rendered it "impossible to obtain that amount of apparatus and external aid which is essential to the advance of letters."[83]

The two shared with Robinson an urgent desire for improved scholarly facilities. The very range of arguments they brought to support their pleas testified that on many levels they thought scholarship an end in itself, rather than an adjunct to piety. They wrote that the quality of theological education would be increased if seminaries were less numerous, so that libraries could be consolidated. Yet this was the age of westward expansion of denominational schools so that the west could be won for Christ through a particular sect. Park and Edwards urged seminaries like their own to raise funds to support their libraries.[84] Better education would increase ecumenism, Park said, because Christians would see that their most venerated ancestors held views unacceptable to the modern age.[85]

Edwards believed better education would improve the quality of government.[86] Everyone would be improved by a higher standard of letters, including lawyers, doctors, and orators.[87]

This passionate reaching out for knowledge created the cosmopolitan community of scholars through which Andover was chiefly distinguished in the 1840s and '50s. The school continued to train more missionaries than philologists, the faculty would not expose the tender minds of the young to too many heretical doctrines, but the range of their intellectual activity, and the depth of their commitment to it, put the scholars in the forefront of the Calvinist renaissance.

The faculty realized that they had a joint mission both to scholarship and the defense and promotion of the gospel of Christ. They saw these as complementary, rather than conflicting goals. In 1850, Park preached a sermon to the gathered clergy of the Massachusetts churches which spelled out the harmony he perceived between piety and intellect. This sermon showed the mature position of Park's theological work.

In preparing "The Theology of the Intellect and That of the Feelings," Park had originally hoped to preach a sermon which would mediate among all the denominations present. He himself realized that the finished product fell far short of his goal.[88] In fact, the sermon touched off a fiery controversy with Charles Hodge (1797–1878), centering on the use of creeds, the authority of the Bible, and the doctrine of imputation.[89] Many of Park's comments did focus on topical problems: the emotional quality of the current revivals; the narrow creedalism displayed by the Presbyterian General Assembly; and so on. But the sermon also reflects his full-grown thought on intellect and feeling, representing an apology for the style of theological training offered at Andover.

Park defended both aspects of religion. The theology of the feelings, he said, expressed the affections of the mind. It was suitable to "the persuasive sermon, to the pleadings of the liturgy, to the songs of Zion."[90] It expressed "sentiments too deep, or too mellow, or too impetuous to be suited with the stiff language of the intellect."[91] On the other hand, theology of the intellect, "comprehends the truth just as it is," expressing it scientifically with the axioms and propositions Park found important.[92]

While making a strong statement for affective religion, the sermon really supported the primacy of the intellect. Park had been developing this argument for several years. In his inaugural address as Abbot professor, he had defended reason as enlarging the realm of the heart, for "feeling shall follow perception."[93] In 1850, he stated the primacy of reason more explicitly. Too many pious people undervalued "the human intellect," Park stated, "for the sake of exalting the affections, as if sin had less to do with the feelings than with the intelligence." As a theologian trained by Taylor, Park believed the mind could accept the Gospel more easily than the corrupted affections. "The will," he asserted, fell *"from* the intellectual powers, while they remain truer than any other to their office." Using the language of Common Sense, Park added that "our speculative tendencies are original, legitimate parts of our constitution which it is irreverent to censure."[94]

Nonetheless, the two modes of faith enlarged each other and protected one another from error. A creed that roused no sentiments in the hearts of Christians must be wrong, the Abbot professor argued. Reason could petrify poetic expressions of the heart to the point where they became false creeds, damaging the unity of Christ's church.

In a tradition established by Stuart, Park wrote that the theology of the feelings expressed with "poetic elegance" ideas which would be false if taken literally.[95] For example, the Bible painted

the unrenewed heart as a stone needing to be exchanged for flesh; and again, not as a stone, but as flesh needing to be turned into spirit; and yet again, neither as stone nor as flesh, but as darkened spirit needing to be illuminated by the light of knowledge.[96]

The mistake theologians made, Park insisted, was in translating such metaphorical portraits into doctrines. The Bible could not always be understood literally.

Hodge attacked this point immediately, but it was not a new one for Park or for Andover. It was Stuart who first taught that literal interpretations of the Bible could lead to ridiculous extremes, that one did not have to understand expressions like the Genesis "water above the heavens" other than poetically. Park merely followed his teacher in explaining to his classes that the Bible taught no false doctrines even though it might contain historical inaccuracies.[97]

Park differed radically from his predecessors in trying to abandon creeds as the rigid expression of metaphorical doctrines. Leonard Woods had defended the use of creeds. The doctrines of faith, he wrote for his own journal, *The Literary and Theological Review*, were the only means by which Christianity could be restored to "its original simplicity." Critics accused the orthodox of "*wasting . . . time and strength in discussing points in theology, and in determining articles of [a] creed.*" But Woods believed devotion to these doctrines should be increased "in our families, schools, and churches . . ."[98]

Park strove to rise above Woods' attitude. He did not want to abandon creeds altogether, but he hoped to see them express a few universally accepted beliefs. When creeds tried to explain every doctrinal detail, they froze Christians into a narrow time frame. Ideas of great beauty and power, Park said, became both ridiculous and sterile when subjected to intellectual debate by parties trying to harden them into doctrines. For instance, the comfort people received from knowing "that our deceased companions still mingle with us, and aid us in our struggles" came from the feelings. The Roman communion petrified this feeling in prose, developing a pantheon of saints to whom Christians prayed instead of God.[99] And once a metaphor was frozen as doctrine, it took years of struggle to free it again.

The heart knows that Christ died and rose again, Park added. On that idea all Christians agreed, despite the great warfare that sectarian leaders fought on the means by which this resurrection saved them.[100] Simple dogmas, which faith and reason could assert together, were the only creeds Park would allow.[101] He believed that he could be in harmony with all Christians who used both heart and mind. He therefore supported the Unitarian Henry Ware of Harvard, who shared Park's rational approach to theology,[102] but he opposed the Trinitarian Hodge, whose narrow intellectualizing (Park thought) stifled the poetry of the Bible.

Park told his audience that religious battles would become rarer and rarer as the progress of science continued to unfold the truth.[103] He believed, like a true Baconian, that he could uncover facts which would command the intellectual assent of all hearers. Like the other Andover scholars, he believed that modern scholarship had placed in his hands the means for finding these facts. While the "Theology of the Intellect" supported religious affections, it really argued for the supremacy of reason over feelings in uncovering the truth. "Holy feelings" served the intellect, Park explained, prompting it "to new discoveries."[104] He could make no clearer statement about Andover's commitment of orthodoxy to the dictates of modern science.

The Knowledge Explosion at Andover

❖ ❖ ❖

Happy is the man who finds wisdom,
And the man who gets understanding,
For the gain from it is better than gain from silver
And its profit better than gold.
— Proverbs 3:13–14

Sir William Jones (1746–1794), the English jurist and India administrator, first recognized the antiquity of Sanskrit and its relation to modern European languages in the 1780s. His work opened up exciting new avenues for study in philology in the early nineteenth century. The Germans, rather than the English, took advantage of Jones' work to produce a scientific study of language. They developed philology in numerous branches—comparative language study, etymology, history of languages, and even histories of nations based on the evolution of their speech.

History also blossomed as a discipline in Germany. As men began cracking different ancient hieroglyphic codes, their research sparked a new interest in ancient civilizations. The textual analyses done by biblical scholars in the eighteenth century helped trigger a revolution in nineteenth-century historical research as well as in philology. In 1811, G. B. Niebuhr published a *History of Rome*. Basing his work on his own ground-breaking decipherment of ancient Latin inscriptions, Niebuhr declared that most of what passed for Roman history in 1800 was inaccurate. He used his inscriptions to write what he considered a better interpretation of the ancient society.

Influenced by Niebuhr's work, Leopold von Ranke began probing into original documents to rewrite Italian and German history of the late fifteenth century. He showed that the contemporary narratives on which most history was based were often factually wrong, and that history could not be written without archival sources.

These were exciting times at the German universities. Scholars came from all over Europe to sit at the feet of von Ranke, Schleiermacher, and other prominent figures. The Americans who trekked to Germany in the 1830s and '40s participated in a major intellectual movement. Their conscious motivation may have been the hope of converting German scholarship to American Christianity, but they were really drawn to the rapidly growing disciplines from a love of learning.

Germany contained as many schools of thought as there were foreigners to hear them. Since auditors often went to five or six universities in two years, they usually returned home with a pretty eclectic intellectual package. Often, a set of warring parties might grow up at home, both based on the new learning. This occurred most obviously in England, where Cambridge and Oxford developed antithetical systems of church history from their exposure to German work.

At Andover, too, pilgrims to Germany brought back varying philosophies of language and history. These differences did not disturb the working relations of the faculty in the 1840s, but they underlay the dissension which developed at the school later in the century. W. G. T. Shedd became an enthusiastic convert to the Platonic interpretation of history developed at Berlin by August Neander (1789–1854). This was also the school adopted at Cambridge (England): in history, as in biblical criticism, Americans tended to follow European scholars. Following Herder and Hegel, Shedd regarded the nation as an organism through which the spirit of history moved. Like the Cambridge scholars, he christened this concept to make progress a spiritual event. Nations might rise and die in a cyclical pattern, but men continued to develop morally, moving towards God's final, inscrutable goal.[1]

Park disagreed with Shedd, for he thought the Platonic approach undermined reliance on Providence.[2] He and Edwards took a more linear view of history, seeing the unfolding of God's purpose in different times as separate from the histories of nations. This view, which had its roots in Augustine's work, said that nations were tools in God's hand, not organic representations of the spirit of history.

Shedd's approach to language also differed from that of his colleagues. He followed Herder and the Grimm brothers in trying to find the organic development of thought, language, and peoples.[3] Edwards and Woolsey studied languages, not language. They did not want to uncover the philosophical relation between thought and speech, but the actual thoughts of the ancients as revealed in a better knowledge of their speech.[4] Their philosophical differences did not divide the faculty, for they also shared many ideas. Perhaps most important, they united in awe of German research. They did not take German philosophy seriously, whereas they generally considered indisputable the facts uncovered by the European scholars.

Andover's deeper involvement in German learning should really be traced to Edward Robinson's first trip abroad in 1826. Robinson probably went at Stuart's urging,[5] to make the trip Stuart's health had always prohibited. Robinson spent four years abroad, primarily at the universities of Halle and Berlin, although he also traveled to Leipsic, Gottingen, and Heidelberg. His ties and interest in German scholarship were strengthened by his 1828 marriage to the daughter of one of the philosophy faculty at Halle. His wife and her father helped make German scholars accessible to Robinson and his friends, and also found a European audience for their writings.

Robinson's own interests were primarily linguistic and hermeneutic. The people who most impressed him were the Hebrew scholar Gesenius and the pietistic theologian August Tholuck at Halle.[6] On his return to Andover, Robinson founded the *American Biblical Repository* as a forum for the many new linguistic ideas he had absorbed abroad. In the single year of his editorship, he published nineteen separate articles. Eight concerned linguistic analysis, eight biblical criticism. Most were translations of articles written by Germans Robinson had met in Europe.

Their involvement in the European knowledge explosion changed the younger men's approach to philology at Andover from that followed by Stuart. Stuart saw language study as an essay into word meanings. The defenses he made both of the Bible and of orthodox doctrines were usually philological, but he equated the science with grammar. His *Chrestomathy* (see pp. 45–46) typified his entire approach to language. His writings addressed one idea: orthodox theology. He learned German in order to understand textual criticism. He took the language of Scripture and subjected it to an intense grammatical analysis out of which he obtained orthodox Calvinistic beliefs. He had only two major approaches to doctrine: grammatical and hortatory. He never seemed to explore an issue from an intrinsic interest in it, but always to prove a doctrinal point. His occasional nongrammatical essays, such as "The Mystical Presence of Christ in the Lord's Supper," read like polemical sermons.[7]

It was the grammatical approach to philology that Stuart taught in the classroom and published in his books and essays. A bibliography of his work contains a vast number of grammars and grammatical studies. These include the six editions of his Hebrew grammar; *A Grammar of the New Testament Dialect*; the *Chrestomathy*; three Hebrew grammars on special aspects of the language; numerous articles on such topics as "The Hebrew Tenses"; "Hebrew Lexicography"; or "Hints and Cautions Respecting the Greek Article." Stuart published many hermeneutical articles exegeting scriptural passages with painstaking grammatical care.

The younger scholars, including Robinson, began using language for non-doctrinal purposes. In addition, they explored doctrines as matters of historical interest, rather than polemically or apologetically. Some of these changes appeared in the early volumes of the *Biblical Repository*. The first volume contained a number of exegetical essays along grammatical lines, mostly by Stuart. He interpreted Romans 8:18–25, and the sixteenth psalm.

However, Robinson also included a number of German articles which began to expand the scope of philological investigation. Among these were a series on the languages spoken in New Testament times. Robinson wrote an introduction, explaining that interest in the question was essential for a biblical critic.[8] These articles relied chiefly on non–New Testament sources for their information, for the authors were trying to analyze New Testament language from other contemporary documents. These were really essays on the history of language, rather than hermeneutical efforts.

Stuart might compare New Testament words to other Greek writings to get the best meaning of a given passage. But he took for granted that the New Testament dialect was the best example of first-century Greek. The Germans, on the contrary, used other early sources to evaluate New Testament Greek. Closely tied to this approach was another new departure: the study of Greek as a classical, not a biblical language. Robinson translated two German articles for the *Repository*, one on a "General View of the Greek Language and Its Dialects," and the other on "Greek Style of the New Testament." In an introduction to both, Robinson wrote of a years'-long debate on whether the New Testament had been written originally in Attic or Hebraicized Greek. This dispute had caused scholars to ignore the real issue, he said, namely the development of a non-Attic Greek outside Greece in the lands of Alexander's conquests. In both articles, Robinson hoped to discuss the nature of provincial post-Alexandrian Greek, a topic irrelevant to the Bible.[9]

Such an interest in language apart from its biblical use absorbed an increasing amount of attention from Christian scholars. As they studied abroad, their involvement in language ranged over a variety of non-biblical topics. They developed in the process a strong sense of yearning for the culture of Europe which enabled its literary men to maintain a sophisticated level of scholarship.

All the younger Christian scholars were adept in the classics. Edwards read Ovid or Virgil every day to reward himself for completing his appointed tasks.[10] In 1843, Edwards, Sears, and C. C. Felton of Harvard published a volume of *Classical Studies* that praised the elegance of mind they all sought. Although everyone agreed with Robinson that philology was "almost an untrodden field in this country,"[11] the three co-authors believed that "classical scholarship in America" was "beginning . . . to be something higher and better than the dry study of words and grammatical forms." It was changing from the approach Stuart had considered important to become "a liberal and elegant pursuit."[12]

The three were disgusted by much in America which they thought classics could correct. In public life, they wrote, Greek and Latin were ignored to the detriment of every profession, whether legal, literary, medical, or political. A knowledge of antiquity would raise the cultural level of every person's life. The classics formed "a common bond," uniting all nations and ages together." The person who neglected them might be learned, or knowledgeable in science and modern languages, but "if he have not imbued his mind with at least a tincture of classical taste," the Christian scholars thought "he will inevitably feel . . . a great defect . . . in his intellectual culture."[13]

The longing for elegant culture was part of the cosmopolitanism that distinguished the new Christian scholars from the seminary's founders, particularly from Stuart's practical philology. Sears, Edwards, and Felton tried to argue that their love of classics had its practical side. They insisted that a lawyer who knew these ancient languages would inevitably understand his profession better, since all occupations originated in classical antiquity. But this was an insubstantial rationalization. In arguing that ministers needed to know Greek and Latin, the scholars' love of language for its own sake became apparent. They justified classical studies for the clergy by saying that "Homer and Herodotus remind the reader in a thousand places of the sweet simplicity and childlike artlessness which delight us in the narratives of the Pentateuch."[14] Yet they saw religion in the Bible, not art. Hebrew poetry drew its readers closer to the grandeur of God, they wrote, but Greek poetry was more beautiful. And it was this beauty which the Christian scholars coveted. Park recalled that Edwards loved the Greek poets, revering their genius. "He was a Grecian," Park said, "not only in his love of the beautiful, but also in his self-control . . ."[15]

Edwards was enchanted with Greek, for the language was "easy, flexible, fashioned to express the subtlest conceptions, and to charm the most practiced ear, . . . copious in its forms, perfect music in its movement."[16]

The index to the *Bibliotheca* for 1843–1873 lists four-and-a-half columns of articles on Greek language, literature, and grammar. Less than half a column of articles appeared on similar topics in Hebrew. The editors wrote on Greek literature, their theater, Greek inscriptions, essays on comparative grammar, manuscripts of the New Testament, and lives of Aristotle and other famous Greeks. They reviewed grammars, lexicons, translations of the great tragedians, modern histories, Herodotus and Thucydides. Roman history and Latin received almost as much attention.

Chapter IV

Woolsey, Edwards, Shedd, and others believed, like Stuart, that philology was a science. Their romantic longings for Greek and Roman culture did not mean they abandoned their predecessors' commitment to Baconian science. Indeed, they thought modern philological science was just beginning to come into its own. Certainly it was more complex than in Stuart's day, for it included comparative grammar and history of languages as well as the straightforward grammar in which the older man had pioneered. The second generation Andover scholars relied as heavily on Reid and the inductive method as their teachers had. Whether they were Platonists like Shedd or Augustinians like Park, the scholars all agreed that Baconian reasoning would unravel the laws of philology.

Common Sense said that a science's basic principles were proved if they could be found in the constitution of the human mind. B. J. Wallace, professor of Greek at Delaware College, wrote in 1847 that the "foundations [of comparative philology] are laid in human nature," or were part of the human constitution. "The philosophical grammarian shows . . . how every branch of a verb, and every vowel-change, follows not caprice, but a natural law . . ."[17] For a grammarian to be philosophical at all meant in this context that he believed in laws of nature revealed by common human experience.

Shedd, trying to show the organic connection between thought and language, believed he could do so because the need to articulate thought had "its origin in human nature."[18] He might have some rather Hegelian notions about the necessity of "formlessness of thought to become form in language,"[19] or the organic nature of language itself,[20] but he sought the universal laws by which philology could be discussed.[21] Another believer in the organic theory wrote even more explicitly that because language was "a living product . . . we may expect to trace its relation with the laws of mind."[22]

Woolsey was not interested in these abstract philosophical issues. He believed that much more careful research had to be made into the roots of words before one could begin theorizing about language. ". . . little has hitherto been settled, and . . . much . . . obscurity remains in Greek etymology," he wrote in 1844. The laws which produced "much of the delicate texture seen in the formation and derivation of words" lay "quite out of sight," he wrote.[23] Woolsey did not doubt that philology was a science following natural laws. Unlike Shedd, however, he thought the facts too incomplete to try to decide what the laws were.

Stuart had found philology synonymous with grammar, while grammar consisted chiefly of analyzing the meanings of words. Edwards added other dimensions. He distinguished between grammar and lexicography, discussing the meanings of words in the first category, and their roots in the second.[24] Woolsey further subdivided lexicography into seven parts, including etymology, statistics, history of words, and rhetoric.[25] The Andover scholars gave a lot of thought to language study. They involved themselves in many aspects of it. Because they followed the Germans so closely, they did a great deal of work in comparative philology. This discipline could not have a solely hermeneutical application. In addition, writers for the *Bibliotheca* might try to compare Semitic languages to Sanskrit to see if they could shed any light on biblical cosmogony. Or articles might treat Hebrew verbs, Greek lexicography, or the structure of Hebrew poetry in the same grammatical fashion as Stuart would.

The definition of philology itself expanded at Andover. When Stuart wrote of "philologizing," he intended to give all the uses and meanings of words in a disputed biblical passage. B. J. Wallace thought that word roots formed the "basis of comparative philology." What words meant might be seen as the end product of the new science. More interesting and important was digging into the past of a word, to find "an ultimate source from which it sprang," Wallace explained. The knowledge that "every word may be reduced to an element" was "the great discovery of our times in philology," he added.[26] The German Bopp laid down principles for investigating word roots. Wallace's article shared this information with the *Bibliotheca*'s readers. This digging into the roots of words was what Woolsey classified as the "historical" element in lexicography. The history of words was a subject which could be applied to exegesis, but its pursuit had little to do with biblical science.

Of course, the Andover scholars continued to justify language study as an interpretive or evangelical tool. Edwards defended the study of comparative philology as an aid to spreading the gospel. The work of German scholars in dividing the world's languages into families had made mastering foreign tongues easier for missionaries, he contended. In 1834, Edwards wrote that the Bible had been translated into 154 languages, a feat possible only because of advances in modern philology.[27]

Much more common uses of linguistic analysis occurred in articles on language itself. These might evaluate different types of lexicons, such as Woolsey prepared for the *Bibliotheca*, or translate ancient inscriptions, or discuss comparative philology. Some people, like the Andover librarian R. D. C. Robbins, continued to write exegetical articles in Stuart's vein. In 1846, for instance, Robbins contributed an article to the *Bibliotheca* on "The Character and Prophecies of Balaam" in which he used Stuart's grammatical techniques to determine the meaning of the story.

Balaam was a heathen soothsayer in the Book of Numbers. When Israel sought to go through the land of Moab, the Moabite King Balak summoned Balaam to curse the Jews. Balaam tried to comply, but the Lord forced him to bless them instead, for they were His chosen people. Robbins hoped to explain how much of the tale should be understood literally and how much figuratively. Specifically, he analyzed seven verses in which Balaam explained to Balak why he could not curse the Israelites. Line by line, Robbins discussed the meaning of each word, giving different versions as they occur in different ancient texts, quoting various German authorities, and finding the best interpretation of each word. The passage begins, "Stand up, Balak, and hear, / Listen to me, son of Zippor." Robbins first considered "stand up," saying that it did not require a "physical action." "Listen to me" was "an urgent request," Robbins said, as Stuart's translation of Roediger's grammar indicated. Robbins quoted translations of the Septuagint into Syriac and Amaritan, referred to Michaelis' interpretation of the Hebrew pronoun, showed where a similar form of it appeared in Exodus and Job, then discussed whether the verb was an obsolete form.[28] He then proceeded to the next line.

For the bulk of the younger scholars, however, as philology became more complex, it ceased being an important exegetical tool. Edwards wrote no exegetical essays in Stuart's format, and Hackett and Stowe wrote only one or two each. The younger men separated philology from hermeneutics. They used history or logic in dealing with the latter, while studying the former as an independent subject.

Typical of the new interpretative approaches were Hackett's essays comparing translations of the synoptic gospels. These were essays in the history of manuscripts, rather than doctrinal histories.[29] H. B. Smith, professor of church history first at Amherst and then Union Theological Seminary, submitted articles analyzing doctrines from an historical standpoint. In 1844, he submitted a piece on the baptismal formula ("I baptize you in the name of the Father, . . ." etc.). He discussed, as Stuart might have, the exact meaning of each word in the formula, offering different translations and German authorities to back up his argument. But there all resemblance to his old master ended. Smith was not trying to prove the validity of some denominational form of baptism, or whether the words mean what we think they do, but to discuss the historical meaning of the rite itself. The person baptized in the name of the Trinity was "declared to be subject to the Father, Son, and Holy Ghost," Smith wrote. This was an oriental custom, and could be seen in other parts of the Bible, where servants took their masters' names. Roman slaves also took the names of their masters, Smith added, and, in the same manner, cult worshippers took the names of their gods. A new name in the old orient could mean elevation to a new dignity, too, a point which Smith quoted various oriental scholars to prove.[30]

This essay was hermeneutical, in the sense that it interpreted a passage of Scripture, but Smith was not interested in the issues which absorbed Stuart and Robbins. They would ask if the passage had actually been divinely authorized, and whether one ought to accept its literal meaning. Smith was interested in what the passage meant historically.

In another type of exegetical article, Edward Robinson tried to decide whether the last supper was in fact the Passover seder. He relied partly on internal evidence from the four gospels, comparing their accounts to see if they disagreed seriously on this question. Up to this point, Stuart might have written the essay. But Robinson went on to compare historical authorities to find out what date and day were generally accepted both for the seder in the year of crucifixion and for the Last Supper itself. He used linguistic analysis a little, trying at points to establish firmly what John said, but he relied more on the logic of Jewish history for his argument.[31] Robinson's essay, like Smith's, could be considered hermeneutic, but it, too, lacked the apologetic element of Stuart's interpretation.

In philology, Americans tended to accept the results of German research unhesitatingly, but no German historians got their unqualified approval. August Neander (1789–1854) came closer than anyone to combining scholarship with piety in an acceptable manner. Robinson studied with Neander in Berlin during his first trip to Germany, and Neander remained a favorite with other Andoverians abroad. At his death, Park tried unsuccessfully to purchase the German's books for Andover; they went to the University of Rochester.[32]

A born Jew who was baptized at the age of seventeen, Neander developed a virulent antipathy to Judaism which considerably distorted his attitude to the history of the early church.[33] This problem combined with his organic developmentalism (enthusiastically embraced by Shedd), kept him suspect in the minds of some Andover scholars, notably Park.[34] However, Neander wholeheartedly accepted the divine inspiration of the New Testament, and more important in Park's eyes, accepted Paul's authorship of the so-called pastoral epistles.

Another church historian of this period whose work the Andover scholars read was Friedrich Christian Baur of Tubingen. The Americans appreciated his painstaking research, but Baur's Hegelianism made him suspect. He believed that each historical epoch rose synthetically out of the preceding, so that the struggle between Jews and Greeks in the first two centuries produced the age of the Fathers in the third and fourth; their struggle with the gnostics and Manicheans produced the authoritarian church of the Middle Ages, and so on. Even worse, Baur assigned the epistles to the Ephesians, Colossians, and Philippians to a period several centuries later than Paul.[35] Baur's work actually laid the foundation for what has become the modern understanding of early Christianity. However, the importance the Christian scholars placed on divine inspiration and the canon of the Bible caused them to reject historical theories put out by men like Baur who disbelieved them.

The development of a mature science of history at Andover is hard to trace. Prior to Robinson's German trip there seems to have been little interest in the subject at all. A narrative of the lives of saints or reformers might be used to illustrate some doctrinal argument, but there is no evidence that essays devoted strictly to historical questions were ever written. Ralph Emerson,[36] appointed to the first professorship in church history in 1824, wrote his earliest published article for a major periodical in 1828.[37] Before developing their own peculiar journals, the Andover faculty wrote chiefly for the *North American Review* and the *Quarterly Christian Spectator* (originally the *Christian Monthly Spectator*). Emerson's essay appeared in the *Christian Spectator*. In it he reviewed an edition of the collected journals of an American explorer, John Ledyard. As the journals had been edited by the Unitarian Jared Sparks (at whose ordination Channing preached in 1819), Emerson's review had doctrinal overtones: he considered it his duty to defend Trinitarianism from all insults, both real and assumed.

Ledyard had been a student at Dartmouth before the Revolution, but abandoned his studies to explore the Connecticut River. Returning to civilization, he sought a license to preach. Sparks condemned the Connecticut clergy in his review for turning down Ledyard's application; Emerson upheld Bellamy and the rest of the New England clergy for refusing to license such an irresponsible young man.[38] Emerson also attacked Sparks for omitting a great deal of Ledyard's writing in his edition, and substituting for it his own summaries. The explorer's language was "better than [Spark's], however elegant and faultless," Emerson contended.[39] This was the closest thing to a historical essay by an Andover man before the *Repository* was started. But it was undertaken with half an eye to the Unitarians. So little interested was Emerson in the details of Ledyard's life that he did not even record the year in which he died.

The one historical essay Stuart seems to have written, "The Creed of Arminius with an Account of His Life and Times," showed his usual meticulous scholarship. It made use of the variety of documents that the younger scholars considered mandatory, but, as usual, Stuart's purpose was primarily apologetic. While he did not try to support a particular party doctrine, he wrote on the subject because American churches were beginning to attack each other as being "Arminian" (i.e., non-predestinarian). The debate centered on free will, a topic Stuart did not address directly; he wanted to make Arminius' beliefs clear to those trying to label others with his name.

In writing the essay, Stuart divided his work into two parts: that of a historian, and that of an evaluator of Arminius doctrines.[40] Later historical essays by the Andover faculty would not combine these two functions. Doctrinal questions might be argued in a historical context, but biographies did not judge doctrinal issues. Stuart, on the other hand, spent a fair amount of space evaluating the relative merit of Calvin's and Arminius' sides of the seventeenth-century debates.

Andover's self-conscious interest in the European historians first appeared in the third volume of the Repository, now under Edwards' editorship. At that point, Edwards had begun translating German historical work for Americans. In this volume, we have the first translation of Neander's work, an article on "Augustine and Pelagius." The essay was actually translated by a seminarian with Edwards' assistance, but the older man wrote a nine-page introduction in which he explained the importance of Neander for Christian scholars. Edwards believed that the new direction in historical methodology followed by Neander deserved particular attention. Former narrators dwelt "on the external history of the church," Edwards explained, "merely arranging and recapitulating the facts preserved in ancient authors." Neander, on the other hand, tried to take a "comprehensive historical survey of the affects produced by Christianity on the human race."[41] Neander strove to discuss "the national views and philosophy of the Jews at the time of our Saviour's appearance, a knowledge of which is to be drawn chiefly from the Bible and Jewish writers." He presented the "philosophical views . . . of the heathen world," the sources for which he found "in the lives and writings of those who embraced or rejected or modified Christianity, viz., the early teachers and fathers of the church, the schools of philosophy, and the ancient heretics." Finally, Edwards said, Neander presented "the various speculative and practical systems, both orthodox and heterodox . . . which are recorded in the . . . decrees and . . . discussions of friends and foes in the Middle Ages."[42]

Above all, Edwards believed, Neander tried to get away from the type of narrative which uncritically accepted contemporary accounts as factually accurate.[43] For Edwards, as for other American scholars, Neander came as a revelation. They considered him the first real church historian, for he was the first to go back to the original sources of Christian history, and the first to discuss the relations between a variety of different peoples and philosophies in the early church.[44]

Edwards' translation of Neander showed the first self-conscious Andover interest in new German methodology. It was important, too, for presenting the idea that the past may be interesting for its own sake, not for any doctrinal argument. Edwards wrote that he selected the article partly to acquaint the American public with Neander, who had not yet been translated into English. Secondly, he wanted to "spread before the public . . . a controversy [between Augustine and Pelagius] which once shook the Church to the Centre . . ."[45] Edwards was not trying to illuminate any New England controversy. Unlike Stuart's essay on Arminius, which obliquely treated a modern dispute, Edwards was interested in Pelagianism in the detached fashion of a scientist.

In 1835, Edwards felt confident enough in the new historical techniques to write an original essay, "Slavery in ancient Greece."[46] The article, which he published in the *Biblical Repository*, was copiously footnoted, relying on a range of documents for its information. These included the Iliad and Odyssey, Demosthenes, Thucydides, and the Greek playwrights, as well as some modern authorities. The essay was factual and non-didactic. Nowhere did it refer to the condition of American slaves. Active in the anti-slavery movement as he was, Edwards still did not try to draw any parallels or morals from ancient Greece to the American condition. He simply discussed reasonably how many slaves each city might have contained, their duties, how they were treated, and how people became enslaved. The concluding pages of the article quoted ancient Greek attitudes towards the institution. In contrast to Stuart, whose essay on Arminius persistently weighed the merits of its subjects' doctrines, Edwards injected no editorial opinions.

Edwards' essay on Greek slavery was the first attempt by a Christian scholar to write a purely historical essay that had no doctrinal message. It displayed some of Andover's critical prejudices, particularly their belief that Homer had actually written down the Iliad and Odyssey (German opinion since the 1790s considered it an orally transmitted work). Still, given Edwards' belief that the Iliad was a historical document on par with Thucydides, he made proper use of it, quoting Homer extensively. "'These are the evils,' we are told in the Iliad, 'that follow the capture of a town;'" Edwards wrote. "'The men are killed; cities burnt to the ground; the women and children of all ranks are carried off for slaves.'" He quoted Homer elsewhere in relating the duties of slaves.[47]

It was in the *Bibliotheca Sacra* that the Christian scholars made their mature expression of history as a science. By this time many of them had studied in Germany and were familiar with German archives and methods. Reflecting on the development of the discipline since 1800, Sears wrote an essay on "Historical Studies" for the *Bibliotheca* in 1846. Published immediately after his return from two years in Germany, the article spelled out Andover's belief in the methodology of Niebuhr and von Ranke as the only approach to the science.

Sears admitted that "the study of history and the historical art itself" were only beginning "to receive from our countrymen a larger and more just share of attention."[48] He clearly stated that the basis of writing history lay in research into original documents. Sears believed that only in the last thirty years—or since the publication of Niebuhr's *Roman History*—had people been writing what he would consider real history. In 1820, comparatively little "was known of the many-sided life of the Greeks," he wrote. The "entire subject of the legal antiquities of Athens, to give but one instance, was a chaos."[49] Sears condemned the antiquarians preceding Niebuhr for indulging only in "rhetorical exhibition and . . . setting forth, by way of ratiocination, vague and uncertain generalities."[50] That day, he said, was fortunately over, for if "men will now write history, they must begin with research, the want of which it is in vain for mere cultivated taste, or even genius to attempt to supply."[51] Research should not be into "secondary sources of information," he warned, for "Niebuhr has shown how little reliance can be placed on much that passes under the name of Roman history." Therefore, if one were going to do research, it must be into original documents written at the time of the subject being studied.[52]

These materials might be found "in manuscript records, documents, and correspondence," Sears suggested.[53] He believed too, in looking up decrees, papal orders, or proceedings of councils—any record which was not hearsay evidence. The historian's ideal, he wrote, "must be the nearest possible approach to a resuscitation [of an age]."[54] History could no longer be written by amateurs, he concluded, but must be studied by professionals.

These principles dominated the Andover approach to history after 1840. In the first volume of the *Bibliotheca*, Emerson submitted an essay on "The Early History of Monasticism from Original Sources."[55] Like his early review of Ledyard's journals, the essay consisted mostly of excerpts from the monastic documents themselves. Unlike his earlier review, however, this one contained no editorial judgments, except in a short introduction in which Emerson explained the importance of using original sources. His documents were autobiographical accounts by the early monks, many of them previously untranslated. Since Emerson hoped to present the philosophy of monasticism by which its early devotees justified the practice, these autobiographies were the best source, he believed. "A mere summary of the facts would be to but little purpose," he wrote, in explaining his methodology. "We must hear the venerable theologian Athanasius tell the stories himself, if we would know how people in his age regarded them." That was the key to his interest in original materials, for they "give us a view of the spirit of the age in some of its most important features which we cannot elsewhere gain."[56] He wrote that he certainly would have preferred summarizing the facts in his own way, "if that would have answered the purpose, than have toiled for the exact import of every Greek sentence, then to have sought for some decent English in which to clothe it."[57]

Emerson opposed monasticism. He believed that the early eremites were frauds, reporting miracles that had not occurred. More seriously, he believed solitary contemplation opposed the communal nature of Christianity. He made these editorial remarks in the introduction, however, and did not allude to them in the article. Instead, he allowed the translations to carry his story, leaving the readers to draw their own philosophical conclusions.

Most of the historical essays in the *Bibliotheca*—and there were a great many—detailed events in ecclesiastical history. There were many biographies of famous reformers, Protestant martyrs, and great epochs in the church. They all followed Sears' general rules, dealing as much as possible with original source material and refraining from moral judgments on the character of their subjects. Articles always began or ended with a list of those documents the scholars had used in their research.

Their participation in the knowledge explosion changed the way in which Christian scholars proved the authenticity and genuineness of the Bible. The scriptural questions in which they were interested were historical or logical. H. B. Smith wrote on the historical significance of the baptismal rite; Robinson did not try to prove or disprove whether New Testament events had actually taken place, but relied on Jewish history to decide what the gospel accounts said. On similar questions, Stuart would have used grammar to prove his point.

Stuart equated interpretation of words with the historical correctness of events. If one rejected a literal understanding of the Bible's first chapter, one could not trust philology "to decide any matter brought before its tribunal," Stuart believed. "It would become a judge partial, or vacillating [*sic*], or cowardly . . ."[58]

Furthermore, for Stuart, philology was the science that saved. His faith in the truth of biblical history was so great that he believed the only possible hermeneutical questions addressed what the Bible's language really meant. That is the approach he took in defending orthodoxy against Channing; he also defended the veracity of the Bible against outside attacks with philology or grammar. This was most apparent in an 1836 article he wrote for the *Biblical Repository* defending the Genesis account of creation from modern geology.

In 1836, Edward Hitchcock, the Amherst geologist who later became its president, had written a three-part essay for the *Repository*, outlining what he considered the most plausible of modern geological theories. Himself an evangelical Christian, Hitchcock wanted to reconcile geology with apparent discrepancies in the Genesis account.[59] Stuart, greatly enraged, responded with "A Critical Examination of Some Passages in Genesis I; with Remarks on Difficulties that Attend some of the Present Modes of Geological Reasoning."

Every Christian writing on alleged discrepancies between the Pentateuch and the rocks agreed that "so strong is the proof of the authenticity and inspiration of the sacred record, that even if a *point-blank* inconsistency" appeared between them, geology "must yield, because it is not sustained by proof as strong as revelation."[60] Hitchcock wrote this in 1836; English geologists agreed, as did a host of Americans, including the eminent Benjamin Silliman. The question was, what constituted a "point-blank" inconsistency. Stuart held that it occurred at the moment one believed something other than those literal truths revealed to Moses by God.

In his classroom lectures, Stuart had assumed that Moses knew the early history of the world either through ancient written accounts, or directly from the mouth of God. The ancient accounts, if any, had been divinely informed, for the creation process was known only to God. This meant that the facts Moses reported must be correct. Since Stuart did not believe in verbal inspiration (that the words themselves were the ones used by God), he did not think one had to take literally the language in which Moses expressed these facts. "Nothing can be more certain," he wrote, "than that the sacred writers did not compose their books with modern sciences in view."[61] Moses was not trying to teach science, but morals, and therefore did not pay much attention to how he described the world. When some physical fact obviously contradicted a biblical figure of speech, faith did not require one to ignore astronomy. For instance, men knew that "waters above the firmament" was a metaphysical, not literal description of where the Noachian flood originated.[62]

But when Moses wrote of the creation, or the deluge, these were historical facts, not open to question.[63] It was beside the point, as far as Stuart was concerned, to bring in geology to decide whether the Pentateuch was correct. Moses was not trying to teach that science, but to relate what he knew had occurred. Hitchcock had complained that those who defended the Genesis account had not studied geology, or they would not take Moses literally. Stuart retorted that that "complaint is [not] well grounded." Geology was a modern development and could not be used to interpret a 3400-year-old document.[64]

Stuart believed that true understanding of Scriptures was enhanced by knowing details of contemporary culture. "The philosophy, science, opinions in any respect, which attended or belonged to any ancient writer" were all "proper and even necessary objects of consideration" in order to understand him, Stuart wrote. But to bring in a modern science of which that writer was ignorant as an interpretative tool, was to read into his words what the modern reader thought they ought to mean.[65]

Philology was the only modern science which could be used to study the Mosaic account, Stuart insisted. Since it tried merely to discover the exact meaning intended by the sacred writers, it was a communications tool, not a modern imposition on the text. "The question, what Moses meant, is one of *philology*," Stuart told Hitchcock,[66] adding that he "despaired of knowing how geology can tell us that."[67]

As Stuart saw it, geology would have to abide by the linguistic analysis of what Moses really meant. Since Hitchcock agreed that geology had to give way to revelation, Stuart stated that whatever he discovered through philology would determine the issue.[68] Stuart was the servant of an inexorable science, which would find out through "usual, well-known, and established principles of interpretation" what the author had said. Even if this overthrew his own beliefs or Hitchcock's, Stuart believed he had no choice but to follow his science.[69]

Stuart analyzed the Hebrew verb "barah" or "created" according to his usual detailed methods, to see whether it should in fact be construed as making something out of nothing. Using Hebrew testimony from other parts of the Bible, he found that "barah" could indeed mean that; logic demanded that it mean create out of nothing in the first verse of Genesis.[70] Similarly, Stuart studied other words, in particular "yom," or "day" to see whether it could mean more than one twenty-four-hour period. He found that it could not. When God created the heavens and the earth, he had taken 144 hours, whether Sedgwick and Hitchcock liked it or not. They would simply have to readjust their theories.

Stuart's students were more cautious in basing scientific judgments on the Bible. The "Bible as originally written contained [no] Historical or Scientific Error," Park told his classes. However, there might be disagreements between science and Scriptures due to "Corruption of the Text; future new interpretations; future new developments in Science, etc."[71] He further stated that the Bible might contain errors if "they pertain to the commonly held historical opinions of the day."[72] It was true on doctrinal matters: "Every religious teaching and impression in the Bible is correct," he told the young men.[73] But its chronicles could be interpreted with a somewhat more liberal mind. Neither Park nor his contemporaries dreamed of questioning divine revelation, or the miracles and other remarkable deeds. They believed the New Testament fulfilled prophecies of the old, and they accepted the Bible's chronology.

Like Stuart, B. B. Edwards thought Old Testament events were validated by passages in the New. In 1849, he questioned the German habit of ignoring New Testament evidence. Surely, he wrote, German historical criticism was "compelled to find some of its most important materials in the records of the New Testament." For "Jesus Christ . . . perfectly obeyed the law of God, was full of grace and truth, . . . and . . . all the words he ever uttered are worthy of the most implicit belief." Therefore, Edwards affirmed, "his declarations in regard to the Old Testament" should be "credited without any misgivings."[74]

In 1850, Edwards wrote on "The Present State of Biblical Science."[75] Here, he showed further agreement with Stuart's faith in the Bible. Stuart had told his classes that the Bible contained material "which is intended to apply to the feelings and sympathies of men, their moral and religious feelings and sympathies." If one were going to understand this document properly, one ought to "possess those feelings and sympathies."[76] Edwards agreed. He wrote that "on one essential point" the Bible "is not analogous to other books. It reveals truths which are to be believed. . . . It speaks with authority to the interpreter himself."[77]

When Stuart spoke of using external evidence to prove the validity of the Bible, he actually meant discovering whether the New Testament supported the deeds of the Old. Or he saw the intimate knowledge of details about Egyptian life in Exodus as external testimony to Moses' having written it. He did not try to find documents contemporary with the Old Testament to corroborate its historical details.

Edwards agreed with his teacher that one had to use the laws of grammar to arrive at the meaning of any biblical text,[78] but he did not use philology as Stuart did in analyzing the truth of the biblical stories. Like Stuart, he argued that as there was no literature contemporary to the Pentateuch, one had to accept its own testimony as to its credibility.[79] Edwards contended that since Tacitus was still accepted as an accurate historian despite obvious errors of fact, the Jewish historians should receive the same respect. Only a desire for skepticism made rationalists give less credence to the Jews than to Romans and Greeks, Edwards maintained: their histories also had no supporting contemporary documents.[80]

Despite his agreement with Stuart on these basic points, Edwards nonetheless argued for the authenticity of the Pentateuch from outside evidence. His acceptance of modern historical methods would not allow him to rest a belief in biblical history simply on faith. He found testimony in a number of areas: the age of alphabetical writing, which made possible the Bible's early composition; the veracity of the Old Testament as a Palestinian guidebook; and the support Egyptian inscriptions gave Old Testament history.

Edwards' arguments for the early existence of alphabetical writing ranged widely. Its usefulness had required its invention, he believed, so that logically we might expect it to be very old.[81] An English authority, J. G. Wilkenson, dated the earliest Egyptian hieroglyphics sometime between Joseph's arrival in Egypt and the enslavement of the Hebrews. In this case, Moses certainly had been acquainted with hieroglyphs, if not the alphabet.[82] The high state of Egyptian art included the invention of paper some 2,000 years before Christ, while newly-discovered Greek fragments showed that the Phoenicians had an alphabet about that same time.[83]

Interest in hieroglyphs began with Napoleon's recovery of the Rosetta stone. G. B. Niebuhr's disciples had then taken up Egyptian monuments with great enthusiasm. They translated hieroglyphics on tombs and monuments and began looking for buried tablets. They were able to push Egyptian history back to around 3300 B.C.

The existence so long ago of a flourishing civilization with well-developed arts and sciences destroyed the idea of a Noachian deluge, according to rationalist critics.[84] The deluge should have occurred at the time kings were ruling happily in Egypt, according to Niebuhr's students. But Edwards found these monuments the best evidence for the Mosaic account, rather than its refutation. "Profounder investigations into ancient history and monuments are undermining the imposing and widespread hypothesis that the Pentateuch was written at the time of the Babylonian captivity," he said.[85]

Edwards brought in some expert testimony on the issue from a German Egyptologist named Bunsen. Edwards reviewed Bunsen's five-volume study for the *Bibliotheca* in 1849. He concluded that "all searches into the ancient history of mankind and into the Egyptian antiquities" gave "the highest credit . . . to the biblical notices [of events]." Egyptian inscriptions had been "subjected to every species of scrutiny and their accuracy, not merely their general but their minute accuracy" had been demonstrated. Investigations of the English scholar Wilkenson in Assyria proved that "the shades of thought, the minute colorings in the dilineations of the Hebrew prophets were wonderfully exact." Nothing on the Egyptian monuments contradicted Scripture history, Edwards reported to his readers.[86] A French authority had further written that "all of the kings of Egypt named in the Bible . . . are found on the Egyptian monuments in the same order of succession and [in] the precise epochs where the sacred writers placed them."[87]

Edwards believed that this type of evidence, verifying a small part of biblical history, proved the truth of the whole. In addition, Edwards said, current researches in Palestine undertaken by such respected scholars as Edward Robinson showed that the Pentateuch was the best guidebook possible to the Middle East. Edwards quoted a number of German authorities who had written that the data of the Pentateuch were "geographically altogether true."[88] Edwards added that "every fresh examination of the topography and geography of places described or alluded to in the Pentateuch" showed "that the writer had that exact local information which could proceed only from personal observation."[89]

Edwards believed in the veracity of the Pentateuch. But he did not use Stuart's argument that a good God would not deceive us by making us believe a false text. Nor did he make great use of Stuart's grammatical methods. In his article on the "Authenticity and Genuineness of the Pentateuch," he did use some word analysis to argue that the five books were older than the books of the prophets. The latter do not differ much from the five in linguistic form. Rational critics in Edwards' time claimed that this proved all the books were written around the same time, perhaps 600 B.C. But the Christian scholars, including Edwards, said uniformity came from the later writers copying the style of the earlier. In just this fashion Luther had frozen the style of written German for centuries, he argued. Edwards spent a few pages picking out archaisms in the prophets which proved they were copying earlier, more ancient texts. A German scholar, Edwards added, had shown "the continued unchanging character of the Arabic language . . . not only during a period of six hundred years, but of a thousand years." Over three widely-separated epochs, "grammatical structure of the Arabic language remains the same." These Arabic writings could all be accurately dated, occurring as they did between about 400 A.D. and 1800 A.D. If this language changed so little even though exposed to foreign influences, Edwards concluded, how much less should one expect Hebrew to change considering the isolation of that people.[90]

Grammatical analysis formed only a small part of Edwards' argument.

Nor could he say, like Stuart, that the New Testament was sufficient proof for the events of the Old, for he had sat at Neander's feet and imbibed the methods of von Ranke. "History is the key to all fulfilled prophecy," he wrote in 1850. One would know whether the prophets had been right if their predictions came to pass. Hence "a searching examination into the remains of antiquity" rather than a simple reliance on the New Testament was "indispensable for one who would be a truly able interpreter of the Prophets."[91] Modern research had opened up whole new vistas on oriental civilization in general. Archeologists who "unveil[ed] the long-buried secrets of the Mesopotamian Plain [threw] new light on the Mosaic and prophetic records," Edwards added.[92]

Edwards was trying to use German historical methods to prove their rationalist critics false. In this way he tied biblical criticism to external authorities, despite his belief in the truth of the entire record. He condemned higher criticism, because it breathed "a spirit of suspicion . . . over all ancient documents." But he thought one ought to be able to sift true from false sections. Here he was much closer to Stuart. Presumably the eye of faith could tell when a copyist's error made the meaning of a passage untenable. But one should not find the entire text "spurious [when] a little flaw has been detected in a trustworthy document."[93]

Edwards did not look at external historical evidence with a rationalist's eyes. He did not try to find in it proof against the miracles or prophecies of the Old Testament. But just as Park had tied theology to modern science in an effort to make it acceptable to the modern age, so Edwards tied biblical criticism to modern history.

CHAPTER V

The Narration of the Creation in Genesis

❖ ❖ ❖

Where were you when I laid the foundation of the earth?
Tell me, if you have understanding. Who determined its measurements
—surely you know!
On what were its bases sunk, or who laid its cornerstone,
When the morning stars sang together,
And all the sons of God shouted for joy?
— Job 37:4–7

Like philology and history, natural philosophy changed rapidly in the first half of the nineteenth century. Inundated by a vast array of data, sciences developed where there had been only science before. In 1802, Yale created the first chair of chemistry in this country. Benjamin Silliman (1779–1864), its first holder, taught mineralogy, geology, and what we call zoology and botany, as well as chemistry. In 1853, the chair was divided into two appointments, and in 1864 divided again.[1] In those sixty years, the body of scientific knowledge had grown so much that four men had to teach material one covered previously. Such a deluge of facts removed science from the hands of the talented amateur. The gentleman naturalist, who tapped rocks or collected plants while pursuing a career in law or religion, could not keep pace with the professionals who did nothing else with their time.[2]

The naturalists of the 1830s agreed with the theologians that their work was described by the principles of Bacon and Newton. As Daniels points out in *American Science in the Age of Jackson*, everyone claimed discipleship to the masters without ever saying precisely what that meant. Their work, however, reveals two major points by which they understood Baconianism: science should be limited to "naming, classifying, and describing," as prescribed by the French anatomist Georges Cuvier; and one should induce laws from known facts, not frame hypotheses for experimental testing.[3]

As new data poured in in all fields, classification became increasingly difficult. Did facts about electro-magnetism belong to chemistry or physics? And once that was decided, how did one classify contradictory phenomenal behavior without framing a hypothesis and testing it experimentally? Most

Americans in the 1830s and '40s contented themselves with simply making as many observations as possible. Others wrestled with unwieldy categorization schemes. Still a third group self-consciously began building hypotheses. A public debate of major proportions grew up between this group and the Baconians, for it included the issue of whether the public should fund research it could not understand. As this argument progressed, it cut sciences off further from the grasp of the educated amateur.

But Andover approached science in this period as if nothing were changing. They saw a stability and harmony in the relationship between the natural world and revealed theology which caused them to ignore new developments for some time. "There are many dark passages in the volume of nature which are illustrated by the book of inspiration," Park wrote in 1846. "The teachings of the former volume are so far informed by the latter, so many of its deficiencies . . . supplied, that the right-minded student of one will feel his knowledge to be incomplete without an acquaintance with the other."[4] Revelation and nature had one author. Logic demanded that the truths of one be visible in the other. The Bible itself could guide the student of nature, Park said: the sacred text explained "many enigmas in the creation"; it "reflected so much light upon nature" as to make easy the study of difficult sciences.[5]

Viewing nature as the handmaiden of religion, Christian scholars took for granted that discoveries in natural science would work into a scheme showing the benevolence of God. They agreed with Paley that the remarkable adaptation of means to ends in nature demonstrated God's existence. They could easily see this agreement in animal behavior, plant structure, and even chemistry. Until the arguments began over the age of the earth, no discoveries directly contradicted the view of cosmogony presented in the Bible. Secure in this belief, Andover did not pay close attention to developments in natural science. Students came no closer to discovering the wonders of nature than might be done by reading Paley.

Americans found geology one of the most absorbing of the new sciences. The digging of the Erie Canal made it increasingly interesting, for the cut bared 300 miles of strata illustrating a variety of geological eras. In addition, Europeans, particularly the English, had made major strides in understanding and classifying rock formations. In geology, as in philology, Americans tended to follow where Europeans led.

The empirical evidence available to those who studied rock formations and fossil remains showed that water and fire were both somehow at work in their creation. The upper rocks close to the earth's surface seemed to be the precipitate of a water solution, while the bizarre angles of some strata and the unstratified rocks in others looked like the result of fire working under intense pressure.

Several schools arose in Europe to defend water and fire respectively as the cause of geological layering. The Vulcanists, led by the Scotsman James Hutton, claimed that rock strata had been created by subterranean volcanic activity, which possessed the heat necessary to melt rock and the pressure to fuse it. The Neptunists, whose chief theoretician was the German mineralogist Gottlieb Werner, claimed that existing land formations were the sediment of a vast precipitation. By 1815, this controversy died down in favor of the Vulcanists. But it gave way to a new argument as to whether the present state of nature had resulted from catastrophic interventions of God through such agencies as the Flood, or from natural causes whose present operation was identical to their past.

William Buckland, an Oxford geologist, led the catastrophist school in the 1820s and '30s. As a devout Christian who reconciled the Mosaic account with the geological, he enjoyed considerable vogue in the United States as well as in England. Charles Lyell was the foremost spokesman for the uniformitarians. Between 1830 and 1835, he published his three-volume *Principles of Geology*, in which he demonstrated that "the former changes of the earth's surface are referrable to causes now in operation."[6] Examining the formation of strata by uniformitarian principles caused Lyell to push the earth's age back by several million years.[7]

Americans were chary of allying themselves too closely with any one European school. The American interior provided damaging evidence against Werner, and no proof for Hutton.[8] However, Americans relied on European theories in formulating their own ideas: they did not develop any independent hypotheses to explain the causes of what they saw. Major American scientists such as Edward Hitchcock (1793–1864) followed Buckland closely, but used the results of Lyell's work as well. Most Americans began their careers as Wernerians and changed as they became more sophisticated.

European interest in American rock formations helped spur American interest in the discipline. Cuts like the Erie Canal, and long fault lines made American strata easier to study than European. Americans were jealous of European scientists stealing their continent for European glory; in geology, as in anthropology, zoology, and botany, they tried to forestall foreigners by making discoveries first.

Another boost to American geology came from state governments wanting to assess their natural resources. This was a most important influence for the development of the new science. While men like Hitchcock had an innate enthusiasm for rock tapping and fossil collecting, geologists were paid by state governments to survey mineral resources. Silliman did his first geological work in response to a plea from Connecticut's governor for a catalog of her mineral resources. Hitchcock performed a similar service for Massachusetts in his first paid geological work.[9]

No matter what European theory one accepted, the evidence of the rocks demonstrated overwhelmingly that the earth was very old indeed. Genesis stated that God had created the heavens and the earth in six days. Counting backward from the birth of Christ through the various genealogies in the Old Testament placed the earth's creation in 4004 B.C. But whether one was a Wernerian, believing the rocks to be the detritus of a great flood, or a Huttonian, seeing in them the remains of violent volcanoes, it was obvious that the process had taken anywhere from 600,000 to 6,000,000 years or more.

Such a discovery might seem a shattering blow to anyone's faith in the Bible. However, there was a group of Christian scientists, just as there were Christian scholars, who tried to reconcile the new knowledge with old beliefs. These men straddled several difficult conflicts. As prominent scientists, they were involved in the debate between Baconians and experimentalists. As evangelical Christians, they were caught between Genesis and geology. When the Christian scholars finally took note of the problems geology offered theology, the Christian scientists mediated between them and the rocks. The mediation itself alienated many scholars.

A number of these people, including Silliman and Hitchcock, became eminent geologists. Silliman had been converted by Dwight in the 1802 revival which turned Stuart from law to the ministry. A lawyer, too, Silliman was picked by the old man to fill Yale's newly-created chair in chemistry. Although he knew no science, his piety and intelligence were both unquestionably high.[10] He spent three years in Edinburgh studying chemistry and returned to New Haven in 1805. He became an outstanding scientist; most of the young geologists of the thirties and forties studied with him.

One of Silliman's most important contributions to the discipline was his *Journal of Science and Arts*, started in 1818. From the outset, the journal was distinguished by its scientific quality. Like the *Bibliotheca*, it reprinted articles from prominent foreign scholars, including Buckland and Lyell. It printed results of U.S. geological surveys, as well as articles from other scientific fields. Silliman resisted the pressure to print popular essays. His *Journal* survives today as the official organ of the American Geological Society.

In addition to his geological work, Silliman kept up a lively interest in evangelical religion. With the help of James Kingsley (1778–1852), Yale's librarian and an amateur meteorologist, he published several articles seeking to reconcile Genesis with geology. In his classes, Silliman repeatedly tried to show that he was "investigating the laws by which the Creator works."[11] He made clear to his students that theology stood at "the head of all sciences; it is the only revealed one, and it is necessary, to give a proper use and direction to all the others." Geology he thought particularly valuable, for it gave "decisive proof of the power, wisdom, and design" of God.[12]

In his scrupulous reconciliation of the Bible and the rocks, Silliman pointed out, as the Christian scholars did, that the Bible gave moral, not scientific instruction. He and Kingsley argued forcefully that the Bible described phenomena as they appear, not necessarily as they operate physically. Thus Scriptures speak of the rising of the sun, the waters above and below the firmament, and a number of other points which no one believed any more. Therefore, Silliman believed, one did not have to take too literally the Mosaic account of creation: it was obviously a metaphor, describing the world as Moses saw it.[13]

The important thing, Silliman said, was that what Moses understood metaphorically coincided with the facts geology had discovered. Both declare that the world had a beginning, indicating the necessary existence of a Creator. Furthermore, the order of creation recorded by Moses corresponded to the order in which life occurred in the fossil record. The lowest strata contained plants, the higher ones increasingly sophisticated animal life remains.[14]

Hitchcock worked even harder to reconcile the two accounts. He had been a Congregational minister before becoming professor of geology at Amherst in 1825, and his ties to evangelical religion remained very strong throughout his life. Indeed, on one trip to England, as a scientist of international renown, he was relieved to find himself sharing a train car with a converted Christian. The two conversed earnestly on the sweet topic of salvation.[15]

Born into a Calvinist family in Deerfield, Massachusetts, Hitchcock had an early interest in science. His first love was astronomy; at the age of sixteen he prepared some observations of a comet which were published by the American Academy of Arts and Sciences.[16] However, an attack of mumps weakened his eyes so much that he was forced to give up all study, particularly astronomy. During two years of enforced idleness, his spirit was humbled, and he was converted. He felt a call to the gospel ministry, "having been led by my trials to feel the infinite importance of eternal things, and the duty of consecrating myself to the promotion of God's glory and man's highest good."[17]

During his two-year hiatus from study, Hitchcock began going on mineralogical expeditions, collecting and classifying rock specimens. In 1816, Hitchcock heard Amos Eaton, one of the fathers of American geology, lecturing at nearby Amherst. Hitchcock became fired with even greater passion for his new hobby. He went on a few limited expeditions with Eaton, acquiring valuable technical information.

The following autumn, he began the course at Andover. In 1821, he accepted a call to the church in Conway, Massachusetts, where he conducted several revivals. After four years at Conway, he wrote, the heavy duties of the ministry had taken an intolerable toll on his health. When Amherst called him to their professorship of natural history and chemistry, Hitchcock petitioned for dismission in the hopes that "the great amount of physical exercise requisite in such a professorship, might enable me to hold out a few years."[18]

As soon as he was released from his parish, Hitchcock went to New Haven to study for a year with Benjamin Silliman. The two struck up a lifelong friendship, collaborating in running the early American Geological Society as well as in defending both Christianity and geology.

From New Haven, Hitchcock went to Amherst, where he spent the rest of his life. He worked to build up Amherst's science departments, developed a large collection of rocks and fossils for the school, and conducted numerous geological surveys. His most important work lay in his collection of fossil footprints.[19] These were dinosaur prints, but were considered tracks of extinct birds during Hitchcock's life. He went everywhere for them, even making casts of flagstones from New York sidewalks which had been quarried from fossiliferous beds.[20]

In addition to his scientific career, Hitchcock remained actively involved in religion, helping conduct numerous revivals at Amherst. His published works totaled 8,000 pages, of which 50 percent were devoted to scientific and 32 percent to religious issues. He wrote not merely on theological issues relating to science, but also on "The Resurrection of the Body," "The Importance of an Early Consecration to Missionary Work,"[21] and a number of attacks on Unitarianism. He was particularly active in the temperance movement, and intermittently a vegetarian.

As a scientist, Hitchcock was a firm Baconian. He relied on patient observation, description, and classification, staying away from experimental hypotheses. His numerous essays in Silliman's *Journal* included descriptions of mineral deposits, classifications of new fungi, and a detailed *Report on the Geology of Massachusetts*. In the *Report*, undertaken at Commonwealth expense, he outlined the state's rock strata and mineralogical composition.

On several occasions, Hitchcock wrote about his beloved fossil footprints, describing in one article some sixteen-inch sandstone tracks. He detailed the type of rock formations in which the tracks were found, then gave details on the size of the prints, comparing toe shapes to find several different species. This essay on "Ornithicnology" (Hitchcock was assuming that the prints were birdtracks), illustrates a number of Hitchcock's beliefs about geology and cosmogony. In the first place, he accepted unquestioningly the vast, unknowable antiquity of the earth. The tracks offered convincing evidence that birds were among the earliest inhabitants of the earth, he said, at a time so remote that the "entire population of the globe has been changed, at least once or twice, and probably several times more."[22] In the same strata with these prints were plant and animal remains of species now extinct. "The number of years that have since elapsed, we cannot even conjecture," he wrote. The Scriptures were silent on that point, "giving us to understand, merely, that a period of indefinite duration" occurred between the beginning of the world and man's appearance on it. Geological remains "clearly point out successive epochs in the natural history of the globe, yet present us with few chronological dates."[23]

In addition to accepting the antiquity of the earth, Hitchcock also showed his ideas on creation in this article. He thought terrestrial history consisted of successive creative interventions by God. The disjointedness of rock strata, particularly apparent in the long Erie Canal cut, gave credence to this view. Each stratum was distinct from the next, not only in the type of rock, but also in the plant and animal life it contained. So in writing that the "entire population of the globe" had been changed several times since his "birds" cast their footprints by the Connecticut river, Hitchcock relied not just on his faith in the divine designer, but on the evidence of the rocks.[24]

The theory of successive creations belonged to the catastrophists, but Hitchcock also believed, in a general way, in Lyell's uniformitarian principles. The bird tracks Hitchcock observed were clearly made by the operation of forces still at work, he wrote. This notion contradicted the usual belief that "early geological changes on the globe" had "taken place in a very different manner, from those which are now going on," he stated.[25]

In another article, an apology for geology written for the *Biblical Repository* in the same year, Hitchcock further clarified his uniformitarian principles. Here he defended the antiquity of fossiliferous rocks, trying to show that they were the result of a long, slow sedimentation. If his readers would merely go "to the banks of a river, and collect some pebbles and sand from its beach" deposited there by the water, and compare these with fossiliferous rocks, they would see that both had been acted on in the same way.[26]

Although Hitchcock discarded biblical dating of the age of the earth without a qualm, he would not let geologists abuse Christianity as a religion. In 1837, Hitchcock censured the Scottish geologist MacCulloch and the American doctor Thomas Cooper for "assail[ing] Christianity" in their work. [27] Their science was sound, he wrote Silliman, but "I have always tried to make it my rule of action not to let private . . . considerations prevent me from a decided vindication of revealed religion from all covert or open attacks." No matter how estimable a man might be, Hitchcock "could not in conscience let a fair opportunity pass . . . of avowing my reliance on a crucified Saviour."[28] Silliman agreed, but thought that Lyell, whom Hitchcock had also attacked, had a "character and mind" which were irreproachable on religious questions.[29]

Like Park, Hitchcock was especially interested in natural theology. While Park concentrated on the existence and attributes of the Deity, Hitchcock devoted himself to the wonders of nature, in the manner of Paley. In his *Reminiscences*, he wrote that the great disappointment of life had been his failure to publish a full-length book on natural theology "in which all its great principles should be stated and fully illustrated by modern science."[30] He had written fragments for the *Bibliotheca*, and a popular exposition in his 1850 Religion of Geology, but the demands of the Amherst presidency kept him from completing the task. He wrote that "scientific reputation was not the culmination of my ambition, but the higher object of making science illustrate the Divine Glory."[31]

His earliest efforts in natural theology were a series of five articles Hitchcock wrote for the *Biblical Repository* in 1835–36. B. B. Edwards had solicited these articles in an early attempt to reconcile the Pentateuch with geology. Hitchcock accepted evidence from both authorities. Unlike Silliman, Hitchcock was trained in biblical philology, and so could analyze the text in Stuart's manner.

In the first article, Hitchcock confined himself to outlining major areas of agreement between the Pentateuch and the evidence of the rocks. One striking coincidence was their accord on "the nature and operation of the agents that have been employed in effecting the changes which have taken place in the matter of the globe since its original creation."[32] These agents were water and fire: the deposition of stratified rocks could not have occurred without water, nor could their elevation and dislocation have occurred without intense heat.[33] Hitchcock found these same agents present as the chief forces mentioned in Scripture. "There can be no doubt but under the term *ohr*, light, Moses includes both light and heat, or fire," the use of which was dramatically apparent in God's causing dry land to appear in the first day. Moses did not describe how this occurred, beyond ascribing it to God's command. "But if there be any fact clearly established in geology, it is, that all dry land on the earth has been elevated by a volcanic agency," Hitchcock commented. "Now how appropriate to represent such an agency in operation as the voice of God's thunder, from which the waters hasted away."[34]

In another remarkable agreement between revelation and geology, both taught that "the work of creation was progressive after the first production of matter in the universe."[35] In revelation this referred to the successive acts of creation. In geology it meant that the same principles are currently in operation which gave us the rock formations, oceans, and rivers, eons ago.[36]

In the next issue of the *Repository*, Hitchcock actually produced proof from the language of Genesis that the two records did not contradict one another. He believed Genesis itself proved that the earth was not 6,000 years old, but at least several hundred thousand, possibly several million.[37] He gave a detailed philological argument for the use of the word *yom*, or day, in the Hebrew text. Just as Stuart might, he examined various Old Testament uses of the word to see whether it could mean a longer period than twenty-four hours. There had always been writers, as far back as Augustine of Hippo, who had given the six days a metaphoric sense, but Hitchcock believed this tradition did not afford enough justification for bending the meaning of time needed by geology.[38] An examination of the word in Genesis, and its obvious metaphoric meanings elsewhere, convinced Hitchcock that it needed a literal interpretation in Genesis I.[39] He therefore decided that the extra time required by the rocks lay between the beginning, and the first day. That was the only place that the meaning of the text did not have to be distorted to meet the needs of science. "The sacred record admits of this interpretation without doing violence to the language," Hitchcock said. The phrase "*in the beginning* is as indefinite with respect to time as language well can be."[40] Hitchcock wrote that God had not specified to Moses when the six demiurgic (creation) days began. He quoted some Hebrew scholars, including a favorite of Stuart's named Rosenmüller, as supporting the interpretation of the first verse as: "In the beginning God created heaven and earth. *Afterwards*, the earth was desolate, etc."[41] Since Moses was interested in the history of the earth only as it affected humans, Hitchcock thought it natural that he would leave out any preceding creations.[42]

With Silliman and Kingsley,[43] Hitchcock believed that geology was an admissible tool for interpreting the sacred record. Since everyone agreed that the Bible taught moral, not scientific truths, Hitchcock agreed that its authors described natural phenomena as they appeared, not as they were. "Facts derived from civil history and astronomy" modified our understanding of the sacred record, Hitchcock wrote. He added that the well-established discoveries of geology demanded that its facts "be admitted equally with civil history and astronomy as aides in interpretation of the Bible."[44] Just as Galileo's work modified the geocentric teachings of Moses, so could the creation story be re-interpreted without loss of faith in its essential truth.[45]

Hitchcock and Silliman, immersed in the rocks, realized that they had to re-interpret the Creation story in some manner or abandon the idea of a divine contriver. Stuart saw the matter completely differently. In 1828, he wrote Silliman for clarification of the latter's views on creation.[46] Receiving them, he objected strenuously, publishing a refutation of the geologist's ideas in his 1829 Hebrew *Chrestomathy*. While agreeing that the "Bible was not designed to teach the Hebrews astronomy or geology,"[47] Stuart also believed it recorded "matters of fact, real verities."[48] Moses wrote about creation in terms intelligible to his readers, Stuart asserted, just as we speak of the rising and setting of the sun. Furthermore, the scholar wrote, if Moses had tried to teach astronomy or geology in all their truth—which he probably knew—the Bible would be incomprehensible, save to the most learned.[49] Moses wrote simply so that complicated scientific work would not frighten uneducated people away from the Bible's moral truths. Nonetheless, his simple version recorded matters of fact.

Perhaps the most important point Stuart made stated that the Mosaic account tallied "well with the mission of God's own Son, to redeem our guilty race."[50] A standard part of Christian doctrine lay in attributing death to Adam's fall. Sin entered the world because of the fall, and sin meant death in this context. If the evidence of the rocks were understood as Hitchcock or Silliman did, many species had undergone corruption and death before man's fall from grace. If death were not connected with man's free will in choosing disobedience, there was no need for Christ to restore perfect obedience.

Silliman did not bother to answer this question, but Hitchcock devoted some careful thought to it. In 1851, in *The Religion of Geology*, Hitchcock published popular lectures reconciling Genesis and geology which he had been delivering for over a decade. In this book, he gave his answer to the question of death. God's foreknowledge let him know that man would sin, so he prepared a fallen world for him to live in.[51] Later, Hitchcock wrote that when God said what he created was good, he meant it was good for a fallen being. ". . . the world in its present state is admirably adapted to be a theater for a display of the work of redemption," he added, "and this seems to have been the grand object for which it was created . . ."[52]

Stuart objected to all such efforts to reorganize either the theology of the Fall or the story of Creation. In 1836, he responded virulently to Hitchcock's reconciliation articles in the *Biblical Repository*. The issue, he wrote, was not whether the rocks could be reconciled to the Mosaic record, but what that record said. Unlike some Christian critics, who refused to believe that fossils really existed, Stuart wrote that they were "real specimens." Yet how these fossils came to be buried so low, the geologists had not explained— indeed, he added witheringly, they offered a bewildering array of conflicting theories.[53] If the uniformitarians Hitchcock quoted were correct, why had these forces not operated in the same fashion everywhere on the globe, Stuart demanded. If fossilized plants under pressure turned into coal, why had this happened only in Newcastle and Pennsylvania, instead of everywhere there had been ancient plantlife?[54]

In addition, the idea that God had created such an earth as Hitchcock conjured up contradicted the Lord's reaction to his creation. God said that the world was "at the Beginning . . . very good." If he found it so, it was not because he intended it to be ruled for millennia by lizards. The eternal Wisdom through which God created rejoiced at the beginning "'in the habitable parts of the earth, and her *delights were with the sons of men*,'" as Solomon rhapsodized.[55] In this case, men must have been present from the start of creation, not after several million years of it. Stuart added as a clincher that "a world without man" would always seem to him like "a body without a head," contemptible, rather than the image of the living God.[56]

Silliman urged Hitchcock not to bother responding to Stuart. The Hebraist was "a poor judge" of geology, Silliman told his friend. "If one had health and time, it might be well to open the subject," he continued, "but I have not, and I shall only talk and write as I think, without regard to the obstinacy of those who will neither listen nor learn."[57] Hitchcock, however, "determined to push ahead, though in seasons of despondency I feel inclined strongly to give over any further scientific efforts."[58]

Hitchcock and Silliman objected to Stuart's singling out geology from other sciences. The theologian insisted the geology could not be used to interpret the ancient record. Yet Stuart also agreed that Galileo and Newton had shown that the Bible's astronomical references, such as to the rising of the sun, were only optical metaphors. Kingsley responded to Stuart "in a masterly manner," Silliman wrote Hitchcock, showing Stuart's inconsistency in letting astronomy, but not geology, interpret Genesis.[59]

The Christian scientists were contemptuous of theologians who refused to accept the findings of geology. Long before debates between Huxley and Wilberforce captured the public mind, Christian scientists skirmished with scientific skeptics. The original issue lay not between science and religion, but was argued by Christians between geology and biblical criticism. As early as 1820, Silliman wrote that "no mere divine, no mere critic in language, can possibly be an adequate judge" of geology. His opinion of "theological gentlemen" did not improve over time. Hitchcock, too, was impatient with those "Protestant divines . . . who are battling the geologists," as he wrote Silliman in 1837. "I am satisfied with you that some of our theologians are determined to wage everlasting war with geology."[60]

As long as people like Stuart insisted on interpreting the earth's history on a biblical timetable, there could be only "everlasting war" with geologists. For men like Silliman and Hitchcock were so persuaded by the evidence of the rocks that the Bible had to conform to science or they could not accept the sacred word. As they saw the matter, many clergy were cutting themselves off from the truth by insisting on a "literal and limited understanding of . . . history."[61] On the other side, Stuart was convinced that geology had nothing to teach him. ". . . those who bear hardly upon others for meddling with their *geology* should keep a good look out how they meddle with Hebrew *philology*," he wrote.[62] Hitchcock sneered because he ignored the rocks, but Hitchcock blatantly distorted the meaning of the text. Stuart said he would applaud geology when her devotees produced a science consonant with the Mosaic text.[63]

The majority of Andover's faculty did not take Stuart's strongly hostile position. For a long time, they ignored the controversy developing in the *Repository*, although Edwards probably invited Hitchcock's articles. The scientist wrote urging him to edit anything which would be too offensive.[64] Edwards usually put editorial disclaimers next to *Repository* articles with which he disagreed. His failure to do so with Hitchcock's essays argues at least that he suspended judgment on the question.

Moreover, Edwards had a private interest in geology. In St. Augustine, Florida, for his health in 1845, he wrote Park about geological sites he had visited, and described in detail the remains of a plesiosaur.[65] The following year, he spent part of his trip to Europe in attending the British Geological Society and visiting its members in their homes.[66] He condemned Oxford for excluding geology, with astronomy, from its required course of study. "This circumstance gave rather a ludicrous aspect to the repeated meetings of the British [Geological] Association at Oxford," he wrote Park, "unless that body acts on the principle of holding its convocations where there is the greatest need of light."[67]

Edwards did not record his views on the age of the earth. It is probable that he agreed with Buckland in attributing fossil remains to the Noachian deluge, since he viewed all ancient history from a biblical timeline. He did not commit himself to any written opinions of Lyell when he visited the Geological Society, although Lyell was a prominent member. He agreed with Park that the Bible and nature served as mutual interpreters, and may have thought he could take descriptions of nature from geology without getting involved in harangues with her devotees. It is probable that he did not see the threat to cosmogony implicit in geology as a serious one. His knowledge and his faith could convince him that the Bible was so true that nothing could overturn it.

Park did not commit himself to the age of the earth, either, but he had a great deal of respect for Hitchcock's scientific judgment on nongeological matters. Writing at one point on the relation of divine providence to physical laws, he quoted Hitchcock as an unquestionable authority on how divine agency operated in nature. Park was reviewing a book by a man who argued that God operated according to a foreordained plan, rather than as events arose. Park reported that Hitchcock said it didn't much matter which view one held. With this argument, Park closed the review.[68]

Lecturing to his classes on science and the Bible, Park said that "no view of Inspiration is to be adopted which will make it necessary to *distort* scientific phenomena or historical facts."[69] Elsewhere he suggested that "the writers of the Bible may have been inspired merely with regard to religious truth."[70] He would not specifically deny the kind of construction Hitchcock placed on the evidence of the rocks.

Park's and Edwards' interest in geology fit in with their general sense that natural science was just one more aspect of the multi-faceted divine truth. Geology was undertaken in a Baconian, i.e., non-experimental fashion; it showed the existence of the Creator; and it was studied by Christians like Buckland for whom they had a high regard.

When the two wrote "Natural Theology" for the Bibliotheca in 1846, they defined the reciprocal relation between science and natural theology. The latter proclaimed design in nature from the fitness of means to ends and cause to effect. Scientists who understood that nature followed a divine design understood the physical world better than those who did not. Cuvier was once given a hundred broken-up skeletons of twenty different kinds of animals, Park recorded. He easily sorted them out because he understood that their parts followed an inherent design.[71] In describing Cuvier's work, Park referred to the fossiliferous rocks in which some of the bones had been found. Fossils were the major source of evidence in arguing the age of the earth, but Park did not discuss that issue. He simply argued that the fossil remains supported the existence of a divine designer.[72]

One sign of the growing concern at Andover over the discoveries of modern science lay in the changing meanings its faculty gave the word between 1844 and 1861. In the early years of the *Bibliotheca*, articles reflected a general application of the word as "knowledge or certain knowledge." Webster's 1832 *American Dictionary* defined science as

a collection of the general principles or leading truths relating to any subject. *Pure* science, as the mathematics, is built on self-evident truth; but the term science is also applied to other subjects founded on generally acknowledged truths, as metaphysics; or on experiment and observation, as chimistry [*sic*] . . .[73]

Here natural science was given secondary attention, after considering the broader framework of any discipline which relied on self-evident truths and inductive reasoning.

For the first decade of the *Bibliotheca*'s existence, its contributors shared Webster's general indifference to natural philosophy. Robinson contributed a report on "Aspects of Literature and Science," but with that sole exception, the *Bibliotheca* did not discuss natural science under that title. Instead, there were essays on "Theological Science and Education in the United States," (Vol. I); an article by Edwards on "The Present State of Biblical Science," (Vol. VII); and one by Philip Schaff on "The Science of Church History," (Vol. VIII).

After 1855, writers for the *Bibliotheca* used "science" almost exclusively in reference to natural science, and then to a natural science by and large at odds with revealed religion. We have "Scripture and Science Not at Variance," (1856); "Science and the Gospel," (1860); and "The Debate between the Church and Science," (1861). From ignoring geology, or casually sweeping its evidence into the argument from design, *Bibliotheca* contributors became increasingly concerned about conflicts between science and religion.

The new disciplines further demonstrated their power by controlling the methodology of the argument with religion. They pulled the debate away from what Genesis actually said to how the Bible could be reconciled with the rocks. In 1836, Hitchcock and Stuart both argued philologically to decide what the Hebrew would support in the way of creation theories. In the 1850s, no one used philology on this topic at Andover. That discipline had definitely been relegated to an exegetical, not a critical tool. Instead, critics tried to find ways of re-interpreting Genesis by logic.

In 1861, a Brooklyn pastor, James McLane, raised one of the few voices still agreeing with Stuart's utter rejection of the evidence of the rocks. McLane wrote angrily that the Christian met the scientist "on his own ground," examining strata and fossils and allowing "them to affect his mind in explaining the Bible." But the Christian had facts, too, McLane said bitterly, "which must be taken into account." These were the facts of revelation, but science ignored them.[74] Even though he agreed with Stuart in believing that geology should not be used to interpret what Moses said, McLane did not analyze the Hebrew of Genesis in his argument. He merely inveighed against geology without offering any positive defense of a traditional biblical cosmogony.

Similarly, an Andover graduate named Means who tried reconciling the two accounts did so by logic, not philology. "We believe this record [Genesis]," Means wrote. "We believe the facts of science. And we believe they are consistent."[75] The two difficulties confronted by theology continued to be what the record really said, and how old the universe actually was.[76] But these two questions were reinterpreted by modern science. Means argued that even those who wanted to dispute the geological record would be forced to accept the evidence of astronomy on the age of the universe. By 1855, enough was known about the velocity of light and the distance of the earth from other galaxies for people to realize that light had been traveling several light years from them to the earth. Evidence obtained by Sir William Herschel indicated that "the nebulae which can now be seen by the most powerful telescopes were in existence, certainly, almost two millions of years ago," Means wrote.[77]

Since the universe was certainly at least as old as the geologists claimed, Means said the real problem was to salvage the Genesis account. The literal interpretation of the demiurgic days as twenty-four hours long was clearly the most pleasing solution philologically. But to stick to this meaning in the face of the geological evidence would mean losing the Bible as a creditable source on other topics. "When the interpretation of the days as indefinite periods seems to be the easiest solution of great difficulties," Means continued, ". . . the man of science says: 'I may want to put this sense upon the term day; will the Bible allow it?'"[78] He may have chosen an unusual meaning, Means agreed, but a plausible one. "It must be acknowledged, interpreting scripture by scripture, that such a meaning of day is allowable," he concluded. And if it were allowable, it should be undertaken in order to save the Bible.[79]

Means selected an interpretation of the Hebrew "yom" which most closely fit his understanding of the rocks. Stuart called this "hineinexigieren" in 1836, reading into the text, rather than out of it. Stuart accused Hitchcock of this intellectual crime. Means did not use grammatical analysis in 1855. Whether he could have or not is an open question: textual analysis no longer seemed to be a good basis for any arguments on the age of the earth or the true meaning of Genesis I.

Christian scholars had not abandoned philology, but they used it in very limited ways. An essay discussing the internal sense of the Bible would still use philology, but it was no longer the apologetic tool which Stuart had developed. Most of the *Bibliotheca's* contributors who wrote on the problems geology posed tried, like Means, to reconcile Genesis with the rocks. In doing so, they inevitably distorted the literal Mosaic account. By abandoning Stuart's position "that the question, what Moses meant, is one of philology," the Christian scholars ceded an important point. Philology had given them the means to judge the other sciences: it was the tool of biblical science, and others could be evaluated according to their agreement with its analysis of the biblical text.

Stuart at least was consistent. His successors tried to keep theology "the queen of the sciences," but gave up her status as an independent arbiter of other disciplines. In 1846, Park had written that natural theology contained the basis "of all other sciences, and crowns all with additional truth."[80] Woods believed that theology headed up all other fields of learning, and could evaluate work in other fields.[81] But in the 1850s, as Christians got more involved in the work of modern geology, they gave up their independent standard for evaluating natural science. This process undermined theology's centrality in the intellectual world.

Austin Phelps, who succeeded Park as Bartlett Professor of Sacred Rhetoric, was acutely aware of this problem. Addressing the Congregational ministers of Massachusetts in 1859, he tried to assure them that the God of nature was the same as the God of revelation. But he was unable to claim that theology crowned the other sciences with distinction. Instead, he compared theologians unfavorably with natural scientists. The latter approached truth in a spirit of humility, content to be persuaded by evidence. Theologians, on the other hand, approached "revealed religion, with preconceived assumptions . . . , not with the upturned eye of faith."[82]

Not only did scientists have a better attitude towards truth than theologians, Phelps continued, but their work spoke with greater authority. Science "affirms its facts with the calm consciousness that they are indisputable," Phelps told his colleagues. "It starts with axioms which it is proof of insanity to deny, and then it deduces its laws with a power of command which is obeyed, because it speaks what it knows."[83]

Theology ought to have the same "definiteness and positiveness of truth," Phelps argued, since the God of nature and revelation were identical. The Bible ought to contain "verities which it is as unphilosophical for a believer in . . . inspiration . . . to deny, as it is for any sane mind to refuse credence to the elementary facts of geology." It ought to command faith as science commands belief in physics.[84]

Instead, Phelps noted, theologians had ceded much of the authority of the Bible in an eagerness to be reconciled with unbelieving scientists. "The argument with unbelief . . . is sometimes too apologetic for the regal character of a revealed theology," Phelps proclaimed. "The difficulties of revelation are allowed to be thrust so confidently in advance of its evidences; its seeming inconsistencies" given so much prominence, and so much sympathy given to infidelity that "doubt comes to be regarded as the normal state, at least of cultivated minds, regarding the teachings of the Bible."[85]

A generation earlier, men calmly described theology as a science. In 1859, Phelps argued that his colleagues needed to prove to the world that they had "a theology which is a science."[86] And where Park found all disciplines subordinated to natural theology in 1846, Phelps could plead only for the equality of theology with other studies. It was as wrong for "natural science to discard the claims of sacred philology, as for philology to attempt to dislodge geology," he told his audience.[87]

Phelps described theology's weakness in confronting the claims of natural science. The fear the Christian scholars had for their diminishing authority was further evident in the measure he proposed as a remedy for the situation. Rather than urging his colleagues on to a vigorous counterattack, as a previous generation had made on the Unitarians, Phelps advocated a laissez-faire policy. Let archeologists go out and uncover ancient civilizations, he told the assembled clergy. Let geologists study rocks, until they "run through the circuit of . . . eighty anti-Mosaic theories . . ." Geology would gradually discard them all and come "in the freshness of its strength to sit at the feet of Moses, and pay its tribute to the cosmogony of . . . Genesis."[88] Let the government support science, Phelps urged, and eventually science would learn to support the Gospel.[89]

Phelps' decision to let time heal all wounds was a solution the Christian scientists had offered for three decades. This approach effectively took from the queen of the sciences the right to oversee its subsidiary fields of knowledge. Phelps divided the two even further by telling his colleagues that Christianity discussed questions of faith, revelation, and redemption, not geology.[90] Theology and geology existed in separate spheres, he said, approaching the truth from separate but converging interests in it. Phelps retreated to this position in an effort to protect theism, but it separated the God of nature further from the God of revelation.

Andover tried to preserve the unity of revelation and creation. One of Park's last acts as editor of the *Bibliotheca* was to commission a series of articles proving that Darwin and Calvin were compatible theorists. But to harmonize theology with geology, the Christian scholars had to reorganize the Mosaic cosmogony in a way that violated the science of philology. All of the reconcilers gave the words a meaning which the text would not support. In this way, they gave up the validity of sacred philology, and hence theology, as sciences equal to geology or astronomy, whose basic tenets were accepted unquestioningly. It was such a posture that upset Phelps, when he discussed the "power of knowledge" natural science possessed compared to theology.

The Christian scientists were placed in as much of a dilemma by the knowledge explosion as the scholars were, but for somewhat different reasons. Like the scholars, the scientists relied on the ultimate unity of God and nature. They gathered more and more data, confident that the underlying truth of God would eventually illuminate their discoveries. However, Hitchcock and Silliman believed that reorganizing the biblical text was the only way they could accept Christianity and geology at the same time. From 1820 on, they denied the right of sacred philology to criticize natural science. Abandoning the Bible because they believed nature would uphold their faith, they were betrayed by the data they collected.

The scientists assumed that if they garnered as many facts as possible, they would induce natural laws enabling them to understand any science completely. Instead, as they became inundated with facts, it became impossible to use taxonomy as a tool for organizing or understanding any science.[91] Moreover, the facts they gathered became the foundation of sciences which denied the design inherent in a god-made creation. The *Origin of Species*, published in 1859, took information Americans like Hitchcock had helped gather, and used it to describe a stochastic universe. Hitchcock rebutted Darwin's thesis, because it overthrew the argument from design, but he conceded that Darwin's observations were correct.[92] However, evolution seriously undermined Hitchcock's theistic solution to creation problems.

After the publication of the *Origin of Species*, Hitchcock retreated somewhat from his uniformitarian position. If change occurred in nature only as the result of the patient working of uniform forces, then there was no strong ground for denying evolution. As long as the geological evidence pointed to repeated acts of creation, Hitchcock's faith was secure. But evolution, or the development hypothesis, obviated the need for successive creations.

Writing in 1863 on "The Law of Nature's Constancy Subordinate to the Higher Law of Change," Hitchcock defended God's miraculous intervention in nature. He stated that while constancy, or uniformitarianism, was supposed "to be the great law of nature that extends to all events," the Christian believed miracles interfered with these established laws.[93] Hitchcock told Stuart that geology did not overturn the Fall or the need for an Incarnation. But the development hypothesis, destroying the need for miraculous creations, did threaten Christianity in Hitchcock's eyes. Evolution obviated the necessity for redemption, because by it, "man cannot be a fallen being . . ." Instead, "he has been continually rising, physically, intellectually, and morally, and is steadily advancing to his culmination." If one believed Darwin, "the doctrine of an incarnate Redeemer and Savior is absurd. For no intervention is needed."[94]

Hitchcock's alternative to Darwin lay in successive interventions by God in nature. His understanding of creation depended on the divine designer, yet he was scarcely a strong ally for biblical Christianity. His faith was independent of the Bible. He knew that Christ had died and risen again, but not even Darwin could move him from his geological beliefs. His defense of Christianity depended on a theory of creation which had no biblical support. It was not contradicted by the rocks, but they did not prove his notion of creation, either.

The Christian scientists could not defend the sacred text because they were too firmly welded to geological evidence. On the other hand, the Christian scholars had tampered with the text to make the form of the creation story agree with external evidence. They no longer had a science which gave them command over the Bible, for they had abandoned Genesis to geology. Ultimately, Stuart's warnings proved correct: by not sticking to sacred philology, and interpreting the words of the text literally, the theologians had allowed geology to interpret the Bible for them.

As both scientists and scholars struggled to maintain a sense of God's sovereignty in a seemingly stochastic universe, they developed new modes of thought in treating revelation and nature. Common Sense, with its strong reliance on induction and taxonomy, was unequal to the task. The next chapter describes some of these efforts at Andover in the 1880s.

——— CHAPTER VI ———

The Breakdown of
Moral Philosophy at Andover

❖ ❖ ❖

Every science has a philosophy, by which the mind
determines the rationale of the facts, and without which science can
neither justify its own laws nor grasp the significance of its own facts.
— Samuel Harris,
"The Theological Department Essential in a University"

In October 1871, Samuel Harris (1814–1899) addressed the topic of science and theology in his inaugural address as Yale's Dwight Professor of Theology. The speech was part apology, part polemic. Its title, "The Theological Department Essential in a University," indicates the defensiveness theology continued to feel in the late nineteenth century. Harris believed that "one of the highest ends of liberal education is to enlarge and liberalize the mind" by creating "an appreciation of all kinds of knowledge . . ." But the creation of specializations by the knowledge explosion had narrowed people's minds: they came to regard their fields "as the only sphere and the only method," and looked on "other spheres of thought with a certain contempt."[1] Harris admitted that theologians, too, had "shown the effects of the tendency inseparable from every special pursuit," but added that "devotion to science subjects [one] to the same danger and needs the same caution . . ."[2] Finally, he warned that "if theology is excluded as not a legitimate subject of knowledge, the exclusion belittles the sphere of human knowledge . . ."[3]

The problems Phelps had warned about in 1859 had grown if anything more acute. Science not only showed no interest in the truths religion had to offer, it threatened to sweep theology from the University altogether.[4] But Harris did not want to give up the synthetic New England theology embodied by Park. Educated at Andover from 1835–1838, he fully accepted Common Sense philosophy, including the division between mind and matter. With mind in the ascendant, theology must also be an important science for elucidating the highest creating mind, that of God. He also believed in the unity of science, religion and philosophy. "We cannot complete the circle of intelligence respecting any object till [*sic*] we know it in the light of science, philosophy, and theology," he told his audience.[5] "There is no conflict [among the] three departments of thought," he affirmed. "It is only when one of them claims to occupy the whole field of thought and . . . knowledge that antagonism appears."[6]

Harris reaffirmed the major points upheld by the Christian scholars in the heyday of moral philosophy. But in 1871 his was a voice crying in the wilderness. As Darwin and evolution increasingly captured the intellectual imagination of the times, theologians like Park made ever more convoluted efforts to synthesize it into Calvinism. But a large group of young men turned their backs on this avenue for relations between science and religion. They chose, instead, to make religion acceptable to the modern age by tying it to evolution, and by tying it in such a way as to make religion subordinate and auxiliary to the new sciences. Unlike Hitchcock, they made no efforts to see whether the Bible supported their interpretation of creation: they took the Bible out of Christianity.

The focus of this new movement lay at Andover. Rapid changes there after the Civil War left Park and Phelps in a lone minority, and the changes disturbed every facet of the seminary, both its structure and its approach to learning.

The new era began innocently enough in 1863, with the appointment of Egbert Coffin Smyth (1829–1904) to succeed Shedd as professor of ecclesiastical history. Smyth belonged to that class of Christian scholars which Park thought he wanted at Andover. A graduate of Bangor Theological Seminary, Smyth had studied theology under Park as a resident licentiate. He taught "natural and revealed religion" at Bowdoin for six years, and then went to Berlin and Halle for additional study in theology and church history.[7]

Smyth's credentials were impeccable, but he was at loggerheads with the older man from the outset. The first issue lay in the relative importance given history by the seminary. Until Smyth's appointment, the discipline had been relegated to a minor spot in the third year of instruction. This reflected the early faculty view that a study of "the various clashing opinions and unauthorized practices which have prevailed among Christians since the apostolic age" might unsettle the faith of the young. "After becoming grounded and settled in . . . the faith once delivered to the saints," one might find it "interesting and instructive" to see how people have reacted to the gospel through time.[8]

Smyth claimed that the study of ecclesiastical history formed an integral part of theology. He therefore wanted to lecture twice a week on church history to the middle class, and have Park give one theology lecture a week to each of the junior and senior classes.[9] Park was outraged. Such a division, called the "parallel course," would be an intolerable disruption of the logical flow of his theology. A presentation once a week to the junior class would make absolutely no impact on them, he stormed. "The Professor of Theology ought, in my opinion, to concentrate his energies on one Class, and not scatter his labors over other classes," he wrote the trustees in 1865. "During the year now closing, all the time which I have spent on the Junior Class has been thrown away."[10]

Smyth prevailed on the trustees to set up the parallel course in 1863–65, while Park was away from the seminary for his health.[11] The time was one of educational experimentation: Harvard and other colleges were trying elective curricula, and the trustees doubtless believed Andover should move with the highly experimental times.

Of course much of Park's objection must be put down to his fear of losing his long-held prominence in the seminary. The lectures to the Middle Year formed a key part of his influence in the school. At the same time, Smyth's views on history contradicted the ideas Park and Edwards had vigorously upheld. Smyth broke down the boundary between ecclesiastical and secular history which even Shedd had maintained.

The early faculty, and Park and Edwards later, had believed that the faith once delivered to the saints contained an unchanging core of doctrine, which orthodox theologians from Augustine to Edwards had increasingly elucidated. Church history merely explained the development or retrogression of Christians in understanding this faith (the long primacy of the Roman church was an example of retrogression). The study of history therefore could not compare to the actual investigation of the Bible itself. And how, Woods asked reasonably, "can the history of the subsequent opinions and actions of men help us to determine the sense of the sacred writings?"[12]

The early scholars accepted the Christian partition of pre- and post-millennial history originally articulated by Augustine. All human history led to the last judgment, and it merely foreshadowed heavenly life.[13]

Such a division made the Bible the only essential document for understanding the past: history reflected the biblical prophecies.[14] God transcended human history. He stood above it, watching it unfold.

Shedd began modifying these attitudes with his organic, quasi-Hegelian approach to the past. Doctrinal developments manifested the growth of church history, rather than refinements in understanding a core of belief.[15] God did not transcend human life; rather, his purpose was immanent in it. Thus ecclesiastical history was not solely a progression to the Last Day, but was itself a manifestation of God.

Shedd maintained the separation between ecclesiastical and secular history. He also carefully united immanent history with orthodox views on sin and redemption. Because of these positions, and because he did not try to expand the history department at Andover, Shedd did not come into conflict with Park. Even so, his views roused enough uneasiness at Andover for him to leave there in 1859 and go to Union Theological Seminary.[16]

Smyth, on the contrary, said no doctrine could be comprehended apart from its history. Instead of believing a body of unchanging truths which theologians must try to understand, Smyth taught that doctrinal truths change as theology develops. He asserted that theology could not be taught independently of church history, for the two were inextricably intertwined. "Theology is essentially a growth and should be studied as a growth," he told the senior class at Andover in 1874.[17] As such, it had no distinct advantage for interpreting other sciences, for it developed at the same rate and under the same circumstances as they did. Indeed, theology was subject to the same higher impersonal laws as they were.

If Smyth had been alone in his beliefs, Park would probably have reacted just as wrathfully, but relegated him to an insignificant position in the seminary. However, Smyth belonged to the majority. Four new chairs were established at the seminary between 1864 and 1878, and they were all filled by men temperamentally and intellectually aligned with Smyth. Separate chairs were created in New and Old Testament Studies, in addition to the Brown professorship. Joseph Thayer and Charles Mead, who held these positions, were Andover graduates educated in Germany. They completely adopted German historical criticism, without bothering to modify it in accord with New England Calvinism. A new chair in biblical theology, filled by Edward Hincks, treated theology as an objective study. The Abbot chair under Park taught students orthodoxy that they were supposed to believe: Hincks essentially taught heterodoxy. Finally, one family endowed a chair in "The Relation of Christianity to the Secular Sciences."

Only Phelps and Park remained of the old faculty. The younger men instituted the Parallel Course, and soon Egbert Smyth took the faculty presidency from Park, who no longer attended faculty meetings. "I do not agree with the members of the Faculty in reference to the mode of conducting the Seminary," Park wrote the trustees in 1871. "The most that can be expected of me is to make no active opposition to measures which I privately think have been injurious to the institution . . ."[18] In 1871, Park stopped attending faculty meetings for a while, he was so exasperated and humiliated at having all his preferences ignored. He pleaded ill health to the trustees when they remonstrated with him.[19] He finally began attending meetings again in 1878, only to resign his chair in 1881. His eyes had failed so much that he could no longer read his own lecture notes,[20] and his sense of isolation was so complete that he no longer had the emotional energy to continue on the faculty.[21]

After Park's retirement, the changes he had fought came quickly. Within a few years, the entire face of New England theology as Andover taught it was remade. Park still had enough influence among the Congregational churches to fight some of the changes in court, but the power of the new faculty was too much for him.

The fight centered initially on the question of Park's successor. Park's choice lighted on Frank Hugh Foster, a favorite pupil whom he had groomed to fill the Abbot chair. Foster was doing doctoral work at Leipzig in 1881, at Park's insistence, since the old man believed that the highest possible standards were essential to the Andover faculty. But as Foster himself wrote, "the simple fact of nomination by [Park] was fatal to the candidacy. The dominating influence with the Trustees had determined on a modernization of Andover."[22]

The trustees therefore elected the choice of the majority faculty, Smyth's younger brother Newman. And Newman Smyth, then a pastor in Quincy, Illinois, subscribed to ideas known as "the New Departure." The "New Departure" claimed a second chance after death for those who had not known Christ in this life.

The fate of great and good men, like Plato and Socrates, who lived before Christ, or those like the Buddha who never heard of him, has always been a theological issue. Luther denied them salvation, while the Catholic Church put them in Limbo. Park adopted a theory of the "essential Christ" which stated that any man, heathen or other, who truly strove to do his duty, and had the same moral attitudes as the believing Christian, would be saved. Such a person believed "essentially," if not formally, Park wrote.[23] The new departure went far beyond essential belief. Based on the work of a German theologian, I. A. Dorner, the theory articulated by Newman Smyth asserted that one came to faith only through a personal relation to the historical Christ. As many people have no exposure to Christ in this life, after death they are granted a second probation, the opportunity to accept or reject the Christ whom they never knew on earth.[24]

Smyth's nomination outraged Park. It was not enough that his own candidate had been rejected, but the trustees preferred one who could not in good conscience affirm the seminary creed. In a last effort to retain his influence, he roused public feeling against Smyth by claiming that second probation "cut the nerve of missions."[25] If the heathen had a chance for a second probation after death, why bother to convert them now? This argument touched a nerve among the missionary minded churches. So many ministers wrote in protesting Smyth's appointment that the Visitors, who had final authority for the Abbot professorship, vetoed it.

The trustees next selected as a compromise candidate George Harris, who affirmed the Andover creed and the Westminster Confession. Some faculty members objected to the creed, but Harris and Egbert Smyth saw it as a way to restructure New England theology. Phelps' replacement as Bartlett professor, William Jewett Tucker, wrote that creed subscription "carried with it the right of interpretation."[26] Harris claimed no "definite opinion" on future probation, although he upheld the right of his colleagues to believe in it.[27]

As a last ditch effort, Park took Harris, Hincks, Egbert Smyth, Tucker, and John Churchill, the professor of elocution, to court. He charged them with violating the creed, and therefore being unable to teach at the seminary. The *North American Review* commented sardonically that Park's "own early experience has failed to satisfy him of the general principle that the serious disapproval of one's predecessor is no disqualification for the Abbot professorship."[28] The suit was overturned. Fighting it took up a great deal of Park's energy. He was an old man; the battles he fought drained him of the ability to complete his systematic theology. He lived until 1899, but spent the last eighteen years of his life removed from the center of intellectual Congregationalism. In 1884, the *Bibliotheca* moved to Oberlin: the seminary was cleared of all trace of Park's generation.

Second probation and church history were only minor areas of the changes that the new Andover faculty undertook. Far more cataclysmic was the destruction of natural theology, moral philosophy, and the delicate balance between reason and revelation. Nature became a thing apart from theology for the new generation. It could instruct and inform the sacred science, but the God of revelation no longer seemed one with the God of nature. In fact, the new faculty would be very circumspect in speaking of a God of creation at all.

George Trumbull Ladd (1842–1921), who lectured at Andover from 1879–82, wrote on some of these issues in 1877. "To the chemist, geologist, physiologist who come back from their spheres and say: 'we find in the laws of affinity, in the deposits of past ages, in the structure of the human frame, no trace or token of God.'" Ladd said, "I simply reply 'I never expected you would.'"[29] Only "obedience and self surrender" could lead one to God, not nature.[30]

The key to the approach taken by Ladd and his colleagues lay in the enthusiastic acceptance of Darwin, Spencer, and the whole issue of evolution. Just as the Christian scientists and scholars had grappled with Lyell and the *Principles of Geology*, so the new generations strove to fit evolution into a modern religious framework. The problems Hitchcock faced in his synthetic attempts had become much more acute, calling for more drastic responses from the religious community.

Darwin did not originate the idea of evolution with *On the Origin of Species, etc.* In fact most of Darwin's key ideas—natural selection, the struggle for scarce resources, and adaptation of organisms to their environments—had been considered by previous naturalists for more than a century.[31] Darwin's extensive and careful observations enabled him to induce the evolutionary process in a way that made it more credible than many other explanations of the origin of species. Natural selection was not even the only evolutionary theory discussed in 1859.

The Christian belief in man's fall had predisposed early naturalists to see change as degenerative: the human race was lower in the present age than in the golden one celebrated by Moses and Ovid.[32] The effort to combine the idea of a developing nature with man as its *summum*, and a degenerating anthropology, was a consistent difficulty for Darwin's predecessors. Darwin removed the valuation of nature from his theory: evolution did not move nature in general or man in particular towards good or evil. There were no moral connotations to natural selection.

Whether it was the convincing nature of his evidence, or his synthesis of a number of vague theories, or the major support his work had from leading British scientists, Darwin's name immediately became associated with evolution as its creator. And his book pushed evolutionary thought into the forefront as an intellectual issue.

Other systems of evolution competed with Darwin's for intellectual acceptance in the late nineteenth century. Some of these were important enough that they also demanded a response at Andover. The most prominent of these was put forward by Herbert Spencer (1820–1907), based on the work of a French naturalist, the Chevalier de Lamarck (1744–1829). Lamarck developed the idea of classifying organisms according to the complexity of their nervous systems. The higher developed from the lower, in his scheme. Lamarck differed from Darwin in thinking the organism changed from choice to adapt to the environment. His most often quoted example was the giraffe, stretching its neck to reach the uppermost branches of trees. Further, Lamarck found progress and development synonymous. Perhaps the major difference between Lamarck and Darwin lay in the use of evidence. Lamarck believed his theory "followed plainly and inevitably from the laws of organic transformation";[33] Darwin amassed thousands of observations from which he induced a hypothesis.

Spencer had been a civil engineer involved in railroad design in the 1830s and '40s. A man of phenomenal curiosity, he explored the countryside he was surveying to find geological specimens. He became interested in Lyell, Lamarck, and other natural historians, reading Lamarck in 1840 while examining fossil remains in railway cuts. Lamarck's theory that "organic forms had arisen 'by progressive modifications physically caused and inherited'" had an "irresistible attraction" for Spencer, he recorded in his autobiography.[34] It transformed his way of thought.

His was a synthetic mind; he wanted to find an underlying principle of evolution which would elucidate human society, the history of the earth, and, indeed, the development of the entire cosmos. Unlike Darwin, Spencer was a philosopher, not a naturalist. He did not seek facts about nature, but principles. Spencer's first book-length work on evolution dealt with human society, not natural history. In *Social Statics*, published in 1850, he argued for the inevitable perfection both of man and of human society, and against all but the most minimal government. Too active a government interfered with the laws of nature at work in society, Spencer believed. He further expressed a belief in the struggle for existence, and what he called the "survival of the fittest" in that struggle.[35]

Darwin and Spencer did not collaborate in any sense of the term. Well acquainted with each other's work, they rejected it owing to their fundamental differences. Darwin, indeed, once wrote that if Spencer "had trained himself to observe more, . . . he would have been a wonderful man";[36] one of Spencer's last major projects was to refute Darwinism.[37] Darwin's theory dealt almost exclusively with copiously documented natural phenomena. Spencer was concerned with metaphysics, the persistence of a Force that made evolution inevitable, the "super-organic evolution" of society out of organic life, and other indemonstrable ideas.[38]

While Spencer is practically unremembered today, he had a tremendous impact on his contemporaries. He was feted on both sides of the Atlantic, his work translated into many languages, and influenced such diverse figures as George Eliot and Mao Tse-Tung.[39] He enjoyed a major vogue in America, striking the universities like lightning, as John Peel put it; his 1882 American tour was a triumphal progress.[40]

Faced with so formidable a movement, Christian scholars and Andover Liberals alike were forced to come to terms with evolution. Those who still adhered to Common Sense philosophy responded from within that framework. They tended to oppose Spencer wholeheartedly. Some, like the famous educator John Bascom (1827–1911) wrote systematically against both Darwin and Spencer. He abhorred their unification of mind and matter, and their rejection of "everything but physical causation."[41]

The *Bibliotheca Sacra*, which continued to be published by the old Andoverians, strongly attacked Spencer on the grounds of positivism, materialism, atheism, and lack of humanitarian beliefs. When the American edition of the *Data of Ethics* appeared in 1880, D. McGregor Means of Middlebury College reviewed it angrily for the *Bibliotheca*.[42] Spencer could not define happiness, Means wrote: he tried to define it from a number of contradictory philosophical bases, including hedonism, stoicism, and utilitarianism. Evolution not only promoted such sloppy thinking, Means asserted, but it was a useless theory on which to build ethics. It claimed to predict the future state of society, but ignored evidence and so predicted only within its narrow theoretical framework.[43] Spencer stated that evil would disappear when society reached its perfect equilibrium. In order to hasten this state, Means believed the Englishman would advocate dispensing with social authority in the present.[44]

Other conservative Andoverians produced stronger attacks on Spencer. George Mooar (1830–1904), an Andover graduate who taught systematic theology at Pacific Theological Seminary, assailed Spencerian sociology. The discipline was one thing, Mooar wrote, when it saw "human action as determined by social conditions alone, and quite another when" it taught that social conditions were "largely determined by spontaneous energies . . ."[45] Spencerian sociologists regarded the discipline as a science describing "the laws in accordance with which the changes occur in human society."

They claimed to be able to describe how any culture arrived at its present state, Mooar said, by elucidating the "interplay of certain factors, internal and external," which existed from the society's beginning and have "continually and progressively modified each other." They say, he quoted Spencer, that a "given society 'has passed from an indefinite, incoherent homogeneity to a definite, coherent heterogeneity.'" Societies are organisms, Spencerians claimed, "and organisms all follow this order of evolution."[46]

This type of statement illustrated Means' frustration with the new philosophy for predicting the future with only a theory and no reliable factual data. Mooar was upset because such a static, deterministic view contradicted his own observations as a missionary. Spencer treated religion as a passing phenomenon in society's development. An evangelical Christian, Mooar thought religion elucidated human social development.[47] Moreover, his own experiences convinced him that Spencer was wrong in describing men as bound by "social conditions . . . determined by spontaneous energies which the individual" could not control. "Few men have more reason than the missionary to emphasize the tremendous power of circumstances and conditions over the will," Mooar asserted.

> Nowhere so much as among the people with whom he labors does he see how prostrate the individual is under disabilities which he inherits or which the custom of his country put upon him. Nevertheless, the missionary has learned that the individual is still a power.[48]

Sociology delighted too much in "resemblances and uniformities," Mooar maintained, taking "too little account of the solitary self."[49] Despite that discipline's decrees, the missionary experience proved that a culture could be transformed within a single generation. Fiji Islanders who as late as 1854 still strangled royal widows were now "honest, upright citizens," in Mooar's experience.[50]

Spencer's sociology did not accurately describe human nature; his ethics was diffuse, contradictory, and incomprehensible. *Bibliotheca Sacra* contributors also objected strenuously to his treatment of religion. The Rev. J. R. Herrick, of Bangor Theological Seminary, complained that Spencerians assumed Christianity was merely "an agent for promoting public morals."[51] Christianity was part of the naturalism which Spencer, Lecky, and others claimed "contain[ed] the whole truth," Herrick wrote. Such an attitude meant that there was no true morality, for "morality will perforce conform to laws by which nature works."[52] Men thus have no capacity for rising above their present situation, a total contradiction of Christianity.[53]

Mooar continued the argument in an article for the *New Englander*, saying that the very history of Christianity disproved Spencer's description of it. Theology might be a progressive science in that it described Christ's life and death more and more fully. But the revelation of Christ himself was a complete act. Even the progressive nineteenth century had to admit "that no one has come after the Son of Man,"[54] wrote Mooar.

Spencer was no problem for the old Andoverians to refute, because his theories were all philosophically grounded. The Christian scholars could refute them by the same logic they had used against materialists for years. Without Darwin to back evolution up with his impressive body of data, they could have dismissed Spencer as just another materialist. As Herrick said, the Spencerians rejected the supernatural, confining men wholly to nature. Christianity then became "an agent for promoting public morals" which could be understood by "look[ing] at the external features of moral development."[55] This was developmentalism of the kind Eichhorn had espoused eighty years earlier. In itself it posed no major threat to the Calvinist system.

Experience with the natural sciences gave the Christian scholars more respect for Darwin's analytical work. To be sure, some remained completely opposed to evolution. One such was Thomas Hill, a mathematician and sometime Harvard president, who attacked Darwin by an awkward application of the favorite Common Sense tool, analogy. In an essay praising Darwin's illustrious grandfather Erasmus,[56] Hill likened living organisms to mathematical figures. Organic beings were distinguished by their different forms in space, Hill wrote. In that way, they resembled conic sectors or other geometric shapes. An ellipse might change in many ways, but could never be other than a conic sector. "It is therefore probable," Hill continued, "that species and genera, which like curves are . . . defined by laws of space, have the like elasticity in some directions, . . . rigidity in others." One could assume that any species might "vary into any [other] but there was no more ground for tracing "a common ancestry . . . between two species taken at random" than for trying to find some such connection between two curves taken at random.[57]

Other objections to Darwin stemmed from a much more serious issue: the downgrading of religious authority in metaphysics. Just as writers in the fifties had objected to geology for ignoring the claims of theology, so later contributors resented evolution. James Bixby, of Meadville Theological School, wrote in 1881 that science's proper position was physics, not metaphysics. Followers of Darwin, however, had lately "assumed absolute authority in the domain of the knowable," ordering "religion into close confinement. The brilliant successes of modern science have made her believe that her favorite methods are the only ones by which anything is to be known."[58]

This point sounds similar to ones Christian scholars had been uttering against geologists for years. The difference was, as Bixby, Samuel Harris and others realized, that science's, or at least Darwin's facts were too well established to be changed for Genesis. Samuel Harris couched his response in old moral philosophical terms, demanding full equality for theology with the new sciences. Others, like McIlvaine took the position Austin Phelps had suggested a quarter century earlier: to stand back from all disputes with science and wait for truth to emerge. If "the Author of nature and of revelation be one and the same infinitely wise and good Being, true science and true religion can never have any quarrel with each other."[59]

Others saw that Darwin's work meant a serious rethinking of their most basic assumptions. One man who addressed this question for the *Biblio-*

theca in the 1870s was Frederic Gardiner, a friend of Park, who taught at the Episcopal seminary in Middleton, Connecticut. In general, he thought theologians did well to stand back from the controversy. The knowledge explosion had progressed at such a pace that theologians could not, like Stuart, try to treat a subject on which they had inadequate knowledge. "As a scientific theory, discussed on scientific grounds, Darwinism must be finally accepted or rejected on scientific evidence," Gardiner wrote judiciously. Besides, he added, theologians had made fools of themselves over the centuries by attacking science.[60]

Writing in 1878 on "The Bearing of Scientific Thought," Gardiner continued the development of his ideas. Theology did not depend on whether evolution was proved true or not, he decided. Indeed, much of the defensiveness exhibited by men like Bixby came from their fear that nothing would be left of Christianity if evolution were true. But for theology, Gardiner wrote "the question between evolution and anti-evolution is simply a question between mediate and intermediate creation."[61] Did God create everything at a word, or did his Word set the forces of development in motion? The answer was undiscoverable. "A self-evolution of the cosmos would indeed be destructive to theology," Gardiner added, but scientific thought actually was tending away from that idea.[62]

Gardiner did object to Darwin and his supporters ignoring Scriptures. However, his argument differed considerably from Stuart's. Stuart had believed that the creation question could be solved philologically. Gardiner recognized that the issue of what the Bible really meant was no longer relevant. However, he said, the Bible had "a purely historical value" for reporting "men's primeval state, [and] . . . the extent and the . . . diffusion of the populations of the world . . ."[63] By ignoring Scriptures, Darwinians limited the degree to which they could uncover the truth, Gardiner argued.

The real problem, as Gardiner saw it, was the position of public trust scientists now occupied. The scientists occupied the position "once held by the religious teacher," he pointed out. If Spencer and Darwin abandoned religion, that could have a great influence on the country at large. "Men have come to rest very implicitly upon the announcements of science," Gardiner said.[64] To counter this influence, he tried to point out some of the scientific problems inherent in Darwin's thought. Proceeding without invective, he reviewed the literature carefully. He highlighted Alfred Russell Wallace's doubts on the application of natural science to man, and suggested places where Darwin or Lyell had misconstrued evidence.[65]

For Gardiner, the best solution would be to find theism inherent in evolutionary thought. Given its strong public influence, evolution could not

Chapter VI

be dislodged by invective or logic. However, if it were theistic, theology would interpret it in light of traditional Christian doctrine. Writing in 1878, Gardiner saw hopeful signs for the unity of theology and natural science. "Time was . . . when scientists who had cut themselves loose from revelation thought they might find nature complete within itself," the theologian remarked.[66] However, as the evolutionists had learned more about the world, they had come upon the God behind it. "Herbert Spencer himself, in the very act of declaring the ultimate cause of all things to be unknowable, . . . actually predicates of [the ultimate cause] omniscience, omnipotence, eternity," Gardiner reported.[67] "Tyndall's account of evolution as a 'power inscrutable to the human intellect' is more just than the congeries of attributes sometimes bestowed upon [God] in metaphysics," he added.[68] Finding signs of religious belief among the evolutionists filled Gardiner with relief. The "self-evolution of the cosmos" would be a terrible thing; fortunately science had abandoned this notion in favor of "an inscrutable Power . . . under whom evolution has been accomplished."[69]

Other Christian scholars made even more extreme efforts to reconcile themselves to evolution. George Frederick Wright, a friend of Park's, wrote five articles for the *Bibliotheca* between 1875 and 1880 reconciling Calvinism and Darwinism. He drew close parallels between the two systems of thought, finding similarities between Darwin's determinism and predestination.[70]

Wright, Samuel Harris, Gardiner, and the other Christian scholars were trying to integrate evolution into the New England theology. Harris upheld the co-equality of science, theology, and philosophy; Gardiner saw hopeful signs of religion among the evolutionists; Wright found Darwinism philosophically akin to Calvinism.

The new faculty at Andover made no such efforts at reconciliation. They rejected Spencer's views on sociology, but they embraced evolution with great enthusiasm. They saw theology as a discipline completely separate from natural science, yet strongly influenced by it. In fact, in an age where evolution was a popular catchword, they set out to make theology a modern study by showing that it followed evolutionary principles. The new men, the Andover liberals, adopted German critical and historical methods without question. They did little or no textual criticism; they took the Bible away from Congregationalism, and based their religion solely on faith.

Once they had Andover to themselves, the Liberals set up their own journal, the *Andover Review*. Unlike the *Bibliotheca Sacra*, which avoided a particular editorial stance, the *Andover Review* was designed from the outset to be a party organ. It publicized the "new departure" from Calvinism on second probation and defended what the liberals called "progressive orthodoxy." The *Review* paid a fair amount of attention to evolution as it affected theology and ethics. Among the articles which merged these subjects were "Theistic Evolution"; "Evolution of the Conscience"; "Evolution and Theology"; and "The Evolution of Truth."

Indeed, the idea that all things change, including theology, lay at the heart of "Progressive Orthodoxy." In the introduction to the first edition of the *Review*, Egbert Smyth explained the changing nature of theology. It was not the gradual development of an ever greater body of truth, but a way of approaching God which changed as the intellectual environment changed. One might think of the adaptation of theology to the needs of the day almost as a metaphysical parallel to the adaptation of species to new environments. The progressives themselves did not expect to build a lasting system of theology. Smyth did not doubt "that every reader of these pages is now holding some belief as part of his Christian faith, some dogmas as a part of his theology, which Christian men of later generations will reject."[71] Elsewhere he wrote that "progressive orthodoxy emphasizes the present state of thought; it seeks no absolutes."[72]

Progressive orthodoxy discussed six major doctrinal features, from the Incarnation and Atonement, through Christian life and a doctrine of the Scriptures. It reinterpreted the nature of the Atonement and Christian life to deal with the pressing urban problems of the day. In dealing with these issues, the *Review* was particularly hostile to Spencer. F. H. Johnson, an Andover clergyman who wrote most of the Review's essays on evolution, Darwin, and Spencer, said "all moral distinctions have grown directly from the conviction that each human individual is a soul."[73] Abandon the soul to Spencer's transcendent force, and one subverted "every high belief."[74]

On these issues, the *Review* and the *Bibliotheca* were as one. But the *Review* did not stop with rejecting Spencer. Instead, they christened evolution and with it transformed theology. F. H. Johnson gave coherent expression to their new departure in "Co-Operative Creation," written for the *Andover Review* in 1885.[75] In this essay, Johnson refuted the old Andover position uniting theology with natural science. This was the science of natural theology, which discovered in the creation of the world a beneficent design, proving its author to be the God of Revelation.

In "Co-Operative Creation," Johnson explicitly espoused a doctrine of evolution in the natural world. ". . . structural or functional modifications of the organism so marked that they lead to a new variety of species," Johnson stated, should be attributed to "the unconscious efforts of the organism in response to its environment."[76] The minister saw evolution's underlying idea of struggle for existence as the unifying principle of Christian thought. In opening his essay, he posed a new beatitude: "Blessed are the fit, for they shall inherit the earth." This saying contradicted the Sermon on the Mount at first glance, Johnson admitted, but closer inspection showed them to be in harmony. He quoted Paul, who said that "unto everyone that hath shall be given, and he shall have abundance: but from him that hath not shall be taken away even that which he hath."[77] Furthermore, no one achieved a high state of spirituality who did not struggle for it. Man was not a help-less puppet in the hands of God, but an active agent in his own salvation. The person who sat back without praying and working to await dumbly divine salvation would never achieve it.[78] In this sense, Johnson said, one ought to view creation as a cooperative process. Man co-operates with God in developing his own capabilities, and working through his own salvation. Similarly, the rest of creation co-operated with God in evolving and grow-ing itself.[79]

Johnson claimed that such an understanding of creation was much more sensible than the argument from design, both as a realistic interpretation of life, and as a confutation of atheism. "On the theory of a sudden and special creation, the Christian argument for design admits only of a one-sided ar-gument," Johnson asserted. It brought together all facts pointing to benefi-cence, but also threw into strong relief those proving a meaningless, evil world.[80] ". . . the strongest points of atheism are drawn directly and natu-rally from the old conception [of design]," he added.[81]

Evolution, on the other hand, first described the realities of existence. While the natural theologians saw in mineral resources, sun, air, and water the action of a beneficent designer, Johnson saw only struggle and pain.

> . . . what obstacles are not placed in the way of man's becoming
> possessed of the world's treasures? The animals which exist for his
> food are swifter of foot than he; and the forests . . . abound also with
> creatures that are as ready to make food of him as he of . . . them.[82]

The process of producing mineral resources in the earth destroyed many forms of life; glaciers which provide much-needed water for today also ruined much fertile farmland with stone deposits. In short, Johnson wrote, all nature was in a constant state of struggle, and that struggle was to pro-duce even higher forms of life, both physiological and spiritual. Indeed, he said, a belief in eternal life was a strong indicator of evolution. For "if life here on earth has been a continual becoming and overcoming, and bears the unmistakeable marks of incompleteness, the anticipation of a continu-ance of the half-finished process is not only natural but unavoidable."[83]

There is a beneficence in nature, Johnson asserted, but not that assumed by natural theology. The beneficence lay in the idea of struggle, or effort itself, for through it man was able to understand God better, draw nearer to him, love him more fully, and exist as a higher moral being.[84]

The Andover progressives not only rejected the argument from design; they considered natural science something that could elucidate theology. This put a completely different construction on the relation between reason and revelation. The Protestant notion of the relation between the two, F. H. Johnson wrote in 1886, found its "perfect analogy in the progressive revelation" in natural science, which "moves onward by hypotheses," he claimed. Biblical theology progressed by the same methods.[85] Theology was a science because it followed the methods of Darwinian biology, not because of its independent position as an interpreter of nature.

Another author made this point even more strongly. He saw "but one outcome" to the antagonism between science and theology. That was for theology to "learn to utilize the facts and apply the methods of science so far as they have any application in the province of religion."[86] He added that science would then become the servant and an ally of religion, a relationship Park would have rejected unhesitatingly. In natural theology, the wonders of nature proclaimed the existence of God; they did not interpret either sacred Scriptures or Christian theology. Yet the *Andover Review* discussed revelation as part "of a natural religion built upon evolution."[87]

The *Bibliotheca Sacra* persisted in trying to reconcile Genesis with modern biology and geology through the 1880s. The *Andover Review* started life with the issue decided in favor of evolution.

The new faculty discarded another important tenet of the prior generation, the close alliance between reason and affection in understanding God. If natural science were to dictate how men understood the world, then the office of logic in finding a good God behind his creation was necessarily lessened. However, the Andover progressives emphasized intuition and feeling to the exclusion of logic. They even saw the early Andover faculty as sharing this proclivity. Reminiscing on changes in theology during his lifetime, George Harris saw them beginning at Andover in 1808. "The New School theology was the dictate of the heart," he wrote in 1914, ". . . more human and humane than Calvinism." Calvinism fell at Andover in its early years because "logic was powerless against the heart."[88] Theology under Park and Taylor did expand the freedom of the human will, but Park considered himself a consistent *Calvinist*. He did not believe in giving untrammeled sway to the heart. As "The theology of the Intellect and That of

Feelings" clearly expressed, he insisted on a balance between the two. The heart without logic to check it could easily blunder into mere emotionalism.

The progressive faculty believed that Park and his generation had tied New England theology to a hide-bound, stultifying scholasticism; they saw Progressive Orthodoxy as a tool for breaking away from that prison.[89]

As a consequence, they undervalued reason relative to what they called experience.

In 1884, George Harris wrote an article for the *Andover Review* defining what he called "Christian Consciousness."[90] In it, he explained how Christians might be sure of the existence of God and of the saving mission of Christ. Everyone knew, Harris stated, that one accepted the effects of Jesus' ministry from the experiences of believers, not from rational proof.[91] Therefore, it was only reasonable to assume that this experience formed the highest proof of God's existence.[92] Not only was collective experience the testimony to God's existence, it stood above biblical interpretation. Harris wrote that "any theories which claim to be confirmed by the Bible, yet against which Christian sentiment protests, should not be accepted." There should be "no assent to opinions against which refined Christian sentiment rebels."[93]

One might enquire how "refined Christian sentiment" was discerned. Harris had some vaguely democratic answers which relied on sensing the majority opinion on issues. The Abbot professor believed the question of second probation was a good example of Christian consciousness in action. As Christians evolved, developing increasingly refined senses "of the very heart of God [and his] love . . . which throbs in sympathy for the whole world," they abandoned the cruel idea of the damnation of millions. Modern Christians had evolved to the point of allowing God's love to apply to everyone.[94]

Christian experience did not abandon reason so much as subordinate it to sentiment. Harris insisted that reason had its place in Christianity, as long as it did not stultify her. Still, he concluded his essay by saying that "those who prefer to stand on the higher grounds of historical reality, conscious experience, sanctified imagination, and the best Christian sentiment, have no quarrel with those who will not climb as high."[95] The only thing that upset these more advanced Christians was having the "rationalists," as Harris called them, try to use "intellectual proofs" instead of appealing to sentiment.[96]

Harris's remarks drew some inevitable protests from Princeton, and from the *Bibliotheca* ("Is Andover Romanizing?" an angry 1884 editorial demanded).[97] But those who abandoned the full equality of theology with natural science seemed to agree that the intellect should take a secondary role in theology. Francis Peabody of Harvard wrote on "The Office of Proof in the Knowledge of God" for the *Andover Review*, expressing much the same sentiments as Harris. "Religious conviction is not the result of any formal proof," Peabody said.[98]

Park, Bela Bates Edwards, or any of their contemporaries would have agreed wholeheartedly that only the heart can be moved to turn away from sin and toward God. But Peabody, with Harris and the Andover Liberals, included proofs of the existence of God in his sweeping statement. "We have swung to [an] extreme of unbelief in any efficacy from such demonstrations," Peabody wrote. They were simultaneously "superfluous and impossible."[99]

The history of New England theology before the Civil War asserted that unbelievers could be converted through logic. That was the thrust of Woods's and Stuart's campaign against the Unitarians, or Park's meticulously argued Natural Theology, or, indeed, of some of their revivals. Right thought would lead to right belief. The time was, mourned the *Bibliotheca* in 1870, when "one or two arguments from scholars, like Butler's *Analogy*, or Paley's *Evidences*, were sufficient to save the cause of truth in that field."[100] But that day was gone.

A final blow the Andover progressives dealt Stuart, Edwards, and Park came in their changed understanding of the authority of the Bible and the interpretation of Scriptures. In his essay on Christian consciousness, Harris had stated that Biblical interpretation must bow to refined Christian conscience. The value of a book should be determined "by the amount of truth it contains concerning Christ," he said, and a consensus of refined Christians would determine that.[101]

The main commentators on biblical criticism for the *Review* were Egbert Smyth and George Trumball Ladd. Ladd is better known today for his work in psychology at Yale. At Andover from 1879–82 as lecturer on Congregationalism, he took the opportunity to write a *Doctrine of Sacred Scriptures* prized at Andover and excoriated by the *Bibliotheca*.

In an essay written for the *Andover Review* in 1885, Ladd presented a digest of some of his major ideas.[102] He began by explaining that the traditional doctrine of inspiration of the Bible could no longer be accepted.

Elements of uncertain traditions entered into historical passages. The original authors did not distinguish among conflicting oral traditions, but left them standing side by side. Not only were there apparent discrepancies in the text, there were real discrepancies in various biblical accounts.[103]

Finally, Ladd asserted, such questions as the authenticity of the Bible belong to historical criticism. The individual Christian could not, as Stuart had assumed, have faith in God's inspiration of the text to make all seeming difficulties come out right in the end. "A theological dogma dictating how these questions *must* be or *ought* to be answered is a worthless impertinence," Ladd stated coldly. "Historical science is obligated to do what it best can to discover how they probably are to be answered."[104] Discrepancies could not be resolved by philology, history, exegesis, or criticism, Ladd concluded. They were irresolvable.[105] The present job of criticism, Ladd argued, was to break away from the falsely inductive reason of Stuart's generation. No one knew what Christians would finally perceive the Bible to mean, but they must break away from the doctrine of inspiration.[106]

Smyth discussed this point in the wider context of a belief in Christian consciousness. Scriptures attested to the revelation of God in Christ, he said, and that testimony was verified by Christian witness. "A genuine Christian doctrine has a subjective as well as objective basis," he wrote in 1884.[107] The doctrine attested to by the Bible and affirmed by experience was true. That which was denied by the Bible was false. But that which the Bible affirmed and consciousness denied was false.[108]

In 1808, Morse, Woods and Pearson established Andover to defend orthodox Calvinism. The development of an intellectual center which would train erudite rivals to Harvard was their cherished dream. As a consequence, Moses Stuart was hired to prepare an intellectual defense of the Scriptures; under him, the tradition of the Christian scholar grew up at Andover. . . . Harris, Ladd, and Smyth were all Andover-trained men whom Andover encouraged to explore the range of intellectual probing of the day.

In the years 1808 to 1850, Andover articulated a major synthesis of theology, philosophy and natural science. All were united by Common Sense philosophy, which provided the methodological tools for joining nature and the Bible. The Andover Liberals overturned this carefully wrought structure. Evolution took the place of Common Sense for them; theology became subordinated to a biological theory. And biblical scholarship ceased being a science. It became dependent, instead, on the intuitive feelings of the mass of Christians.

"Of all the seeming antagonism between science and theology, there can be but one outcome," E. A. Lawrence wrote for the *Andover Review* in 1887. "Theology will learn to utilize the facts and employ the methods of science . . . in the province of religion."[109] Theology was no longer a science in its own right, with axioms, facts, and relationships. In the eyes of the Andover Liberals, theology had no coherent structure of its own. It was amorphous;

it should change with the changing times. And modern science would determine its direction.

The distance between the Liberals and Park's generation was light-years wide. In 1846, Park and Edwards had written that "Natural Theology augments our interest in the revealed word, as well as in the sciences of matter and the mind." Natural theology, the umbrella for moral philosophy and natural philosophy, was "the crown of all sciences." Theology dominated other sciences in Park's system. Yet "they are not more subordinate to it, than itself is a tributary to Revelation."[110] The Christian scholars could not conceive of a theology which was not dependent on the Bible. The Andover Liberals would not turn to Scriptures even to justify their religious ideas. The heart alone would tell them if they were correct. "Historical reality, conscious experience, and [a] sanctified imagination" were far better than "logical methods and intellectual proof," the Liberals believed.[111] The Christian scholars needed both.

Edwards and Park believed that they could only strengthen Christianity by exposing it to modern scholarship. They had a supreme faith, not just in the unifying power of Common Sense philosophy, but in the Bible itself. No teaching, however bizarre, could prove the Bible false. They sent dozens of students abroad to prepare at German universities so that they might bring the best knowledge to the aid of Christianity. With Park counteracting atheistical arguments in his theology lectures, they saw no harm in the young men learning rationalist-based criticism. Perhaps they argued that they themselves had gone abroad, sat at the feet of the Hegelians, and come home all the more eager to defend Congregational Christianity.

The third generation of Andover faculty overturned the notion of Christian scholarship. In denying the balance of reason and revelation, they removed the basis for a Christian scholarship. In fact, the Liberals removed both reason and revelation from the foundations of their work. Because the Bible could not be reconciled with evolution, unless by logical contortions such as Wright underwent, they jettisoned the Bible. Stuart would have asked them how they could be sure of the existence of Christ, without a Bible. The Liberals relied only on their collective consciousness. But Stuart and Edwards had a document whose truth was supported by reason, while the eye of faith understood the deeper realities behind it.

The Christian scholars opened the doors on history, languages, and criticism for American students. Through that door came the skepticism predicted by the Andover trustees in 1825. The Liberals abandoned Park, abandoned the New England theology, abandoned a rationally-based faith. They should at least have paid homage to Stuart, Edwards, and Park who made it possible for them to acquire the learning on which they based progressive orthodoxy. The Liberals downgraded reason as a theological tool. But the educated reason by which they overturned Park's system was the hallmark of Andover's scholars: Progressive orthodoxy in the end was a tribute to the seminary's constant involvement in the frontiers of learning.

AFTERWORD

❖ ❖ ❖

As readers of this remarkable work learn, Andover Seminary supported a cadre of Christian scholars who helped revolutionize intellectual life in nineteenth-century New England. Attending to the breakdown of moral philosophy that resulted from historical and scientific projects these scholars pursued, Sara Paretsky's 1977 dissertation describes the creative process of intellectual outreach that more familiar narratives of theological declension during this period fail to capture. Authored by an intellectual historian who turned to crime fiction instead of building an academic career, this work invites readers to take up where Paretsky's inquiries into post-Calvinist American intellectual life left off, perhaps with the independent spirit of Paretsky's feminist detective V. I. Warshawski.

Focusing on "the Calvinist Renaissance" at Andover Seminary from the 1830s through the 1850s, Paretsky describes the passion for historical and scientific research that engaged biblical scholar Moses Stuart and his influential students. A new breed of "Christian scholars," these Andover men were Christian intellectuals devoted less to pastoral duty than to research and writing. Inspired by the challenge of showing how biblical revelation could be integrated with new discoveries in philology, history, and geology, their faith that reverence for divine sovereignty would stand and even be strengthened by scientific knowledge led them to consequences they did not foresee. Through various stages of intellectual development, the Christian scholars at Andover began to evaluate the Bible historically and scientifically, slowly overturning their understanding of theology's relationship to science. Ironically, faith in the durability of Calvinist theology and its hospitality to historical and scientific knowledge launched a broad-ranging, step-by-step dismantling of that theology.

The important thrust of Paretsky's argument can be appreciated by comparing it to the thrust of arguments crafted by Mark Noll, the best-known historian of American Calvinism in the late twentieth and early twenty-first centuries. In his popular and prize-winning *Scandal of the Evangelical Mind* (1994), Noll identified the Reformed tradition of New England Calvinism as the intellectual foundation for American evangelicalism, and he chastised evangelicals for selling out Calvinism. Seduced by the apparent certainties of Enlightenment rationalism, Noll argues, evangelicals set Calvinism on its intellectual course toward the dead end of fundamentalism. In his subsequent magisterial work, *America's God: From Jonathan Edwards to Abraham Lincoln* (2002), Noll showed how the self-centered moralism of evangelical rationalism escalated in the context of dispute over the nature of republican government, leading to a religious war between northern and southern evangelicals in which both sides arrogantly claimed to have God on their side. In Noll's reading of antebellum theology, evangelicals on both sides of the sectional conflict lost sight of the transcendent God revered by Jonathan Edwards and his puritan predecessors.

Noll's cautionary narratives about the lure of Enlightenment rationalism, the contested implications of evangelical theology for American government, and the collapse of evangelicalism into fundamentalism offer much new insight. At the same time, they echo an older tradition of historical interpretation in relation to which Paretsky's dissertation offered an alternative path. Rooted in the neo-orthodox theology popular among protestant intellectuals in the early twentieth century, and best exemplified by Joseph Haroutunian's 1932 work, *Piety versus Moralism: The Passing of the New England Theology from Edwards to Taylor*, this older historiographic tradition supported a declension narrative about New England theology. It also contributed to the animus toward both fundamentalism and liberalism for which many later Christian scholars became known.

Paretsky's 1977 work offered an alternative interpretation of New England theology. Today, her work takes on new value as an alternative to Noll's reading of the transformation of American Calvinism. Unlike Noll, Paretsky has no ax to grind with evangelicals for abandoning their true Calvinist intellectual heritage or any apparent interest in making evangelicalism more intellectually robust. Indeed, Paretsky is not concerned with evangelicalism, exactly, but with the breakdown of New England Calvinism itself and the intellectual ferment within that process.

Paretsky follows the Andover faculty through their enthusiasm for German scholarship and into their turn toward the "God of evolution" driving nature and history. The difficulties these men faced in defending protestant theology in this intellectual context after the Civil War, and the rear-guard loyalty to orthodoxy traced by Daniel Day Williams in his *Andover Liberals* (1941), were not Paretsky's primary focus. She was more interested in the Andover scholars' passionate thirst for knowledge than in their defensiveness. No one has told their stories as fully or so well.

Readers of Paretsky's crime fiction may be struck by the resonance between the quest for knowledge evident in these nineteenth-century Americans and Paretsky's fictional detective, the redoubtable V. I. Warshawski. The fictional detective braves danger and often goes without sleep or reimbursement in her headlong dive into mounds of data and recondite bodies of possibly relevant scientific literature. She investigates people's lives to uncover their secrets and find out what really happened. Much to the irritation of anyone standing in her way, V. I. shakes any tree that seems likely to yield fruit. While not unaware of threats to herself in the course of dangerous investigations or the possibility that painful truths may be exposed, the characters around her come, sooner or later, to respect the fact that nothing short of an ambush can hold her back. Beyond the more obvious similarities between detective work and the work of a historian and between the skills involved in constructing compelling narratives in fiction and in fact, the character V. I. embodies some of the same qualities that Paretsky found in the Christian scholars at Andover Seminary. Unlike some of their more worried and less creative successors, these men did not fear the consequences of investigation enough to stop what they were doing. Something visceral motivated them. And that something cannot be entirely explained by the naive optimism (or stubborn arrogance) of Enlightenment rationalism.

Readers interested in new topics for historical investigation may find some interesting clues here. The family networks at Andover merit further study, especially the lives and intellectual contributions of the wives and daughters of Andover men. We learn that the families of the two most prominent Andover scholars in the 1840s—Edwards A. Park and Bela Bates Edwards—were closely intertwined and that Paretsky found a "fascinating collection" of Park family papers held by Park family descendants. Readers familiar with the novels of Elizabeth Stuart Phelps and with Phelps's interest in feminism and spiritualism will recognize Moses Stuart's erudite daughter. As these tantalizing breadcrumbs of information may suggest, investigation into the rich intellectual life growing out of the breakdown of Calvinist moral philosophy at Andover is far from complete. The publication of Paretsky's work may open an important new chapter.

Amanda Porterfield

NOTES

PREFACE

1. Frank Wilczek and Betsy Devine, *Longing for the Harmonies: Themes and Variations from Modern Physics* (New York: W.W. Norton, 1987).

2. Charlotte Brontë, *Jane Eyre.*

3. For a concise discussion of the formidable obstacles facing the Civil Rights Movement in Chicago, see Taylor Branch, *At Canaan's Edge* (New York: Simon & Schuster, 2007). Elizabeth Taylor and Adam Cohen's study of Richard J. Daley, *American Pharaoh* (New York: Little Brown and Company, 2000), includes a major analysis of race in Chicago.

4. I wrote in detail about my Chicago summer in my memoir, *Writing in an Age of Silence* (London: Verso Press, 2007).

5. *Science* is a portmanteau word here for evidence-based natural research. The word didn't have the same meaning in the nineteenth century, when scholars were more likely to talk about natural philosophy or natural history.

6. I wrote newsletters and helped run conferences for Fortune 1000 companies on how to implement Title VII and its executive orders. Ironic.

7. The department notoriously gave little support to students of any sex in their job search. A visiting site committee in 1970 or 1971 wrote scathingly that Chicago students were left to sink or swim on their own as best they could.

8. Melville to Hawthorne, June 1851. (The exact date is unclear; it is probably June 1.) Melville believed the grass-growing place was where a "man ought always to compose," but I believe it's true for women as well, or at least for me.

INTRODUCTION

1. Lewis Simpson, *The Man of Letters in New England and the South* (Baton Rouge: Louisiana State University Press, 1973), p. 22.

2. George Schmidt, *The Old-time College President* (New York: Columbia University Press, 1930), p. 112.

3. Ibid, p. 109.

4. Daniel Day Williams, *The Andover Liberals* (New York: King's Crown Press, 1941); and Laurence R. Veysey, *Emergence of the American University* (Chicago: University of Chicago Press, 1965).

5. Leonard Bacon, *Discourse . . . at the Ordination of Theodore Woolsey, . . .* (New Haven: B. L. Hamlin, 1846).

6. Edward Hitchcock, *Reminiscences of Amherst College* (Northhampton, Mass: Bridgeman & Childs, 1863), p. 295.

CHAPTER I

1. Edwards A. Park, "The New England Theology," *Bibliotheca Sacra*, IX (1852), 191.

2. William Sprague, *Annals of the American Pulpit*, 9 vols. (New York: Carter & Brothers, 1858–1869), I, 548.

3. Ibid., II, 693.

4. Samuel Hopkins, *Sketches of the Life of the Late Rev. Samuel Hopkins* (Hartford: Stephen West, D.D., 1805), pp. 28–37.

5. According to the Old Calvinists, Adam's sin came to us in two ways, first through our own lack of personal righteousness, due to his transgression; and secondly, through imputation. Because Adam was the federal head of the human race, the whole race participated in his fall from grace as if it had been their own. Old Calvinists drew a parallel between Adam's loss of righteousness, and Christ's total righteousness, so that they perceived certain parallels in the way in which sinners inherited sinfulness and the just received grace. Hopkins differed from the Old Calvinists in saying there could be no imputed sinfulness since that meant that man could achieve righteousness by imputation. He also differed from the Old Calvinists in saying that we have a moral, not a natural impediment to regeneration. The only way in which we differ from Adam's pre-lapsarian state, according to Hopkins, is in the removal of the Holy Spirit from our acts of decision, making them totally corrupt. Thus *natural* ability (the will and the understanding) were still intact. The Old Calvinists held that during conversion the Holy Spirit operated on the will to enable the sinner to repent of his sin and choose God. The Hopkinsians believed that repentance preceded the infusion of grace, because man could choose God through his unimpaired natural ability.

6. Frank Hugh Foster, *A Genetic History of the New England Theology* (Chicago: University of Chicago Press, 1907), p. 168.

7. Leonard Woods, *A History of Andover Theological Seminary* (Boston: James R. Osgood & Co., 1885), p. 454.

8. Ibid., p. 52.

9. Ibid.

10. Edwards A. Park's undated notes for his memorial of Pearson, Edwards A. Park's Papers, Yale University Library, New Haven, Conn.

11. Morse to Woods, 21 October 1806, in Woods, *History*, p. 462.

12. Woods to Isaac Warren, 23 August 1797, Leonard Woods' Letters to Isaac Warren, Syracuse University Library, Syracuse, N.Y.

13. Woods, *History*, p. 72.

14. Ibid., pp. 75–76.

15. "Last Will & Testament of Samuel Abbot," 31 December 1806, Park's Papers, Yale.

16. Woods, *History*, p. 57.

17. Pearson to Morse, 2 May 1807, Park's Papers, Yale.

18. "General Principles of Union," 17 September 1807, Park's Papers, Yale.

19. "Last Will & Testament of Samuel Abbot."

20. Data gathered from Andover Theological Seminary, *General Catalogue*, 1808–1908. These figures note only where men spent a significant part of their professional lives. Those who taught for a year prior to or during their ministerial training were not counted as educators, only those who taught in colleges or academies for more than a year on concluding theological study.

21. Abiel Abbot to Sprague, 21 September 1853, in Sprague, *Annals*, II, 129.

22. Woods, *History*, p. 146.

23. Ibid.

24. Woods, *History*, p. 103.

25. From the *Dictionary of American Biography*, 1st ed., s.v. "Griffin, Edward."

26. Orville Dewey to Sprague, in Sprague, *Annals*, II, 360.

27. Foster, *Genetic History*, pp. 304–5.

28. Woods to Isaac Warren, 26 January 1798, Leonard Wood's Letters.

29. Flagg and Gould, who published most of the seminary faculty's work for half a century.

30. Edwards A. Park, "Moses Stuart," in *Memorial Collection of Sermons* (Boston: Pilgrim's Press, 1902), pp. 191–96; and Sidney Mead, *Nathaniel William Taylor* (Chicago: University of Chicago Press, 1944), pp. 55–56.

31. Park, "Moses Stuart," pp. 195–96; and Mead, *Nathaniel William Taylor*, pp. 55–56. Stuart had been called to supplant the Rev. James Dana, whose congregation wanted a more revival-oriented preacher. Dana resigned under considerable pressure. Thus it was with some embarrassment that Stuart sought his own dismission a scant three years later.

32. Stuart to Pearson, 25 November 1809, Park's Papers, Yale.

33. Stuart to Everett, 14 October 1813, 20 Letters from Stuart to Everett, 1813–1815, Edward Everett Collection, Massachusetts Historical Society, Boston, Mass.

34. Park, "Moses Stuart," p. 197.

35. Stuart to Everett, 13 February 1813, Everett Collection.

36. Quoted in Park, "Moses Stuart," p. 209.

37. Woods, *History*, p. 134.

38. Morse to Woods, 21 October 1806, ibid, p. 462.

39. Constitution and Statutes of the Andover Theological Seminary (Boston: Farrard, Mallory, & Co., 1808).

40. Samuel Hubbard to Samuel Farrar (two trustees), 23 December 1841, sending him written professions of the creed from the faculty, Park's Papers, Yale.

41. "The Constitution and Statutes of the Theological Seminary in Andover," *Monthly Anthology and Boston Review*, V (1808), 612.

42. Ibid., p. 614.

43. Quoted in Daniel Walker Howe, *The Unitarian Conscience* (Cambridge: Harvard University Press, 1970), pp. 2–3.

44. Constitution of Andover, pp. 14–15.

45. Howe, *Unitarian Conscience*, p. 84.

46. Ibid., p. 88.

47. Leonard Woods, "Letters to Young Ministers," *Spirit of the Pilgrims*, V (1832), Letter No. 1, 132–33.

48. Ibid., Letter No. 4, p. 249.

49. Ibid., Letter No. 5, p. 308.

50. Ibid., pp. 314–15.

51. Ibid., Letter No. 2, p. 138.

52. "Review of 'The Christian Preacher's Commission,'" *Spirit of the Pilgrims*, V (1832), 35.

53. Ibid., p. 38.

54. Terrence Martin, *The Instructed Vision* (Bloomington: University of Indiana Press, 1961), p. 6.

55. Sydney Ahlstrom, "Scottish Philosophy and American Theology," *Church History*, XXIV (1955), 262.

56. Ibid., p. 268.

57. David Hume, *A Treatise of Human Nature*, ed. L. A. Selby-Brigge (Oxford: Clarendon Press, 1888), p. 83. This and subsequent discussion derived in part from Stephen Grave, *The Scottish Philosophy of Common Sense* (Oxford: Clarendon Press, 1960); Joseph Haven, *Moral Philosophy* (Boston: Gould & Lincoln, 1859); Howe, *Unitarian Conscience*; and James McCosh, *The Scottish Philosophy* (New York: Robert Carter & Brothers, 1880).

58. Grave, *Scottish Philosophy*, pp. 119–20.

59. Ibid., pp. 134–35.

60. Thomas Reid, *Works*, ed. Dugald Stewart, 4 vols. (New York: E. Duyckinck, Collins, and Hannay and R. and W. A. Barton, 1822), III, 234–42.

61. McCosh, *Scottish Philosophy*, p. 2.

62. Reid, *Works*, I, 135.

63. Park, "New England Theology," p. 191.

64. Edwards A. Park, "Review of Stewart's *Active and Moral Powers*," *Bibliotheca Sacra*, VII (1850), 191–93.

65. Foster, *A Genetic History*, pp. 245 ff; and Nathaniel William Taylor, *Essays, Lectures, etc., upon Select Subjects in Revealed Theology* (New York: Clark, Austin, & Smith, 1859), pp. 262–68, passim.

66. Ralph Henry Gabriel, *Religion and Learning at Yale* (New Haven: Yale University Press, 1958), p. 135.

67. Indeed, the Princeton theologian Charles Hodge boasted in 1835 that no new ideas had found their way into Princeton for fifty years, or since they had taken on Common Sense. Placing a book on a reading list did not mean the faculty accepted its views: Andover students also read Hume, who was a skeptic and an atheist. Wilson Smith, whose *Professors and Public Ethics* (Ithaca, N.Y.: Cornell University Press, 1956) is one of the few studies treating the dominance of moral philosophy in this period, bases his work on the use of Paley's utilitarian moral philosophy. The *Christian Spectator* (Yale), and the *Christian Repertory* (Princeton), both published strong criticisms of Paley in 1835, the latter saying that "no man . . . has done more to corrupt the true theory of morals than Dr. Paley." Park at Andover claimed that "Paley's definition of virtue [was] a definition of total depravity!" William Paley's *Natural Theology* (London: J. & G. Robinson, G. Offar, and J. Evans & Co., 1824) was generally accepted, because it used analogy to reason from creation to the Creator. Its utilitarian aspects were presumably ignored.

68. Woods, "Letters to Young Ministers," Letter No. 3, p. 192.

69. George Daniels, *American Science in the Age of Jackson* (New York: King's Crown Press, 1968), p. 65.

70. Ibid., p. 66.

71. Ibid., p. 82.

72. Leonard Woods, *Collected Works*, 5 vols. (Andover: Flagg & Gould, 1859), II, 58.

73. The subtitle of Paley's work on natural theology.

74. Howe, *Unitarian Conscience*, pp. 73–74.

75. B. B. Edwards and Edwards A. Park, "Natural Theology," *Bibliotheca Sacra*, III (1846), 243.

76. Timothy Dwight, *Theology Explained and Defended*, 4 vols. (New York: Harper & Brothers, 1847), I, 75–277.

77. Paley, *Natural Theology*, pp. 236–53, passim.

78. Ibid., p. 236.

79. Daniels, *American Science*, p. 181.

80. Ibid., p. 182.

81. Woods, *Works*, II, 57.

CHAPTER II

1. Moses Stuart, "Letter to the Editor on the Study of German," *Christian Review*, VI (1841), 459.

2. Barnas Sears, "German Literature; — Its Religious Character and Influence," *Christian Review*, VI (1841), 269–84, passim.

3. Jerry Wayne Brown, *The Rise of Biblical Criticism in America* (Middleton, Conn.: Wesleyan University Press, 1969), p. 16.

4. Stuart, "Letter on German," p. 457.

5. The discussion of Buckminster was derived from Brown, *Rise of Biblical Criticism*, pp. 11–15.

6. Ibid., p. 29.

7. Andrews Norton, "Defense of Liberal Christianity," *General Repository and Review*, I (1812), 2.

8. Ibid., pp. 16, 25.

9. Ibid., p. 16.

10. Ibid., passim.

11. Stuart, "Letter on German," p. 448.

12. Ibid., p. 457.

13. Stuart to Everett, 25 December 1813, Everett Collection.

14. Ibid.

15. Moses Stuart, "Lectures on Hermeneutics," Microfilm of Stuart's Lectures and Sermons, Andover-Newton Theological Seminary, Newton Center, Mass. (Hereafter AMF.) The lectures are numbered, but placed randomly in Stuart's papers, possibly in the order that he completed them. Some biographers refer to them by number for quick reference, but I prefer to use their titles. Stuart's teaching method was to begin with the theory of hermeneutics, then defend the Old Testament canon, and finally to appraise each book in order as it appears in canon.

16. John Giltner, "Moses Stuart" (Ph.D. dissertation, Yale University, 1956).

17. Stuart, "Hermeneutics," AMF.

18. Ibid.

19. Moses Stuart, "Are the Same Principles of Interpretation to be Applied to Scriptures as to Other Books?" *Biblical Repository*, II (1832), 138.

20. Stuart, "Hermeneutics," AMF.

21. Moses Stuart, "Lecture on the Principles of Exegesis," AMF.

22. Stuart, "Principles of Interpretation," p. 129.

23. Stuart to Pearson, 12 December 1813, in Giltner, "Moses Stuart," p. 161.

24. Moses Stuart, *Chrestomathy* (Andover: Flagg & Gould, 1829), pp. viii, 101. Those students too indolent to study Hebrew, Stuart wrote, should "keep away from our public seminaries . . . and prepare in another way for the ministry, where their sloth and irresolution can be more creditably indulged."

25. Ibid., pp. 119–29.

26. Ibid.

27. Moses Stuart, "Of the Book of Chronicles," AMF.

28. Stuart, "Principles of Interpretation," p. 137.

29. Stuart, "Of the Book of Chronicles."

30. Moses Stuart, "Genuineness of the Old Testament," AMF.

31. Ibid.

32. Moses Stuart, "Of the Old Testament Canon," AMF.

33. Ibid.

34. Moses Stuart, "On the Book of Job," AMF. Porter was Professor of Sacred Rhetoric.

35. Stuart, "Of the Old Testament Canon."

36. Moses Stuart, "Authenticity and Genuineness of the Pentateuch," AMF.

37. Moses Stuart, "Was Moses the Author of the Pentateuch?" AMF.

38. Moses Stuart, "Time and Manner in which the Pentateuch Was Composed," AMF.

39. Ibid.

40. Ibid.

41. Stuart, "Genuineness of the Pentateuch."

42. Ibid.

43. Moses Stuart, "Of the Book of Joshua," AMF.

44. Ibid.

45. Moses Stuart, "Of the Psalms," AMF.

46. Moses Stuart, "Of Ezra and Nehemiah," AMF.

47. Stuart, "Of the Book of Chronicles."

48. Stuart, "Of the Book of Joshua."

49. Stuart, "Of the Old Testament Canon."

50. Ibid.

51. Stuart, "Letter on German," p. 451.

52. Ibid., p. 455.

53. Woods, *History*, p. 174.

54. Brown, *Rise of Biblical Criticism*, p. 61.

55. Ibid.

56. George Ellis, *A Half-Century of the Unitarian Controversy* (Boston: Cooshy, Nichols, & Co., 1857), p. x.

57. Ibid.

58. Brown, *Rise of Biblical Criticism*, pp. 62–63.

59. Brown, *Rise of Biblical Criticism*, p. 63; Giltner, "Moses Stuart," pp. 304–6.

60. William Ellery Channing, *Sermon Delivered at the Ordination of Jared Sparks* (Baltimore: n.p., 1819), p. 4.

61. Ibid., pp. 13–14.

62. Ibid., p. 21.

63. Ibid., p. 24.

64. Ibid., p. 20.

65. Leonard Woods, *Letters to Unitarians . . .* (Andover: Flagg & Gould, 1820), p. 5.

66. Brown, *Rise of Biblical Criticism*, pp. 65–66.

67. Moses Stuart, Letters to the Rev. Wm. E. Channing, containing remarks on his sermon, recently preached and published at Baltimore (Andover: Flagg & Gould, 1819), p. 4.

68. Ibid., p. 11.

69. Ibid., p. 9.

70. Ibid., pp. 13–15.

71. Ibid., p. 10.

72. Ibid., p. 151.

73. Ibid., p. 156.

74. Brown, *Rise of Biblical Criticism*, p. 74.

75. Andrews Norton, *Statement of Reasons for Not Believing the Doctrine of the Trinity* (Boston: American Unitarian Association, 1875), p. 153.

76. Brown, *Rise of Biblical Criticism*, p. 72.

77. Joseph Haroutunian, *Piety Versus Moralism* (Chicago: University of Chicago Press, 1933), pp. xiv–xx. Emerson's "Wonderful One-Hoss Shay," the description of Calvinism falling apart suddenly one day, probably has helped color the attitude that it was a negative force in the nineteenth century.

78. Park, "Moses Stuart," p. 201.

79. Woods, *History*, p. 174.

80. Ibid., p. 178.

81. Ibid., p. 177.

82. Stuart, "Letter on German," p. 468.

83. Ibid.

84. Woods, *History*, p. 178.

85. Sears to Park, 1842, Mellon Chamberlain Correspondence, Boston Public Library, Boston, Mass.

86. Brown, *Rise of Biblical Criticism*, p. 118.

87. Sears, "German Literature."

88. George Park Fisher to Park, 1 January 1853, Mellon Chamberlain Correspondence.

89. Edward Robinson, "Theological Education in Germany," *Biblical Repository*, I (1831), 48.

90. Ibid., p. 49.

91. Moses Stuart, "Commencement Address," 1846, AMF.

92. A Brown, *Rise of Biblical Criticism*, p. 116.

CHAPTER III

1. Park, "Moses Stuart," p. 206.

2. Ibid., p. 207.

3. Correspondence is extensive and widely-scattered. About 150 letters to Park strictly on the *Bibliotheca*'s editorial business are in the Mellon Chamberlin Collection of the Boston Public Library. Others are at Yale in the Park, Woolsey, Bacon, and Whitney Family Papers. Still more are in Nashville in the private collection of the C. R. Park family.

4. A German title roughly equivalent to the modern associate professor.

5. George Whittemore, ed., *Memorials of Horatio Balch Hackett* (Rochester, N.Y.: n.p., 1876), pp. 17–32.

6. Ibid.

7. Ibid., pp. 50–67, passim

8. *Dictionary of American Biography*, 1st ed., s.v. "Woolsey, Theodore Dwight."

9. Ibid.

10. Edwards to Woolsey, 7 October 1842, Woolsey Family Papers, Yale University Library, New Haven, Conn.

11. Park to Woolsey, 17 May 1852, Woolsey Family Papers.

12. Woolsey to Park, 20 September 1845, Mellon Chamberlin Correspondence.

13. *American Quarterly Register*, I (1833), 224–25.

14. E.g., Robinson to Park, 5 December 1834, Park's Papers, Yale; Edwards to Park, 26 November 1845, Park Family Papers in possession of Drs. Jane and Charles Park, Nashville, Tenn.; C. E. Taylor to Edwards, 31 December 1846, discussing Edwards' search for books for the seminary while in Europe, Park Family Papers, Nashville; Park and Phelps to the trustees, 1 September 1854, pleading for a library appropriation equivalent to Union's $1,000/annum, Phillips-Andover Preparatory School Archives, Andover, Mass.

15. Armstrong to Farrar, 16 August 1833, Park's Papers, Yale.

16. Bannister to Farrar, 6 July 1837, ibid.

17. Whittemore, ed., *Memorial of Hackett*, p. 55.

18. *Dictionary of American Biography*, 1st ed., s.v. "Stowe, Calvin Ellis."

19. Ibid.

20. Edwards to Park, 1 January 1835, Park Family Papers, Nashville.

21. See B. B. Edwards, *Address Delivered at the Fourth Anniversary of the Mount Holyoke Female Seminary* (Andover: Allen, Morrill, and Wardwell, 1841). His daughter was educated in Switzerland at Edwards' insistence, so that she might be proficient in French. After Edwards' death, she and her mother ran a girls' school in Andover, where they taught Greek, Latin, French, trigonometry, astronomy, English literature, and physiology. Sarah's marriage to William Park ended her literary career: he accepted a pastorate in a small town in western New York. However, she taught her own two children, and her daughter Marian was one of the early women Ph.D.'s in classics at Yale. Marian later was president of Bryn Mawr.

22. Quoted in Edwards A. Park, ed., *Writings of Prof. B. B. Edwards, with a Memoir*, 2 vols. (Boston: John P. Jewett & Co., 1853), I, 172–73.

23. Ibid.

24. Ibid., p. 339.

25. *Rules of the American Education Society*, published by the Board of Directors, August, 1808, p. 18.

26. Ibid., p. 14.

27. Ibid., p. 2.

28. Park, ed., *Writings of Edwards*, p. 70.

29. Edwards to Park, 3 November 1832, Park Family Papers, Nashville.

30. Edwards A. Park, "Life and Services of Prof. B. B. Edwards," *Bibliotheca Sacra*, IX (1852), 793.

31. Park, ed., *Writings of Edwards*, p. 83.

32. Ibid., p. 111.

33. Ibid., p. 301.

34. Ibid., p. 133.

35. Ibid.

36. Ibid.

37. Ibid., p. 134.

38. Ibid., pp. 123–24.

39. Ibid., p. 298.

40. Anthony Clay Cecil, "The Theological Development of Edwards Amasa Park, Last of the Consistent Calvinists" (Ph.D. dissertation, Yale University, 1972), p. 22.

41. *Dictionary of American Biography*, 1st ed., s.v. "Park, Edwards Amasa"; Elizabeth Stuart Phelps (Ward), *Chapters from a Life* (Cambridge: Riverside Press, 1896), p. 38.

42. *Dictionary of American Biography*, "Park."

43. Frank Hugh Foster, *The Life of Edward Amasa Park* (New York: Fleming H. Revell Co., 1936), p. 31.

44. Richard Salter Storrs, *Edwards A. Park, Memorial Address* (Boston: Samuel Usher, 1910), p. 30.

45. Ibid.

46. Cecil, "Theological Development of Park," p. 18.

47. Ibid., pp. 33–35.

48. Ibid.

49. Advanced study after completing the regular three-year course.

50. E. A. to C. E. Park, August 1835, Park Family Papers, Nashville.

51. Phelps, *Chapters from a Life*; Foster, *Life of Park*, p. 118.

52. Park to Trustees, 31 August 1846, Park's Papers, Yale.

53. Park to Edwards, 20 October 1846, Park Family Papers, Nashville.

54. Dana to the Trustees, 3 June 1847, Phillips–Andover Archives.

55. Edwards to Park, 19 April 1847, Park Family Papers, Nashville.

56. Park and Edwards, "Natural Theology," p. 242.

57. Ibid., p. 257.

58. Ibid., p. 263.

59. Ibid., p. 264; Lecture notes of William Ladd Ropes, 1849–50, on the benevolence of God, Phillips–Andover Archives, Andover, Mass.

60. Ropes, Lecture notes; Foster, *Genetic History*, pp. 480–85.

61. Foster, *Genetic History*, p. 487; Park and Edwards, "Natural Theology," p. 278.

62. Ropes, Lecture notes.

63. Miscellaneous documents, Park Family Papers, Nashville.

64. Andover Theological Seminary, *General Catalog*, 1844, gives reading lists for different courses.

65. Park to Trustees, 1 September 1851, Phillips–Andover Archives.

66. Edwards to Trustees, 20 September 1851, ibid.

67. E.g., Eullmann, professor of Theology at Heidelberg, to Edwards, asked for a paper on American theology, 20 June 1843, Park Family Papers, Nashville.

68. Princeton was known for its insularity from the scholarship exciting the rest of New England at this time.

69. Whedon to Park, 24 May 1862, Mellon Chamberlin Correspondence.

70. Robinson wrote Edwards in 1847, telling him the *Bibliotheca* was doomed to fail under his editing because it had too many similar competitors (Park Family Papers, Nashville). However, the magazine survived at Andover until 1884, and was published continuously until 1956. Edwards had relinquished the *Repository* to a New York Presbyterian in 1838. When the man (Absalom Peters) no longer felt able to publish it, Edwards took over the subscription lists for the *Bibliotheca*.

71. Leonard Bacon, "Prolegomena," *New Englander*, I (1843), 5.

72. Frank Luther Mott, *A History of American Magazines* (New York: D. Appleton and Co., 1930), p. 740.

73. E. A. Park, "Note to the Subscribers of the *Bibliotheca Sacra*," *Bibliotheca Sacra*, XIV (1857), 460.

74. Mott, *History of American Magazines*, p. 367.

75. Correspondence between Mrs. Park and Mrs. Edwards, in the Nashville collection, shows that they, too, were active supporters of the journal, doing a fair amount of Hebrew translation for Hackett's and Edwards' articles.

76. Edwards to Park, from St. Augustine, Florida, 28 January 1845, Park Family Papers, Nashville.

77. Park and Edwards began renumbering the journal with volume I in 1844.

78. Edward Robinson, "The Aspect of Literature and Science in the United States, as Compared with Europe," *Bibliotheca Sacra*, I (1844), 8.

79. E. A. Park and B. B. Edwards, "Thoughts on the State of Theological Sciences and Education in Our Country," *Bibliotheca Sacra*, I (1844), 766.

80. Ibid., p. 767.

81. Stuart, "Letter on the Study of German," p. 461.

82. Park and Edwards, "Theological Education," p. 741.

83. Ibid., pp. 762–63.

84. In September, 1853, Phelps and Park petitioned the trustees to begin fund-raising for Andover's library so that the seminary would be attractive to eminent scholars. Phillips-Andover Archives.

85. Park and Edwards, "Theological Education," p. 749.

86. B. B. Edwards, Barnas Sears, and C. C. Felton, *Classical Studies* (Boston: Gould, Kendall, & Lincoln, 1843), Introduction, p. iv.

87. Ibid.

88. Edwards A. Park, "The Theology of the Intellect and That of the Feelings," printed in the *Bibliotheca Sacra*, VII (1850), 533.

89. This conflict has been well documented by Cecil, in "Theological Development of Park"; Foster's *Genetic History*; and others.

90. Park, "Theology of the Intellect," p. 537.

91. Ibid., p. 538.

92. Ibid., p. 535.

93. Cecil, "Theological Development of Park," p. 95.

94. Park, "Theology of the Intellect," p. 547.

95. Ibid., pp. 547–51, passim; cf. Moses Stuart, *Exegetical Essays on Several Words Relating to Future Punishment* (Andover: Flagg & Gould, 1830), p. 121.

96. Park, "Theology of the Intellect," p. 543.

97. Ropes, Lecture notes.

98. Leonard Woods, "Introductory Article," *Literary and Theological Review*, I (1834), 12 (italics in the original).

99. Park, "Theology of the Intellect," pp. 557–60, passim.

100. Ibid., pp. 560–61.

101. Ibid., p. 554.

102. Ware had recently attacked Ralph Waldo Emerson for his vague, "feeling-supported" beliefs. Park applauded Ware.

103. Park, "Theology of the Intellect," p. 539.

104. Ibid., p. 564.

CHAPTER IV

1. Duncan Forbes, *The Liberal Anglican Idea of History* (Cambridge: University Press, 1952), p. 65; W. G. T. Shedd, *Lectures on the Philosophy of History* (Andover: Flagg & Gould, 1856).

2. Cecil, "Theological Development of Park," pp. 73–76.

3. E.g., W. G. T. Shedd, "The Relation of Language to the Laws of Thought," *Bibliotheca Sacra*, V (1848), 651.

4. I am indebted to Arnoldo Momigliano of the University of London for suggesting the rough outline of the historical and philological research of this period and its impact on biblical studies. He also pointed out the general European-American involvement in Germany. He suggested a number of sources, including Christian Mackauer's "Ranke," in *A Teacher at His Best* (Chicago: University of Chicago Press, 1973); G. P. Gooch, *Studies in German History* (London: Longmann, Green, & Co., 1948); and Forbes, *Anglican Idea of History*. Also see Hans Aarsleff, *The Study of Language in England* (Princeton: Princeton University Press, 1967), pp. 115–62.

5. Brown, *Rise of Biblical Criticism*, p. 112.

6. Ibid., p. 113.

7. Moses Stuart, "The Presence of Christ in the Lord's Supper," *Bibliotheca Sacra*, I (1844), 110–52 and 225–79.

8. Edward Robinson, "On the Language of Palestine in the Age of Christ and the Apostles," *Biblical Repository*, I (1831), 309.

9. Edward Robinson, trans., "Greek Style of the New Testament," *Bibliotheca Sacra*, I (1831), 641.

10. Park, ed., *Writings, of Edwards*, I, 85.

11. Robinson, "Aspect of Literature and Science," p. 34.

12. Edwards, Sears, and Felton, *Classical Studies*, p. iv.

13. Ibid., p. vii.

14. Ibid., p. ix.

15. Park, ed., *Writings of Edwards*, I, 291.

16. Edwards, Sears, and Felton, *Classical Studies*, p. xii.

17. B. J. Wallace, "The Sanskrit Language in Its Relation to Comparative Philology," *Bibliotheca Sacra*, IV (1847), 671–72.

18. Shedd, "Relation of Language to Thought," p. 651.

19. Ibid.

20. Ibid., pp. 659 and 661.

21. Ibid., p. 661.

22. F. A. Adams, "Collocation of Words in the Greek and Latin Languages, Examined in Relation to the Laws of Thought," *Bibliotheca Sacra*, I (1844), 712.

23. T. D. Woolsey, "Greek Lexicography," *Bibliotheca Sacra*, I (1844), 619.

24. B. B. Edwards, "Sources of Hebrew Philology and Lexicography," *Biblical Repository*, III (1833), 2.

25. T. D. Woolsey, "Principles of Latin Lexicography," *Bibliotheca Sacra*, II (1845), 80–81.

26. Wallace, "Sanskrit Language," p. 681.

27. B. B. Edwards, "The Obligations of Literature, Particularly of Philology, to Modern Missionary Efforts," *Bibliotheca Sacra* VII (1836), 185.

28. R. D. C. Robbins, "The Character and Prophecies of Balaam," *Bibliotheca Sacra*, III (1846), 700–701.

29. E.g., Horatio B. Hackett, "Synoptical Study of the Gospels," *Bibliotheca Sacra*, III (1846), 1–21.

30. Henry B. Smith, "Interpretation of the Baptismal Formula," *Bibliotheca Sacra*, I (1844), 703–8.

31. Edward Robinson, "Alleged Discrepancy between John and the Other Evangelists Respecting Our Lord's Last Passover," *Bibliotheca Sacra*, II (1845), 405–6.

32. Park and Phelps to the Trustees, 1 September 1855, Phillips-Andover Archives.

33. From reviews in: *Princeton Review*, Vol. XVI (1835); *American Church Review*, Vol. III (1836), (Episcopalian, published at New Haven); and the *Bibliotheca Sacra*, Vol. IV (1847), and Vol. VIII (1851).

34. Cecil, "Theological Development of Park," p. 73.

35. Henry B. Smith, "The History of Doctrines," *Bibliotheca Sacra*, IV (1847), 577.

36. A distant relative of Ralph Waldo Emerson.

37. As far as I can gather from Poole's *Index*. I had hoped to be able to trace a development of historical methodology through Emerson's work, but this is so sparse that it was not possible.

38. Ralph Emerson, "Sparks' Life of Ledyard," *Quarterly Christian Spectator*, 2d series, II (1828), 318.

39. Ibid., p. 376.

40. Moses Stuart, "The Creed of Arminius, with an Account of His Life and Times," *Bibliotheca Sacra*, I (1831), 239–40.

41. August Neander, "Augustine and Pelagius," trans. L. Woods, Jr., with an Introduction by B. B. Edwards, *Biblical Repository*, III (1833), 68.

42. Ibid., p. 69.

43. Ibid.

44. Philip Schaff, *St. Augustine, Melancthon, and Neander* (New York: Funk and Wagnalls, 1886), pp. 128–37, passim. Schaff was a German who Park met in Berlin in 1842. The two struck up a lifelong friendship. Schaff came to Andover after the revolution of 1848 before taking a permanent position at Union. He wrote frequently for the *Bibliotheca*, usually on church history.

45. Ibid., p. 73.

46. B. B. Edwards, "Slavery in Ancient Greece," *Biblical Repository*, V (1835), 138–63.

47. Ibid., p. 73.

48. Bamas Sears, "Historical Studies," *Bibliotheca Sacra*, III (1846), 579.

49. Ibid., p. 581.

50. Ibid.

51. Ibid.

52. Ibid., p. 580.

53. Ibid., p. 584.

54. Ibid., p. 595.

55. Ralph Emerson, "The Early History of Monasticism from Original Sources," *Bibliotheca Sacra*, I (1844), 209–24 and 464–22.

56. Ibid., p. 314.

57. Ibid.

58. Moses Stuart, "A Critical Examination of Some Passages in Genesis I; . . . ," *Biblical Repository*, VII (1836), 81.

59. Hitchcock's career will be discussed in detail in chapter 5.

60. Edward Hitchcock, "The Connection between Geology and the Mosaic History of Creation," *Biblical Repository*, first series, VI (1835), 327.

61. Stuart, "Critical Examination of Genesis I," p. 49.

62. Ibid., p. 51.

63. Ibid., p. 52.

64. Ibid.

65. Ibid., p. 53.

66. Ibid., p. 52.

67. Ibid., p. 54.

68. Ibid.

69. Ibid., p. 55.

70. Ibid., p. 58.

71. Ropes, Lecture notes.

72. Ibid., p. 13.

73. Ibid., p. 7.

74. B. B. Edwards, "Remarks on Certain Erroneous Methods and Principles in Biblical Criticism," *Bibliotheca Sacra*, VI (1849), 195.

75. B. B. Edwards, "Present State of Biblical Science," *Bibliotheca Sacra*, VII (1850), 1–12.

76. Stuart, "Hermeneutics," AMF.

77. Edwards, "Present State of Biblical Science, p. 9.

78. Stuart, "Critical Examination of Genesis I," p. 58.

79. Edwards, "Present State of Biblical Science," p. 3.

80. Edwards, "Remarks on the Authenticity and Genuineness of the Pentateuch," *Bibliotheca Sacra*, II (1845), 361.

81. Ibid., p. 375.

82. Ibid., p. 376.

83. Ibid., pp. 385–87. Modern scholarship dates these fragments only to about 800 B.C. However, the development of accurate dating of inscriptions and fragments was an arduous process, depending in part on C^{14}, but also on enough fragments that one could begin to rely on internal style, and internal cross-references to known events. The Egyptian chronologies were easier, because a Ptolemaic scribe had actually listed the three Kingdoms and their various pharaohs. These inscriptions had been translated by the time Edwards was defending the authenticity of the Pentateuch.

84. M. P. Case, "Elements of Culture in the Early Ages," *Bibliotheca Sacra*, IX (1852), 691; and B. B. Edwards, "Bunsen's Late Work on Egypt," *Bibliotheca Sacra*, VI (1847), 713.

85. Edwards, "Authenticity and Genuineness of the Pentateuch," pp. 364–65.

86. Edwards, "Bunsen's Work," p. 714.

87. Ibid.

88. Edwards, "Authenticity and Genuineness of the Pentateuch," p. 371.

89. Ibid., p. 370.

90. Ibid., p. 398.

91. Edwards, "Present State of Biblical Science," p. 5.

92. Ibid., p. 6.

93. Edwards, "Remarks on Biblical Criticism," p. 191.

CHAPTER V

1. Daniels, *American Science*, p. 35.

2. Ibid., pp. 34–35.

3. Ibid., p. 65.

4. Edwards and Park, "Natural Theology," p. 273.

5. Ibid., p. 274.

6. From the title page of Charles Lyell's *Principles of Geology* (Philadelphia: James Kay & Brother, June, 1837).

7. This brief discussion is based on R. H. Dott, Jr., "James Hutton and the Concept of a Dynamic Earth," in *Towards a History of Geology*, ed. Cecil J. Schneer (Cambridge: M.I.T. Press, 1969); M. J. S. Eudwick, "Hutton and Werner Compared: George Greenough's Geological Tour of Scotland in 1805," *British Journal for the History of Science*, I (1962), 117–35; Leonard J. Wilson, "The Intellectual Background to Charles Lyell's *Principles of Geology*," in *Towards a History of Geology*; and Charles Coulston Gillispie's *Genesis and Geology* (New York: Harper and Brothers, 1959). Gillispie's book is excellent, but he is too anxious to have the religious geologists defeated, and so sees all geology as looking forward to Darwin, giving an unfortunate distortion to the weight he places on men like Buckland. He dismisses Lyell's references to God as having been written "tongue in cheek," on which point there is no evidence, but which is most unlikely.

8. Daniels, *American Science*, pp. 10–12.

9. George P. Merrill, *First One Hundred Years of American Geology* (New Haven: Yale University Press, 1930), p. 30.

10. Dirk J. Struik, *Yankee Science in the Making* (New York: Macmillan Co., 1948; revised edition, 1968), p. 124.

11. Conrad Wright, "The Religion of Geology," *New England Quarterly*, XIV (1941), 339.

12. Ibid.

13. Ibid., p. 340.

14. Ibid.

15. Hitchcock, *Reminiscences*, p. 344.

16. Ibid., p. 284.

17. Ibid., p. 286.

18. Ibid., p. 287.

19. Daniels, *American Science*, p. 213.

20. Hitchcock, *Reminiscences*, p. 85. "A large crowd had gathered when I took the first cast, and I was told afterwards that all that saved me from being voted a fit subject for the lunatic assylum was the testimony of a young lady . . . who had attended my lectures on geology at Amherst, and who testified that I was no more deranged than such men usually are."

21. Edward Hitchcock, "The Resurrection of the Body," *Bibliotheca Sacra*, Vol. XVII (1860); and idem, "The Importance of an Early Consecration to Missionary Work," *Christian Spectator*, 3d series, Vol. X (1838).

22. Edward Hitchcock, "Ornithicnology," *American Journal of Sciences and Arts*, XXIX (1836), 337.

23. Ibid.

24. Even Darwin agreed that the rocks gave no evidence of evolution.

25. Hitchcock, "Ornithicnology," p. 332.

26. Hitchcock, "Connection between Geology and Mosaic History," p. 275.

27. Correspondence reprinted in George Park Fisher, *Life of Benjamin Silliman*, 2 vols. (New York: Charles Scribner & Co., 1866), II, 144.

28. Ibid., p. 143.

29. Ibid., p. 144.

30. Hitchcock, *Reminiscences*, p. 295.

31. Ibid.

32. Edward Hitchcock, "Geology and Revelation," *Biblical Repository*, 1st series, V (1835), 444.

33. Ibid. Here Hitchcock neatly agrees with both Werner and Hutton.

34. Ibid., pp. 444–45.

35. Ibid., p. 447.

36. Ibid., p. 448.

37. Hitchcock, "Connection between Geology and Mosaic History," pp. 262–65.

38. Ibid., pp. 287–88.

39. Ibid., p. 292.

40. Ibid., p. 315.

41. Ibid. Italics in the original.

42. Edward Hitchcock, "Remarks on Professor Stuart's Examination of Genesis I in Reference to Geology," *Biblical Repository*, VII (1836), 318.

43. Wright, "Religion of Geology," pp. 339–41, passim.

44. Hitchcock, "Connection between Geology and Mosaic History," p. 267.

45. Hitchcock, "Remarks on Professor Stuart," pp. 452–53.

46. Fisher, *Life of Silliman*, 11, 115.

47. Stuart, *Chrestomathy*, p. 116.

48. Ibid., p. 115.

49. Ibid., p. 117.

50. Ibid., p. 118.

51. Wright, "Religion of Geology," p. 347.

52. Edward Hitchcock, "The Cross in Nature and Nature in the Cross," *Bibliotheca Sacra*, XVIII (1861), 255.

53. Stuart, "Critical Examination of Genesis I," p. 94.

54. Ibid., pp. 90–91.

55. Ibid., p. 100. Italics in the original.

56. Ibid., p. 102.

57. In Fisher, *Life of Silliman*, II, 139.

58. Ibid., p. 142

59. Ibid., pp. 140–141.

60. Ibid., p. 145.

61. Ibid., p. 144.

62. Stuart, "Critical Examination of Genesis I," p. 103.

63. Ibid., p. 106.

64. Hitchcock to Edwards, 15 February 1836, Park's Papers, Yale. "I . . . cheerfully submit to your judgment to correct a bad spirit in any part of the article on the meaning of Genesis I."

65. Edwards to Park, 26 January 1845, Park Family Papers, Nashville.

66. Park, ed., *Writings of Edwards*, I, 187.

67. Ibid., p. 233.

68. Edwards A. Park "The Relation of Divine Providence to Physical Laws," *Bibliotheca Sacra*, XII (1855), 195.

69. Ropes, Lecture notes, I, 14.

70. Anonymous, Lecture notes, 1856, Andover-Newton Archives, Newton Center, Mass.

71. Edwards, and Park, "Natural Theology," p. 268. Park and Edwards wrote separate parts of the article which they recorded in the index.

72. Ibid., pp. 267–69.

73. *An American Dictionary of the English Language*, 1828 edition; revised, 1832.

74. James McLane, "Speculation and the Bible," *Bibliotheca Sacra*, XVIII (1861), 345.

75. John O Means, "The Narrative of the Creation in Genesis," *Bibliotheca Sacra*, XII (1855), 85.

76. Ibid., p. 100.

77. Ibid., p. 102.

78. Ibid., p. 122.

79. Ibid.

80. Edwards and Park, "Natural Theology," p. 261.

81. Woods, *Works*, II, 57, and elsewhere.

82. Austin Phelps, "Oneness of God in Revelation and In Nature," printed in *Bibliotheca Sacra*, XVI (1859), 838.

83. Ibid., pp. 841–42.

84. Ibid., pp. 843–44.

85. Ibid., p. 845.

86. Ibid.

87. Ibid., p. 847.

88. Ibid., p. 849.

89. Ibid., p. 850.

90. Ibid.

91. Daniels, *American Science*.

92. [Edward Hitchcock], "Discussion between Two Readers of Darwin's Treatise on the *Origin of Species* . . . ," *American Journal of Science and Arts*, 2d series, XXX (1860), 226–39.

93. Edward Hitchcock, "The Law of Nature's Constancy Subordinate, to the Higher Law of Change," *Bibliotheca Sacra*, XX (1863), 489.

94. Ibid., p. 523.

CHAPTER VI

1. Samuel Harris, "The Theological Department Essential in a University," *New Englander*, XXXI (1872), 53.

2. Ibid., pp. 54–55.

3. Ibid., p. 55.

4. Ibid.

5. Ibid., p. 39.

6. Ibid., p. 42.

7. *Dictionary of American Biography*, 1st ed., s.v. "Smyth, Egbert Coffin."

8. Woods, *History*, pp. 188–89.

9. Foster, *Life of Park*, pp. 233–34.

10. Park to Trustees, 1865, Phillips-Andover Archives.

11. Park really did overtax his health, lecturing six days a week, preaching 109 times a year, and making a great many public appearances on behalf of the seminary.

12. Woods, *History*, p. 188.

13. Cushing Stout, "Faith and History: The Mind of W. G. T. Shedd," *Journal of the History of Ideas*, XV (1954), 156–57.

14. Ibid., p. 157.

15. Cecil, "Theological Development of Park," p. 74.

16. Foster, *Life of Park*, p. 233.

17. Quoted by Cecil in "Theological Development of Park," p. 157.

18. Park to the Trustees, 11 April 1871, Phillips-Andover Archives.

19. Ibid.

20. Park to Trustees, 1881, Phillips-Andover Archives.

21. Foster, *Life of Park*, p. 236.

22. Ibid.

23. Paraphrased ibid., p. 237.

24. Ibid.; Cecil, "Theological Development of Park," pp. 171–72.

25. Foster, *Life of Park*, p. 239.

26. William Jewett Tucker, *My Generation* (Boston: Houghton Mifflin, 1919), p. 122.

27. Ibid., p. 121.

28. L. W. Brown, "Andover and Creed Subscription," *North American Review*, LXXXIV (1882), 559.

29. George T. Ladd, "The Origin of the Concept of God," *Bibliotheca Sacra*, XXXIV (1877), 11.

30. Ibid.

31. There is an extensive literature on pre-Darwinian evolutionary ideas. Cf. Loren Eiseley, *Darwin's Century* (New York: Doubleday & Co., 1961); John C. Greene, *The Death of Adam* (Ames: Iowa State University Press, 1959); and J. W. Burrow, *Evolution and Society* (London: Cambridge University Press, 1966). An American physician, William Wells, first articulated the idea of natural selection in 1818 (Greene, *The Death of Adam*, p. 220).

32. Greene, *The Death of Adam*, p. 222.

33. Ibid., p. 162.

34. Quoted in Derek Freeman, "The Evolutionary Theories of Charles Darwin and Herbert Spencer," *Current Anthropology*, XV (1974), 215.

35. Ibid.; James Allen Rogers, "Darwinism and Social Darwinism," *Journal of the History of Ideas*, XXXIII (1972), 277–80. Darwin apparently adopted "survival of the fittest" in the 5th edition of the *Origin of Species* because of its wide acceptance from Spencer's writings: the latter definitely coined the phrase.

36. In Rogers, "Darwinism and Social Darwinism," p. 279.

37. Freeman, "Darwin and Spencer," p. 216.

38. Ibid., p. 230.

39. J. D. Y. Peel, *Herbert Spencer* (New York: Basic Books, 1971), pp. 2–3.

40. Ibid.; Richard Hofstadter, *Social Darwinism in American Thought* (Boston: Beacon Press, 1967), pp. 31–35.

41. Robert A. Jones, "John Bascom: Antipositivism and Intuitionism in American Sociology," *American Quarterly*, XXIV (1972), 507–8. Bascom was an Andover graduate who taught at Williams before going to the University of Wisconsin. Like T. D. Woolsey, he was an authority in many of the new social sciences.

42. D. McGregor Means, "The Data of Ethics," *Bibliotheca Sacra*, XXXVII (1880), 471–503.

43. Ibid., passim.

44. Ibid., p. 501.

45. George Mooar, "Sociology and Christian Missions," *Bibliotheca Sacra*, XL (1883), 639.

46. Ibid., p. 630.

47. Ibid.

48. Ibid., p. 639.

49. Ibid.

50. Ibid., pp. 640–42.

51. J. R. Herrick, "Lecky on Morals," *Bibliotheca Sacra*, XXIX (1872), 210.

52. Ibid.

53. Ibid.

54. George Mooar, "The Pilgrim Line of Theological Progress," *New Englander*, V (1883), 119.

55. Herrick, "Lecky on Morals," p. 210.

56. Thomas Hill, "Erasmus Darwin," *Bibliotheca Sacra*, XXXV (1878), 461–81.

57. Ibid., p. 475.

58. James Bixby, "The Know-Nothing Position in Religion," *Bibliotheca Sacra*, XXXVIII (1881), 435.

59. J. H. McIlvaine, "Revelation and Science," *Bibliotheca Sacra*, XXXIV (1877), 262–63.

60. Frederic Gardiner, "Darwinism," *Bibliotheca Sacra*, XXIX (1872), 247.

61. Frederic Gardiner, "The Bearing of Recent Scientific Thought upon Theology," *Bibliotheca Sacra*, XXXV (1878), 67.

62. Ibid.

63. Gardiner, "Darwinism," p. 245.

64. Ibid., p. 247.

65. Ibid., p. 279.

66. Gardiner, "The Bearing of Scientific Thought," p. 60.

67. Ibid., p. 61.

68. Ibid.

69. Ibid., p. 67.

70. George Frederick Wright, "Recent Works Bearing on the Relation of Science to Religion; No. V—Some Analogies between Calvinism and Darwinism," *Bibliotheca Sacra*, XXXVIII (1880), 48–76.

71. Egbert C. Smyth, "The Theological Purpose of the *Review*," *Andover Review*, I (1884), 6.

72. Egbert C. Smyth, "On Atonement," *Andover Review*, IV (1884), 66.

73. Quoted in Williams, *Andover Liberals*, p. 34.

74. F. H. Johnson, "Mechanical Evolution," *Andover Review*, I (1884), 631.

75. F. H. Johnson, "Co-Operative Creation," *Andover Review*, III (1885), 326–46, 436–55.

76. Ibid., p. 440. With the Lamarckians, Johnson accepted the inheritance of acquired characteristics.

77. Ibid., p. 326.

78. Ibid., pp. 328–29.

79. Ibid., pp. 329–30.

80. Ibid., p. 330.

81. Ibid., p. 334.

82. Ibid., p. 331.

83. Ibid., p. 334.

84. Ibid., pp. 454–55.

85. F. H. Johnson, "Reason and Revelation," *Andover Review*, V (1886), 248.

86. Edward A. Lawrence, "Natural Law in the Spiritual World," *Andover Review*, VI (1886), 22.

87. Johnson, "Reason and Revelation," p. 230.

88. George T. Harris, *A Century's Change in Religion* (Boston: Houghton Mifflin Co., 1914), p. 41. Harris succeeded Park as Abbot professor.

89. Williams, *Andover Liberals*, p. 95, pp. 40–42.

90. George T. Harris, "Function of Christian Consciousness," *Andover Review*, II (1884), 338–52.

91. Ibid., p. 339.

92. Ibid., p. 340.

93. Ibid., p. 348.

94. Ibid.

95. Ibid., p. 351.

96. Ibid.

97. Williams, *Andover Liberals*, p. 95.

98. A Francis Peabody, "Office of Proof," *Andover Review*, II (1884), 1.

99. Ibid., p. 3.

100. Joseph Cook, "A Fourth Year of Study in the Courses of Theological Seminaries," *Bibliotheca Sacra*, XXVII (1870), 252.

101. Harris, "Christian Consciousness," p. 349.

102. George T. Ladd, "The Question Restated," *Andover Review*, IV (1885), 1–18.

103. Ibid., p. 6.

104. Ibid.

105. Ibid., p. 8.

106. Ibid., p. 16.

107. Smyth, "Theological Purpose of the *Review*," p. 2.

108. Ibid., and Harris, "Christian Consciousness," p. 348.

109. Lawrence, "Natural Law," p. 22.

110. Edwards and Park, "Natural Theology," p. 273.

111. Harris, "Christian Consciousness," p. 351.

BIBLIOGRAPHY

❖ ❖ ❖

BOOKS AND ARTICLES

Primary Sources

Adams, F. A. "Collocation of Words in the Greek and Latin Languages, Examined in Relation to the Laws of Thought." *Bibliotheca Sacra*, I (1844), 708–25.

Andover Theological Seminary. General Catalogue, 1808–1908.

An American Dictionary of the English Language, 1828 edition; revised, 1832.

Bacon, Leonard. *Discourse and Addresses at the Ordination of the Rev. Theodore Dwight Woolsey to the Ministry of the Gospel, and His Inauguration as President of Yale College.* New Haven: B.L. Hamlin, 1846.

———. "Prolegomena." *New Englander*, I (1843), 4–6.

Barrows, E. P. "The Mosaic Narrative of the Creation Considered Grammatically and in Its Relation to Science." *Bibliotheca Sacra*, XIII (1856), 743–89.

Bartlett, S. C. "The Historic Character of the Pentateuch." *Bibliotheca Sacra*, XX (1863), 381–431.

Bascom, John. "The Synthetic Cosmic Philosophy." *Bibliotheca Sacra*, XXXIII (1876), 618–55.

Benedict, W. R. "Theism and Evolution." *Andover Review*, VI (1886), 337–50.

Bixby, James T. "Immortality and Science." *Bibliotheca Sacra*, XLI (1884), 44–67.

———. "The Know-Nothing Position in Religion." *Bibliotheca Sacra*, XXXVIII (1881), 435–60.

Brown, L. W. "Andover and Creed Subscription." *North American Review*, LXXXIV (1882), 551–61.

Brown, Thomas. *Lectures on the Philosophy of the Human Mind*. Edinburgh: Ward C. Tait, 1820.

Case, M. P. "Elements of Culture in the Early Ages." *Bibliotheca Sacra*, IX (1852), 686–700.

Channing, William Ellery. *Sermon Delivered at the Ordination of Jared Sparks.* Baltimore: n.p., 1819.

Constitution and Statutes of the Andover Theological Seminary. Boston: Farrard, Mallory, & Co., 1808.

"The Constitution and Statutes of the Theological Seminary in Andover." *Monthly Anthology and Boston Review*, V (1808), 610–14.

Cook, Joseph. "A Fourth Year of Study in the Courses of Theological Seminaries." *Bibliotheca Sacra*, XXVII (1870), 244–61.

"Creation." *Andover Review*, V (1886), 299–300.

Dana, James D. "Science and the Bible." *Bibliotheca Sacra*, XIII (1856), 80–130, 631–56.

Dana, J. Jay. "The Religion of Geology." *Bibliotheca Sacra*, X (1853), 505–22.

Day, Jeremiah. "The Christian Preachers' Commission." *Spirit of the Pilgrims*, Vol. V (1832).

Dwight, Timothy. *Theology Explained and Defended.* 4 vols. New York: Harper & Brothers, 1847.

Dwinell, I. E. "Queries about Figure Probation." *Bibliotheca Sacra*, XLIII (1886), 33–56.

Edwards, Bela Bates. "Bunsen's Late Work on Egypt." *Bibliotheca Sacra*, VI (1847), 709–18.

———. "The Obligations of Literature, Particularly of Philology, to Modern Missionary Efforts." *Biblical Repository*, VII (1836), 161–86.

———. "Present State of Biblical Science." *Bibliotheca Sacra*, VII (1850), 1–12.

———. "Remarks on Certain Erroneous Methods and Principles in Biblical Criticism." *Bibliotheca Sacra*, VI (1849), 185–96.

———. "Remarks on the Authenticity and Genuineness of the Pentateuch." *Bibliotheca Sacra*, II (1845), 356–98.

———. "Slavery in Ancient Greece." *Biblical Repository*, V (1835), 138–63.

———. "Sources of Hebrew Philology and Lexicography." *Biblical Repository*, III (1833), 1–44.

———. "The Structure of Hebrew Grammar." *Bibliotheca Sacra*, IV (1847), 171–81.

Edwards, Bela Bates; and Park, Edwards Amasa. "Natural Theology." *Bibliotheca Sacra*, III (1846), 241–84.

Edwards, Bela Bates; Sears, Bamas; and Felton, C. C. *Classical Studies.* Boston: Gould, Kendall, & Lincoln, 1843.

Ellis, George. *A Half-Century of the Unitarian Controversy.* Boston: Cooshy, Nichols, & Co., 1857.

Emerson, Ralph. "History of Monasticism." *Bibliotheca Sacra*, I (1844), 309–24, 464–522.

———. "Spark's Life of Ledyard." *Quarterly Christian Spectator*, 2d series, II (182 8), 317–27.

Fairchild, James A. "Probation—Its Conditions and Limitations." *Bibliotheca Sacra*, XLIII (1886), 423–42.

Fisher, George Park. *Life of Benjamin Silliman.* New York: Charles Scribner & Co., 1866.

Foster, Frank Hugh. "The Argument from Christian Experience for the Inspiration of the Bible." *Bibliotheca Sacra*, XL (1883), 97–138.

———. *A Genetic History of the New England Theology.* Chicago: University of Chicago Press, 1907.

Gardiner, Frederic. "The Bearing of Recent Scientific Thought upon Theology." *Bibliotheca Sacra*, XXXV (1878), 46–75.

———. "Darwinism." *Bibliotheca Sacra*, XXIX (1872), 240–89.

———. "'Errors' of the Scriptures." *Bibliotheca Sacra*, XXXVI, (1879), 496–534.

Gould, Ezra P. "The Duration of Future Punishment." *Bibliotheca Sacra*, XXXVII (1880), 221–48.

Hackett, Horatio B. "Critique on Sharp's *Life of Jesus.*" *Bibliotheca Sacra*, II (1845), 48–79.

———. "The First Eleven Chapters of Genesis Attested by Their Content." *Bibliotheca Sacra*, XXII (1865), 188–96.

———. "The Greek Version of the Pentateuch." *Bibliotheca Sacra*, Vol. IV (1847).

———. "Synoptical Study of the Gospels." *Bibliotheca Sacra*, III (1846), 1–22.

Harris, George T. *A Century's Change in Religion*. Boston: Houghton Mifflin Co., 1914.

———. "Function of the Christian Consciousness." *Andover Review*, II, (1884), 338–52.

Harris, Samuel. "The Theological Department Essential in a University." *New Englander*, XXXI (1872), 36–56.

Haven, Joseph. *Moral Philosophy*. Boston: Gould & Lincoln, 1859.

———. "The Philosophy of fir William Hamilton, and Its Recent Theological Applications." *Bibliotheca Sacra*, XVIII (1861), 94–142.

Herrick, J. R. "Lecky on Morals." *Bibliotheca Sacra*, XXIX (1872), 209–39.

Hill, Thomas. "Erasmus Darwin." *Bibliotheca Sacra*, XXXV (1878), 461–81.

———. "Organic Form." *Bibliotheca Sacra*, XXXVI (1879), 1–22.

Hitchcock, Edward. "The Connection between Geology and the Mosaic History of the Creation." *Biblical Repository*, 1st series, VI (1835), 261–332, 439–52.

———. "The Connection between Geology and Natural Religion." *Biblical Repository*, V (1835), 113–38.

———. "The Cross in Nature and Nature in the Cross." *Bibliotheca Sacra*, XVIII (1861), 252–84.

[———]. "Discussion between Two Readers of Darwin's Treatise on the *Origin of Species*." *American Journal of Science and Arts*, 2d series, XXX (1860), 226–39.

———. "Exegesis I, Corinthians 15:35-44." *Bibliotheca Sacra*, XVII (1860), 303–12.

———. "The Law of Nature's Constancy Subordinate to the Higher Law of Change." *Bibliotheca Sacra*, XX (1863), 489–561.

———. "Ornithicnology." *American Journal of Science and Arts*, XXIX (1836), 307–40.

———. "The Religion of Geology." *Bibliotheca Sacra*, XVII (1860), 673–709.

———. *Reminiscences of Amherst College*. Northhampton, Mass.: Bridgeman and Childs, 1863.

———. "Remarks on Professor Stuart's Examination of Genesis I in Reference to Geology." *Biblical Repository*, VII (1836), 448–87.

Hopkins, Samuel. *Sketches of the Life of the Late Rev. Samuel Hopkins*. Hartford: Stephen West, D.D., 1805.

Hume, David. *A Treatise on Human Nature*. Edited by L. A. Selby-Brigge. Oxford: Clarendon Press, 1888.

Johnson, F. H. "Co-Operative Creation." *Andover Review*, III (1885), 326–46, 436–55.

Johnson, F. H. "Mechanical Evolution." *Andover Review*, I (1884), 631–49.

———. "Positivism as a Working System." *Bibliotheca Sacra*, XXXIX (1882), 674–721.

———. "Reason and Revelation." *Andover Review*, V (1886), 229–49.

Ladd, George T. "The Concept of God as the Ground of Progress." *Bibliotheca Sacra*, XXXV (1878), 619–55.

———. "Final Purpose in Nature." *New Englander*, XXXVIII (1879), 677–700.

———. "The Origin of the Concept of God." *Bibliotheca Sacra*, XXXIV (1877), 1–36.

———. "The Question Restated." *Andover Review*, IV (1885), 1–18.

Lawrence, Edward A. "Natural Law in the Spiritual World." *Andover Review*, VI (1886), 22–34.

Lyell, Charles. *Principles of Geology*. Philadelphia: James Kay & Brother, June, 1837.

McCosh, James. *The Scottish Philosophy*. New York: Robert Carter & Brothers, 1880.

McIlvaine, J. H. "Revelation and Science." *Bibliotheca Sacra*, XXXIV (1877), 259–83.

McLane, James W. "Speculation and the Bible." *Bibliotheca Sacra*, XVIII (1861), 338–57.

Means, D. McGregor. "The Data of Ethics." *Bibliotheca Sacra*, XXXVII (1880), 471–503.

Means, John O. "The Narrative of the Creation in Genesis." *Bibliotheca Sacra*, XII (1855), 83–130, 323–38.

Mooar, George. "Sociology and Christian Missions." *Bibliotheca Sacra*, XL (1883), 630–42.

———. "The Pilgrim Line of Theological Progress." *New Englander*, V (1883), 113–25.

Morgan, John. "Theories of Atonement." *Bibliotheca Sacra*, XXXV (1878), 114–47.

Neander, August. "Augustine and Pelagius." Translated by L. Woods, Jr. Introduction by B. B. Edwards. *Biblical Repository*, III (1833), 66–129.

Norton, Andrews. "Defense of Liberal Christianity." *General Repository and Review*, I (1812), 1–25.

Norton, Andrews. *Statement of Reasons for Not Believing the Doctrine of the Trinity*. Boston: American Unitarian Association, 1875.

"On the Atonement and Creation." *Andover Review*, IV (1885), 56–68.

An Outline or Course of Study in the Department of Christian Theology. Andover: Flagg & Gould, 1822.

Paley, William. *Natural Theology*. London: J. & G. Robinson, G. Offar, & J. Evans & Co., 1824.

Park, Edwards Amasa. "Life and Services of Professor B. B. Edwards." *Bibliotheca Sacra*, IX (1852), 783–820.

———. *Memorial Collection of Sermons*. Boston: Pilgrim's Press, 1902.

———. "Memorial of James Murdoch." *Bibliotheca Sacra*, XV (1857), 888.

———. "The New England Theology." *Bibliotheca Sacra*, IX (1852), 170–219.

———. "Note to the Subscribers of *Bibliotheca Sacra*." *Bibliotheca Sacra*, XIV (1857), 460–61.

———. "The Relation of Divine Providence to Physical Laws." *Bibliotheca Sacra*, XII (1855), 179–204.

———. "The Relation of Theology to Other Sciences." *Bibliotheca Sacra*, XXXIII (1876), 288–92.

———. "Review of Stuart's *Active and Moral Powers*." *Bibliotheca Sacra*, VII (1850), 191–93.

———. "The Theology of the Intellect and That of the Feelings." *Bibliotheca Sacra*, VII (1850), 533–69.

———. "What Can Be Done for Augmenting the Number of Christian Ministers." *Bibliotheca Sacra*, XXVIII (1871), 60–97.

———, ed. *Writings of Professor B. B. Edwards, with a Memoir*. 2 vols. Boston: John P. Jewett & Co., 1853.

Park, Edwards Amasa; and Edwards, Bela Bates. "Thoughts on the State of Theological Sciences and Education in Our Country." *Bibliotheca Sacra*, I (1844), 735–67.

Patton, Francis L. "Is Andover Romanizing?" *Forum*, III (1887), 327–33.

Peabody, Francis. "Office of Proof in the Knowledge of God." *Andover Review*, II (1884), 1.

Phelps, Austin. "The Oneness of God in Revelation and in Nature." *Bibliotheca Sacra*, XVI (1859), 836–63.

Phelps (Ward), Elizabeth Stuart. *Chapters from a Life*. Cambridge: Riverside Press, 1896.

Redd, Thomas. *Works.* Edited by Dugald Stewart. 4 vols. New York: E. Duyckinck, Collins, & Hannay and R. & W.A. Barton, 1822.

Robbins, R. D. C. "The Character and Prophecies of Balaam." *Bibliotheca Sacra,* III (1846), 347–67, 699–742.

———. "The Song of Deborah—Judges, Chapter V." *Bibliotheca Sacra,* XII (1855), 597–642.

Robinson, Edward. "Alleged Discrepancy between John and the Other Evangelists, Respecting Our Lord's Last Passover." *Bibliotheca Sacra,* II (1845), 405–36.

———. "The Aspect of Literature and Science in the United States, as Compared with Europe." *Bibliotheca Sacra,* I (1844), 1–39.

———. "On the Language of Palestine in the Age of Christ and the Apostles." *Biblical Repository,* I (1831), 309–17.

———. "Theological Education in Germany." *Biblical Repository,* I (1831), 1–50, 201–25.

———, trans. "Greek Style of the New Testament." *Biblical Repository,* I (1831), 638–58.

Rules of the American Education Society. N.p.: Board of Directors, August, 1808.

Salisbury, Edward E. "The Himyaritic Language: Foster's Pretended Discovery of a Key to the Himyaritic Inscriptions." *Bibliotheca Sacra,* II (1845), 237–60.

Schaff, Philip. *St. Augustine, Melancthon, and Neander.* New York: Funk & Wagnalls, 1886.

Sears, Bamas. "German Literature;—Its Religious Character and Influence." *Christian Review,* VI (1841), 269–84.

———. "Historical Studies." *Bibliotheca Sacra,* III (1846), 579–604.

———. "Historical Studies in College: Their Degree of Importance and the Best Way of Conducting Them." *Bibliotheca Sacra,* XXII (1865), 251–84.

Shedd, W. G. T. *Lectures on the Philosophy of History.* Andover: Flagg & Gould, 1856.

———. "The Relation of Language to the Laws of Thought." *Bibliotheca Sacra,* V (1848), 650–63.

Smith, Henry B. "The History of Doctrines." *Bibliotheca Sacra,* IV (1847), 552–81.

———. "Interpretation of the Baptismal Formula." *Bibliotheca Sacra,* I (1844), 703–8.

———. "A Sketch of German Philosophy." *Bibliotheca Sacra,* II (1845), 260–92.

Smyth, Egbert C. "On Atonement." *Andover Review,* IV (1884), 56–68.

———. "The Theological Purpose of the *Review.*" *Andover Review,* I (1884), 1–13.

Sprague, William. *Annals of the American Pulpit.* 9 vols. New York: Carter & Brothers, 1858–1869.

Storrs, Richard Salter. *Edwards A. Park, Memorial Address.* Boston: Samuel Usher, 1910.

Stuart, Moses. "Are the Same Principles of Interpretation to be Applied to Scriptures as to Other Books?" *Biblical Repository,* II (1832), 124–38.

———. *Chrestomathy.* Andover: Flagg & Gould, 1829.

———. "The Creed of Arminius, with an Account of his Life and Times." *Biblical Repository,* I (1831), 226–308.

———. "A Critical Examination of Some Passages in Genesis I; with Remarks on Difficulties that Attend Some of the Present Modes of Geological Reasoning." *Biblical Repository,* VII (1836), 46–106.

———. *Critical History and Defense of the Old Testament Canon.* Andover: Allen, Morrill, & Wardwell, 1845.

———. *Exegetical Essays on Several Words Relating to Future Punishment.* Andover: Flagg & Gould, 1830.

———. *A Farewell Sermon, Preached at New Haven, January 28, 1810.* New Haven: Sidney's Press: 1810.

———. "Letter to the Editor on the Study of German." *Christian Review*, VI (1841), 459.

———. *Letters to Rev. William E. Channing Containing Remarks on His Sermon Recently Published in Baltimore.* Andover: Flagg & Gould, 1819.

———. "Presence of Christ in the Lord's Supper." *Bibliotheca Sacra*, I (1844), 110–51, 225–79.

———. "Remarks on 'A Critical Examination of Genesis I; etc.' by Moses Stuart in *Biblical Repository* for January, 1836." *American Journal of Science and Arts*, XXX (1836), 114–30.

Stuart, Moses. *A Sermon, Preached before the Administration of the Lord's Supper to the First Congregational Church, in New Haven, January 14, A.D. 1810.* New Haven: Sidney's Press, 1810.

———. *A Sermon Preached in the Tabernacle Church, Salem, November 5, 1818.* Andover: Flagg & Gould, 1818.

———. *Two Discourses on the Atonement.* Andover: Flagg & Gould, 1824.

Taylor, Nathaniel William. *Essays, Lectures, etc., upon Select Subjects in Revealed Theology.* New York: Clark, Austin, & Smith, 1859.

Wallace, B. J. "The Sanskrit Language in Its Relation to Comparative Philology." *Bibliotheca Sacra*, IV (1847), 671–95.

Whittemore, George, ed. *Memorials of Horatio Balch Hackett.* Rochester, N.Y.: n.p., 1876.

Woods, Leonard. *Collected Works.* 5 vols. Andover: Flagg & Gould, 1859.

———. *A History of Andover Theological Seminary.* Boston: James R. Osgood & Co., 1885.

———. "Introductory Article." *Literary and Theological Review*, I (1834), 1–31.

———. *Letters to Unitarians Occasioned by the Sermon of the Reverend William E. Channing, at the Ordination of the Rev. J. Sparks.* Andover: Flagg & Gould, 1820.

———. "Letters to Young Ministers." *Spirit of the Pilgrims*, V (1832), 78–377.

Woolsey, Theodore Dwight. "Greek Lexicography." *Bibliotheca Sacra*, (1844), 613–32.

———. "Principles of Latin Lexicography." *Bibliotheca Sacra*, II (1845), 7–107.

Wright, George Frederick. "Recent Works Bearing on the Relation of Science to Religion, No. II—The Divine Method of Producing Living Species." *Bibliotheca Sacra*, XXXIII (1876), 448–93.

———. "Recent Works Bearing on the Relation of Science to Religion, No. III-T—Objections to Darwinism and the Rejoinders of Its Advocates." *Bibliotheca Sacra*, XXXIII (1876), 656–94.

———. "Recent Works Bearing on the Relation of Science to Religion, No. IV—Concerning the Time Doctrine Of Final Cause or Design in Nature." *Bibliotheca Sacra*, XXXIV (1877), 355–87.

Wright, George Frederick. "Recent Works Bearing on the Relation of Science to

Religion, No. V—Some Analogies between Calvinism and Darwinism." *Bibliotheca Sacra*, XXXVIII (1880), 48–76.

Secondary Sources

Aarsleff, Hans. *The Study of Language in England*. Princeton: Princeton University Press, 1967.

Ahlstrom, Sydney. "Scottish Philosophy and American Theology." *Church History*, XXIV (1955), 262.

Brazill, William J. *The Young Hegelians*. New Haven: Yale University Press, 1970.

Brown, Jerry Wayne. *The Rise of Biblical Criticism in America*. Middleton, Conn.: Wesleyan University Press, 1969.

Burrow, J. W. *Evolution and Society*. London: Cambridge University Press, 1966.

Cecil, Anthony Clay, Jr. "The Theological Development of Edwards Amasa Park: Last of the Consistent Calvinists." Ph.D. dissertation, Yale University, 1973.

Daniels, George. *American Science in the Age of Jackson*. New York: King's Crown Press, 1968.

Dictionary of American Biography, 1st edition, 1928–36.

Dott, R. H., Jr. "James Hutton and the Concept of a Dynamic Earth." In *Towards a History of Geology*. Edited by Cecil J. Schneer. Cambridge: M.I.T. Press, 1969.

Eiseley, Loren. *Darwin's Century*. New York: Doubleday & Co., 1961.

Forbes, Duncan. *The Liberal Anglican Idea of History*. Cambridge: University Press, 1952.

Foster, Frank Hugh. *The Life of Edwards Amasa Park*. New York: Fleming H. Revell Co., 1936.

Freeman, Derek. "The Evolutionary Theories of Charles Darwin and Herbert Spencer." *Current Anthropology*, XV (1974), 211–39.

Gabriel, Ralph Henry. *Religion and Learning at Yale*. New Haven: Yale University Press, 1958.

Gillespie, Charles Coulston. *Genesis and Geology*. New York: Harper & Brothers, 1959.

Giltner, John. "Moses Stuart." Ph.D. dissertation, Yale University, 1956.

Gooch, G. P. *Studies in German History*. London: Longmann, Green, & Co., 1948.

Grave, Stephen. *The Scottish Philosophy of Common Sense*. Oxford: Clarendon Press, 1960.

Greene, John C. *The Death of Adam*. Ames: Iowa State Press, 1959.

Haroutunian, Joseph. *Piety Versus Moralism*. Chicago: University Of Chicago Press, 1933.

Hofstadter, Richard. *Social Darwinism in American Thought*. Boston: Beacon Press, 1967; revised from 1944 edition.

Howe, Daniel Walker. *The Unitarian Conscience*. Cambridge: Harvard University Press, 1970.

Jones, Robert A. "John Bascom: Antipositivism and Intuitionism in American Sociology." *American Quarterly*, XXIV (1972), 501–22.

Mackauer, Christian. "Ranke." In *A Teacher at His Best*. Chicago: University of Chicago Press, 1973.

Martin, Terence. *The Instructed Vision*. Bloomington: University of Indiana Press, 1961.

Mead, Sidney. *Nathaniel William Taylor*. Chicago: University of Chicago Press, 1944.

Merrill, George P. *First One Hundred Years of American Geology*. New Haven: Yale University Press, 1930.

Mott, Frank Luther. *A History of American Magazines*. New York: D. Appleton & Co., 1930.

Peel, J. D. Y. *Herbert Spencer*. New York: Basic Books, 1971.

Rogers, James Allen. "Darwinism and Social Darwinism." *Journal of the History of Ideas*, XXXIII (1972), 265–81.

Rudwick, M. J. S. "Hutton and Werner Compared: George Greenough's Geological Tour of Scotland in 1805." *British Journal for the History of Science*, I (1962), 117–35.

Schmidt, George. *The Old-time College President*. New York: Columbia University Press, 1930.

Simpson, Lewis. *The Man of Letters in New England and the South*. Baton Rouge: Louisiana State University Press, 1973.

Stout, Cushing. "Faith and History: The Mind of W. G. T. Shedd." *Journal of the History of Ideas*, XV (1954), 153–63.

Struik, Dirk J. *Yankee Science in the Making*. New York: Macmillan Co., 1948; revised edition, 1968.

Tucker, William Jewett. *My Generation*. Boston: Houghton Mifflin, 1919.

Williams, Daniel Day. *The Andover Liberals*. New York: King's Crown Press, 1941.

Wilson, Leonard J. "The Intellectual Background to Charles Lyell's *Principles of Geology*." In *Towards a History of Geology*. Edited by Cecil J. Schneer. Cambridge: M.I.T. Press, 1969.

Wright, Conrad. "The Religion of Geology." *New England Quarterly*, XIV (1941), 335–58.

MANUSCRIPT COLLECTIONS

Andover, Mass. Phillips-Andover Preparatory School. Archives. Reports from Andover faculty to the trustees, 1815–1885.

Boston, Mass. Boston Public Library. Mellon Chamberlin Correspondence. Letters to Edwards Amasa Park.

———. Massachusetts Historical Society. Edward Everett Collection. 20 letters from Stuart to Everett, 1813–1815.

Nashville, Tenn. Park Family Papers in the possession of Drs. Charles and Jane Park.

New Haven, Conn. Yale University Library. Edwards A. Park's Papers. Woolsey Family Papers. Bacon Family Papers.

Newton Center, Mass. Andover-Newton Theological Seminary. Notes on sermons of Edwards Amasa Park and Bela Bates Edwards. 5 vols.

Syracuse, N.Y. Syracuse University Library. Leonard Woods' Letters to Isaac Warren.

INDEX

❖ ❖ ❖

Athanasius, 77
atheism, 111
Athens (Greece), 76
"Augustine and Pelagius" (Edwards), 74
Augustine of Hippo, 65, 75, 92, 105
"Authenticity and Genuineness of the
 Pentateuch" (Stuart), 82

Backus, Charles, 9–10, 14
Bacon, Francis, 21, 23, 84
Bacon, Leonard, 3, 44, 58
Baconianism, 2, 36, 55–56, 69, 84–85,
 87
Bannister, William, 47
Bartlett, 57
Bascom, John, 111, 146n41
Bates, Ann, 49
Baur, Friedrich Christian, 72–73
"Bearing of Scientific Thought, The"
 (Gardiner), 114
Bible, 6, 56, 61–62, 70, 100, 104–5, 114–
 15, 125; authenticity of, 77–79, 121; as
 authoritative, 39, 120; errors in, 80;
 and evolution, 5, 122; and geology,
 87–88, 93, 96–98, 101–2; and herme-
 neutics, 37; meaning of, 16; as myth,
 4; and nature, 37, 85, 101; and reason,
 37–39; and theology, 1; understanding of, 37; veracity of, 78–79. *See also*
 Book of Chronicles; Creation story;
 Genesis; Great Flood; Moses; New
 Testament; Old Testament; Pentateuch
biblical criticism, 3, 18, 83, 121; Christian
 consciousness, 120; and geology, 95
Biblical Repository (journal), 31, 42,
 51, 58, 67, 74–75, 78, 90–92, 94–95,
 137n70. See also *Biblotheca*
Biblical Repository and Classical Review
 (journal), 50
biblical studies, 35–36, 42–44; German
 scholarship, 26–27
Bibliotheca (journal), 58, 68, 70, 76–77,
 81, 87, 91, 96–97, 99, 101, 108, 111,
 113–16, 119–20, 137n70, 140n44. See
 also *Biblical Repository*
Bibliotheca Sacra (journal), 42, 44,

46–47, 51, 54–55, 57–60, 75, 111–12,
 115, 118
Bixby, James, 113
Book of Chronicles, 32, 35–36
Bowdoin College, 47
Brager, James, 24
Brattle Street Church, 28
British Geological Society, 95–96
Brown, Jerry Wayne, 39–40, 43
Brown University, 1–2, 6
Buckland, William, 86–87, 96, 142n7
Buckminster, Joseph Stevens, 28–29
Buddha, 107
Bunsen, 81
Butler, Joseph, 22, 120

Calvin, John, 14, 74, 101
Calvinism, 2, 4, 6, 44, 113, 115, 118, 121;
 and the Creed, 16; Edwardsean Cal-
 vinism, 52; and evolution, 104; and
 moral philosophy, 56; New England
 Calvinism, 3, 5–6, 106, 125–26; and
 Old Calvinists, 8, 10, 14, 16, 130n5;
 and orthodox Calvinism, 12; total de-
 pravity doctrine, 18; Unitarianism,
 conflict with, 40–41, 43
Canada, 44
Catholic Church, 107
Channing, William E., 28, 37–38, 40–41,
 57, 73, 78; Old Testament, rejection
 of, 39
"Character and Prophecies of Balaam,
 The" (Robbins), 70
Chicago Theological Seminary, 6
Chrestomathy (Stuart), 31, 66, 93
Christianity, 39, 62, 65, 73–74, 77, 91,
 102, 104, 114, 122; and geology, 89,
 100–101; and public morals, 112–13
*Christian Monthly Spectator. See Quar-
 terly Christian Spectator*
"Christian Preacher's Commission, The"
 (sermon), 19
Christian Repertory (journal), 132n67
Christian scholars, 3, 6, 24–25, 73, 77,
 82, 87–88, 101–2, 112, 121–22, 125–26;
 classics, scholarship of, 67–68; dimin-
 ishing authority, fear of, 100; and

evolution, 110, 113, 115; geology, and biblical criticism, 95; language study, interest in, 67; moral philosophy, 2, 4, 104; natural science, 85; New England intellectual activity, 2; Orthodoxy, emergence from, 1; and philology, 99; unworthiness, question of, 46. *See also* Andover Seminary

Christian Spectator (journal), 73, 132n67

Churchill, John, 108

Classical Studies (Fenton, Edwards, and Sears), 47, 67

classification, 84–85

Common Sense philosophy, 14, 19, 21, 28, 30, 55–56, 69, 102–3, 110–11, 113, 121–22, 132n67; analogy, use of in, 24; and Congregationalism, 22; induction, use of, 21; moral sense, as *a priori*, 21; as Newtonians, 20–21; obligation, principle of, 23; weakness of, 21. *See also* Scottish Realism

Congregationalism, 3–4, 14, 27, 43, 108, 115; Common Sense philosophy, role of in, 22; and moral philosophy, 2; Trinitarian Congregationalists, 37, 46–47, 57, 73

Connecticut, 5, 8, 87

Conway (Massachusetts), 89

Cooper, Thomas, 91

"Co-Operative Criticism" (Johnson), 116–17

Creation story, 34, 93–94, 102

creed, 10–11, 16, 29, 61–62, 107–8; as medieval vestige, 17

"Creed of Arminius with an Account of His Life and Times, The" (Stuart), 73

"Critical Examination of Some Passages in Genesis I, A" (Stuart), 78

Cuvier, Georges, 23, 84, 96–97

Dana, Daniel, 54–55

Dane, Rev. James, 131n31

Daniels, George, 23, 84

Darwin, Charles, 101–2, 104, 109–12, 114, 116, 142n7; objections to, 113; "survival of the fittest" phrase, 145n35

Darwinism, 110, 114, 118; Calvinism, as akin to, 115

Data of Ethics (Means), 111

Day, Jeremiah, 19

"Debate between the Church and Science, The," 97

Defense of the Old Testament Canon (Stuart), 42

Deists, 18

Demosthenes, 75

depravity, 24–25

developmentalism, 113

Dexter, Samuel, 28

divine design, 5, 24, 55, 86–97, 101–2, 116–18

Doctrine of Sacred Scriptures (Ladd), 120

Dorner, I. A., 107

Dwight, Timothy, 8–9, 14–15, 20–22, 24, 46, 87

"Early History of Monasticism from Original Sources, The" (Emerson), 76

Eaton, Amos, 89

ecumenism, 57–58

Edward, Justin, 41

Edwards, Bela Bates, 4–5, 14, 42–47, 50, 52–54, 55, 57–60, 65, 67–71, 74–75, 80, 83, 91, 105, 120, 122, 127, 137n70, 141n83; as Christian scholar, exemplifying, 48–49; classical learning, love of, 51; death of, 49; geology, interest in, 95–96; Mosaic account, 81; Pentateuch, veracity, belief of, 81–82; sin, obsession over, 48–49, 51

Edwards, Elisha, 49

Edwards, Jonathan, 126

Edwards, Jonathan (the younger), 12

Edwards, Mrs., 46

Edwards, Sarah, 48, 136n21

Egypt, 33–34, 82; hieroglyphs, interest in, 81

Eichhorn, Johann Gottfried, 26–27, 29–30, 32–36, 38, 57, 113

Eliot, George, 110

Elizabeth I, 7

Ellis, George, 37

reconciliation between, 88–89, 92–94; and natural theology, 91; and nature, 91; Pentateuch, and geology, 91; revivals, conducting of, 89; uniformitarian principles of, 90–91, 101

Hodge, Charles, 57, 59, 61–62, 132n67

Homer, 51, 75

Hopkins, Samuel, 7; and Hopkinsians, 8–10, 13, 16, 130n5; regeneration, views on, 8

Howe, Daniel Walker, 41

Hume, David, 20, 42, 57, 132n67

Hutton, James, 86–87

Huxley, Thomas Henry, 95

Iliad (Homer), 35, 75

"Importance of an Early Consecration to Missionary Work, The" (Hitchcock), 89

Introduction to the Old Testament (Eichhorn), 29

Jesus, 10, 17, 27–29, 33–34, 37–38, 49, 80, 119

Johnson, F. H., 116–18

Jones, William, 64

Journal of Science and the Arts (journal), 87, 89

Judaism, 72

Kingsley, James, 88, 93–95

Ladd, George Trumbull, 108–9, 120–21

Lamarck, Chevalier de, 109–10

"Law of Nature's Constancy Subordinate to the Higher Law of Change, the" (Hitchcock), 102

Lawrence, E. A., 121

Lecky, William Edward Hartpole, 112

Ledyard, John, 73, 76

Letters to the Rev. Wm. E. Channing, containing remarks on his sermon, recently preached and published at Baltimore (Stuart), 38, 40–41

"Letters to Young Ministers" (Woods), 18–19, 22

liberalism, 126

Liberals, 1, 3, 38; creed, attack on, 16–17; Deists, in opposition to, 18; and textual criticism, 27–29; and Unitarianism, 37. *See also* Unitarianism

"Life of Henry Martyn" (Edwards), 44

Literary and Theological Review, The (journal), 62

Locke, John, 8, 20, 28

logic, 52, 71–72, 77, 79, 81, 85, 98, 105, 112, 114–15, 119–20, 122; and intuition, 118

Luther, Martin, 82, 107

Lyell, Charles, 86–87, 91, 96, 109–10, 114, 142n7; uniformitarian principles, 90

MacCulloch, John, 91

Man of Letters in New England and the South, The (Simpson), 1

Mao Tse-Tung, 110

Massachusetts, 5, 8, 87, 90, 99

Massachusetts Home Missionary Journal, The (journal), 10

materialism, 111

Mayhew, Jonathan, 8

McIlvaine, J. H., 113

McLane, James, 98

Mead, Charles, 41, 106

Means, D. McGregor, 98–99, 111

Melville, Herman, 129n8

Michaelis, J. D., 26, 28, 42, 71

Momigliano, Arnoldo, 139n4

Monbodo, Lord, 57

Monthly Anthology and Boston Review (journal), 17

Mooar, George, 111–12

moral philosophy, 56, 122, 125; and Christian scholars, 2, 4, 104; as defined, 2

Morse, Jedidiah, 8, 13, 16, 37, 121; as Old Calvinist, 9

Mosaic account, 34–35, 79, 86, 88, 93–95, 99, 101; and philology, 79, 101

Moses, 16, 33–34, 38, 78–79, 80–81, 88, 92–93, 98–100, 109

Murdock, James, 13, 17

"Mystical Presence of Christ in the Lord's Supper, The" (Stuart), 66

Napoleon, 81

Nathaniel William Taylor (Mead), 41

natural laws, 24, 69, 101

natural philosophy, 84

natural science, 4, 114, 120; analogy, use of in, 24; and Baconianism approach, 23

natural selection, 109

natural theology, 18, 23, 91, 99, 118, 120; analogy, use of in, 24; and moral philosophy, 24, 122; and science, 96

Natural Theology (Paley), 24

"Natural Theology" (Park and Edwards), 96

nature, 2, 24, 26, 30, 33, 37–40, 69, 86, 91, 108–10, 112, 115–18, 126; and Bible, 96, 121; religion, as handmaiden of, 85; and revelation, 85, 99–102, 113; and science, 23

Neander, August, 45, 51, 65, 72, 74–75, 83

Neptunists, 86

New Departure, 107

New England, 4, 20, 38, 44, 52, 58; and Common Sense philosophy, 14; New England Calvinism, 3, 5–6, 106, 125–26; New England intellectualism, Baconianism approach to, 23; New England religious orthodoxy, 1–3; New England theology, 115, 119, 120, 122, 126; New England thought, 23, 25

New Englander (journal), 112

"New England Theology" (Park), 21

New Testament, 32–33, 35, 38, 67, 72, 80, 83; New Testament studies, 106

Newton, Isaac, 21, 23, 55–56, 84, 94

Newton Center (Massachusetts), 5, 45

New York (New York), 5

Niebuhr, G. B., 64, 76, 81

Noll, Mark, 125–26

Norris, William, 10

North American Review (journal), 73

Norton, Andrews, 16, 28–29, 40–41

Oberlin College, 5, 108

Odyssey, The (Homer) 75

"Office of Proof in the Knowledge of God, The" (Peabody), 120

Old Testament, 32–39, 80, 83, 87, 92; defense of, 34–35; Old Testament studies, 106

On the Origin of Species (Darwin), 101, 109, 145n35

Optics (Newton), 21

"Ornithicnology" (Hitchcock), 90

Ovid, 67, 109

Pacific Theological Seminary, 6

Palestine, 82

Paley, William, 56, 85, 91, 120, 132n67; analogy, use of, 24

Panoplist, The (journal), 8, 10

Park, Calvin, 53–54

Park, Edwards A., 4–5, 7, 21, 24, 41–42, 44–49, 51, 59–60, 68–69, 72, 79–80, 83, 85, 91, 95–97, 100–101, 103–5, 114–15, 118, 120, 122–23, 127, 138n84, 140n44; Andover faculty, tension between, 54–55; Common Sense philosophy, reliance on, 22, 55; creedal lawsuit of, 108; essential Christ, theory of, 107; failing health of, 106–7, 145n11; family members, friction between, 54; geology, interest in, 96; Hodge, debate with, 57–58, 61–62; language, approach to, 65; modern science, reliance on, 56; moral philosophy, use of, 56; natural theology, use of, 55–56, 99; as pulpit orator, 52, 54; resignation of, 106; Scottish Realism, use of, 54–56; sin and salvation, preoccupation with, 53; successor of, 107–8; Taylor theology, conversion to, 54–55; theology, rational approach to, 62–63

Park, Marian, 136n21

Park, William, 136n21

Park Street Church, 12

Peabody, Francis, 120

Pearson, Eliphalet, 10, 13–15, 121; as Old Calvinist, 9; as perfectionist, 11; resignation of, 12

Peel, John, 110
Pelagius, 75
Pentateuch, 27, 34–35, 68, 78–82, 91
"Perils of Romanism" (lecture), 47
Peters, Absalom, 137n70
Phelps, Austin, 42, 48, 58, 99–101, 103–4, 106, 108, 113, 138n84
Phelps, Elizabeth Stuart, 127
Phillips Academy, 5, 9–10
philology, 71–72, 77, 85, 98, 102, 125; biblical science, as tool of, 99; and grammar, 69–70; Mosaic account, 79, 101
physics, 24; and philosophy, 21
Piety versus Moralism: The Passing of the New England Theology from Edwards to Taylor (Haroutunian), 41, 126
Plato, 46, 107
Porter, Ebenezer, 12–13, 34, 41, 50
Porter, Noah, 46
positivism, 111
"Present State of Biblical Science, The" (Edwards), 80, 97
Princeton University, 57, 119, 132n67; Scottish Realism at, 22
"Principles of Exegesis, The" (lecture), 30
Principles of Geology (Lyell), 86, 109
Professors and Public Ethics (Smith), 132n67
progressive orthodoxy, 119, 123; Bible, authority of, 120; doctrinal features of, 116
Protestantism, 17

Quarterly Christian Spectator (journal), 73

rationalism, 18, 29, 36, 57
reason, 61–63, 123; and Bible, 36–39; Christian experience, 119; and revelation, 2, 18–20, 24, 30, 37, 118
Reformation, 42
regeneration, 14
Reid, Thomas, 20–22, 69
Religion of Geology, The (Hitchcock), 91, 93
Reminiscences (Hitchcock), 91

Report on the Geology of Massachusetts (Hitchcock), 90
"Resurrection of the Body, The" (Hitchcock), 89
revelation, and nature, 85, 99–100, 102, 108
Rise of Biblical Criticism (Brown), 39
Robbins, R. D. C., 70–72
Robinson, Edward, 4, 42, 45–47, 51, 58–59, 67, 73, 77, 82, 97, 137n70; German scholarship, interest in, 65–66, 72
Roman History (Niebuhr), 76
Rosetta stone, 81

Scandals of the Evangelical Mind (Noll), 125
Schaff, Philip, 97, 140n44
Schleiermacher, Friedrich, 64
science: and educated amateurs, 85; public trust in, 114; and religion, 104; and theology, 103, 118, 121–22
"Science and the Gospel," 97
"Science of Church History, The" (Schaff), 97
Scottish Realism, 2, 23–24, 54–56; New England theology, importance of to, 20. *See also* Common Sense philosophy
"Scripture and Science Not at Variance," 97
Sears, Barnas, 26, 42, 45, 47–48, 58, 67–68, 76–77
Shedd, W. G. T., 45, 48, 69, 72, 104–6; Platonic approach of, 65
Silliman, Benjamin, 4–5, 15, 78, 84, 89, 91, 93–95, 101; geology and Bible, reconciliation between, 87–88
Simpson, Lewis, 1
sin, 9, 18–19, 22–23, 46, 48–49, 51, 53, 56, 59, 61, 106, 120; and Adam's fall, 27, 32, 55, 93–94, 130n5; and grace, 8
"Slavery in Ancient Greece" (Edwards), 75
Smith, H. B., 22, 71–72, 77
Smith, Wilson, 132n67

Smyth, Egbert Coffin, 104–8, 116, 120
Smyth, Newman, 107
Social Statics (Spencer), 110
sociology, 112, 115
Socrates, 107
Sparks, Jared, 73
Spencer, Herbert, 109, 114–16; impact of, 110; opposition to, 111–12; "survival of the fittest" phrase, coinage of, 145n35
Spirit of the Pilgrims (journal), 18–19
Sprague, William, 7
Spring, Samuel, 9–10, 15
Stewart, Dugald, 22
stoicism, 111
Stowe, Calvin, 42, 45, 48, 58, 71
Stuart, Moses, 3–4, 14, 17, 27, 32–33, 37–38, 40–41, 43, 47, 52, 55, 57–59, 61–62, 67–73, 75, 77, 80–83, 87, 91–92, 97–98, 102, 114, 120–21, 125, 127, 131n31; Arminius doctrines, 74; Bible, as authoritative, 39; Bible, meaning of, as inspired, 16; Bible, veracity of, defense of, 78–79; biblical studies, perplexity over, 35–36; Calvinist thought, 16; exegetical principles of, 30–31; German influence, 36, 42; German language, study of, 29, 66; German scholarship, hostility toward, 26; Hebrew grammar, study of, 29–31; language study, 66; Mosaic account authorship, 34–35, 79, 93–95, 99; as pulpit orator, 15; pupils of, 42, 44–45
Sumatra, 11
Swedenborgianism, 57
System of Doctrines (Hopkins), 8

Tacitus, 80–81
taxonomy, 101
Taylor, E. R. A., 58
Taylor, Nathaniel William, 14, 18–19, 21, 53–55, 61, 118; moral agency, 22; Scottish philosophy, importance of to, 22
temperance movement, 89
Thayer, Joseph, 106

"Theological Department Essential in a University, The" (Harris), 103
"Theological Education in the United States" (Park and Edwards), 59
"Theological Science and Education in the United States," 97
theology, 99–100, 103; and evolution, 114; and geology, 101; and natural science, 115–16, 118, 120
"Theology of the Intellect and That of the Feelings, The" (sermon), 4, 60, 63, 118–19
Tholuck, August, 16, 45, 51, 66
Thucydides, 68, 75
Transcendentalists, 1, 57
Trinity, 38–39; attack on, 40
Tucker, William Jewett, 108
Tyndall, John, 115

"Unitarian Christianity" (sermon), 37–38
Unitarian Conscience, The (Howe), 41
Unitarianism, 1, 3–4, 36–37, 40–41, 47, 53, 57, 73, 89, 100, 120; and German scholarship, 27. *See also* Liberals
United States, 4–5, 11, 14, 20, 42, 59, 67–68, 86, 110
utilitarianism, 111

Veysey, Laurence, 2
Virgil, 67
von Ranke, Leopold, 64, 76, 83
Vulcanists, 86

Wallace, Alfred Russell, 114
Wallace, B. J., 69–70
Ware, Abigail, 53
Ware, Henry, 8–9, 18, 21, 40–41, 62
Warshawski, V. I., 125–27
Wayland, Francis, 44–45
Webber, Samuel, 9
Werner, Gottlieb, 86–87
Whedon, Daniel Day, 58
Wilberforce, William, 95
Wilkenson, J. G., 81–82
Williams, Daniel Day, 2, 126

Williams College, 2
Witherspoon, John, 20
Woods, Leonard, 9–12, 18–19, 21, 23, 27, 30, 36, 38, 40–42, 47, 53–54, 56, 62, 99, 105, 120–21; and depravity, 24–25; induction, reliance on, 22; resignation of, 13; self-discipline of, 14

Woolsey, Theodore Dwight, 3, 46, 51–52, 58, 65, 69–70, 146n41
Wright, George Frederick, 115, 122

Yale University, 1–2, 5–6, 14–15, 22, 24–25, 84, 87, 103; Andover, dissension between, 41; library of, 47